Abbas Alnasrawi is professor of economics at the University of Vermont. He is the author of two books, Financing Economic Development in Iraq *and* Arab Oil and United States Energy Requirements, *and numerous articles.*

OPEC in a Changing World Economy

OPEC in a Changing World Economy

ABBAS ALNASRAWI

THE JOHNS HOPKINS UNIVERSITY PRESS

Baltimore and London

© 1985 by The Johns Hopkins University Press
All rights reserved
Printed in the United States of America

The Johns Hopkins University Press, Baltimore, Maryland 21218
The Johns Hopkins Press Ltd., London

The paper in this book is acid-free and meets the guidelines for per-
manence and durability of the Committee on Production Guidelines
for Book Longevity of the Council of Library Resources.

Library of Congress Cataloging in Publication Data

Alnasrawi, Abbas.
    OPEC in a changing world economy.

    Bibliography: p. 175
    Includes index.
    1. Petroleum industry and trade.   2. Organization of
Petroleum Exporting Countries.   I. Title.   II. Title:
O.P.E.C. in a changing world economy.
HD9560.5.A5153   1984   341.7'54722820601   84–7196
ISBN 0–8018–3216–0

To the memory of my mother

Contents

Tables

Acknowledgments

It gives me great pleasure to acknowledge the assistance and support I received in the process of writing this book. The publication of the book would not have taken place at this time had it not been for a sabbatical leave granted to me by the University of Vermont. Members of the staff of the library at the University of Vermont, especially Ann Gould, Nancy Crane, William Dunlop, and Milton Crouch, were most helpful. I owe Gwendolyn Hilberg a special debt of gratitude for her patience and understanding as she typed more than one version of the manuscript. Thanks are also due to Molly Ruzicka for her excellent copy editing and for the numerous suggestions she made.

I greatly benefited from Professor Loring Allen, who read the entire work and pointed out certain weaknesses and made important suggestions.

At The Johns Hopkins University Press I am grateful to my editor, Jane Warth, for her meticulous guidance of the book at the various phases of publication.

I am particularly indebted to Anders Richter, Editorial Director of the Press, for his support of the project from its inception, for his encouragement, and for his wise counsel.

The patience and tolerance shown by Susan, Leyla, and Kara are beyond recognition.

I alone, of course, am responsible for the errors that remain.

OPEC in a Changing World Economy

CHAPTER 1

OPEC and Its Member Countries

In August 1960 the major multinational oil companies reduced the prices of crude oil exported from the Middle East. This action produced a countervailing action by the governments of the oil-producing countries, which decided, in September 1960, to create the Organization of Petroleum Exporting Countries (OPEC). The founding members of the new organization—Iraq, Iran, Kuwait, Saudi Arabia, and Venezuela—declared that the price reductions should be rescinded and that future changes in the prices should be effected in consultation with the individual governments. Neither of these objectives was heeded by the oil companies at the time. It was not until 1971 that these two policy objectives became the subject of negotiations between the oil companies and the governments within the context of the celebrated Tehran Price Agreement.[1]

The Tehran Price Agreement introduced for the first time in the long petroleum-producing history of these countries the principle that their governments were codeterminants, with the oil companies, of the prices of crude oil. In 1972 and 1973 OPEC and the multinational oil companies concluded three other agreements that tended to solidify the position of the member countries in the international oil industry.

Two of these agreements, The Geneva Devaluation Agreement (Geneva I, signed in January 1972) and the Supplemental Agreement (Geneva II, signed in June 1973) adjusted the prices of crude oil upward to reflect the depreciation and devaluation of the dollar with respect both to other major currencies and to gold. The other agreement, the General Participation Agreement reached in December 1972, introduced yet another principle, that of allowing the governments to acquire a majority interest in the concession of their operating companies over a period of ten years.

The effects of both the Participation Agreement and the Tehran Agreement were swept aside by the events of the last quarter of 1973. During October, November, and December of 1973 important structural changes were introduced by OPEC actions in the international oil industry, which affected not only the relative positions of the parties in the industry but the world economy for years to come.

In the early days of October 1973 OPEC entered into another set of negotiations with the major oil companies to raise the prices of crude oil. OPEC's position was that official or posted prices (the basis for the calculation of the governments' tax revenues) should be raised from $3 to $5 per barrel, in alignment with the market price. The oil companies and their governments refused such a demand, some offering only 15¢ more per barrel. And even when the oil companies attempted among themselves to reach an agreement at a higher price, the governments refused to approve the companies' position.

These negotiations occurred during the time of the October 1973 Arab-Israeli war. As the war continued, the Arab ministers of oil—not OPEC—decided on a reduction in output and an embargo on exports to the United States and the Netherlands. The day after that decision, OPEC decided to raise posted prices unilaterally in such a manner as to yield $5 per barrel of revenue to the government.

The embargo and cutbacks created an artificial shortage, which led to a sharp rise in market prices for oil. This difference between posted prices and market prices prompted Iran to lead OPEC in another doubling of the price, which became effective in January 1974.

This confluence of events ushered in a new era in the oil industry and also introduced into the media terms such as *energy crisis* and *OPEC cartel*. The abnormal market conditions, together with the sudden visibility of OPEC, made it easy for economists to deduce that the energy crisis—typified by higher prices and lower quantities—was caused by the behavior of a newly born cartel.

The "cartelization" of OPEC, as described in economic analyses and textbooks (Mansfield 1982, 347–48; Samuelson 1976, 812–13; see also Bibliography) had a spillover application in economic policy analysis. Since the "cartel" was perceived responsible for an energy crisis that plunged the world economy into its severest recession since the Great Depression, it was presumed that solving the energy crisis—in other words, lower prices and larger output—would provide the answer to the problems of the advanced countries' economies.

This, in a nutshell, was the diagnosis and the solution proffered for a number of difficulties that plagued the world economy in the 1970s (and that still exist). Yet the analysis suffers from a severe misunderstanding of the nature of OPEC, of its history, its structure, its decision-making process, the role of its members, and its impact on the world economy.

At the heart of OPEC and at the root of the misunderstanding is the fact that each OPEC member attaches far more weight to the idea of the "sovereignty of the state" than to any intergovernmental agency such as OPEC. The centrality of sovereignty in the eyes of member countries cannot be overemphasized, and any attempt to study OPEC behavior must concentrate on the conflicts and compromises that have shaped the actions of OPEC and its member countries, within the framework of each member country's national interests.

Once it is understood that many of the policy actions attributed to OPEC actually originated in the policy actions of one or another member, several current notions lose their force, requiring that another context for analysis and explanation of policy be developed. In other words, it must be recognized that the character and direction of OPEC policy is determined not by what OPEC has done or intended to do but failed to do, but by what each member government has done or proposes to do. And furthermore, that a member government's behavior is determined by the complex of economic, political, and social objectives of that government rather than by its participation in the collective decision-making process of OPEC.

The history of OPEC is replete both with cases in which OPEC actions were inspired by decisions already taken by individual members, as well as by instances in which individual members opted to disregard decisions made by OPEC. The divergence between a member's interest and that of the group as a whole should not be interpreted as meaning that there are no common interests and objectives among member countries, because of course there are. The point to be stressed here is that such interests may or may not always coincide. To the extent that the goals (economic and political) of a given country conform to those of the group, there will be a commonality of interests and a uniformity of application. The moment the perception exists that an individual country's interests and goals are not served by an OPEC decision, however, the interests of that country can be expected to supersede those of the organization's common objectives.

EVOLUTION OF OPEC'S OBJECTIVES

Before the creation of OPEC and almost until 1972, OPEC-member countries' petroleum policies tended to have three objectives. These were:

1. An increase in the revenue per barrel that would accrue to the member country or at least the arrest of decline in such revenue.

2. Equality of treatment by multinational oil companies of member governments.

3. Expansion of the level of output.

These three goals were to be expected, given the nature of the concession system under which oil resources were developed. The system of exploitation accorded the oil companies a legal concession that lasted several decades and covered most if not all the territory of the oil-producing nation; it gave the oil companies the right to pricing and output decisions; and it allowed the host government to receive a certain percentage of the difference between the production cost and the price of crude oil.

Since oil revenues were of primary importance as a source of foreign exchange and domestic finance, it was inevitable that ordinary and development spending, as well as import programs, would be intimately dependent on the revenues from this one source. And since the revenues were a function chiefly of price, it was natural for a government to push for an increase in the per-unit revenue.

Another aspect of the concession system was the fact that most oil deposits in most countries were developed by a core of a few large multinational oil companies. Usually a company had an investment in more than one country and, along with other companies, held joint concessions in these countries. This system of joint ownership gave rise to two sources of friction between governments and companies. The first related to the determination of the level of output from each country; and the second related to the fiscal terms for the extraction of oil from each country. The first source of friction was a logical outcome of the way the oil industry was organized, as contrasted with the way the nation states were organized. Basically, the organization of the oil industry was characterized by a few large firms that had vertically integrated their operations worldwide. Within this broad network, the output from each oil-producing country had to be funneled. Yet, the same output represented the mainstay of each of these host countries and, by extension, it dictated the nature of their political systems. The second source of friction arose because the character of the relationships between an operating company and a host country made it possible for the companies either to extend certain benefits to the host country or to withhold these benefits. In other words, the concession holders had the power to engage in cerain discriminatory practices against a particular government that might result in benefits to other governments.

To avoid such practices and to guard against one government's interest being sacrificed for the benefit of another, the principle of equal treatment was thus a strongly sought OPEC objective. This principle found its clearest application in fiscal matters, in that whenever one government received a particular fiscal benefit the oil companies were induced to extend the benefit to other governments. This equal-treatment clause was an objective that OPEC successfully helped member countries to understand and achieve.

The third policy objective to be embraced by OPEC-member countries involved the question of the level of output from each producing country. As indicated earlier, such output was determined by the worldwide needs of the multinational oil companies, but the output also represented the main economic support of the host countries. Since the oil-producing governments prior to 1973 had no say in determining the price at which oil was sold, it was only natural for them to press the companies to increase their output. But for a company to increase output from any one source had to be at the expense of output from another source. During this era, the oil companies thus played the important role of balancing the demands of various host governments with the companies' own needs for oil throughout the world. The task of regulating output among producing countries and companies was a crucial function of the system prior to 1973.

As could be deduced in light of this summary of the objectives of the oil-producing countries, the concession system resulted in a number of problems between the host country and the company operating there. These problems revolved around the level of output, the components of the cost of production, employment of nationals, the relinquishment of area not utilized by the companies, and of course the price of crude oil.

It should be noted that while each country had a number of conflicts with its producing company, the conflicts varied and usually occurred at different times from country to country. Owing to the nature of the output system, which allowed the oil companies to meet their oil requirements from several countries, host governments had no credible threat to resort to in order to achieve a given objective. For example, although a host government could deny an oil company access to the oil fields, such an act could not have been adopted without far-reaching and damaging consequences for the host government.

It was only in the area of price that governments found themselves facing the companies at the same time. This was unavoidable, since any price change had to be announced to all customers and effected at all export points. In addition to the immediate impact on all governments of any price change, there was the question of sovereignty. A price change—and especially a price reduction—taken uniformly by the companies without consultation with the individual governments came to be regarded as an infringement of the prerogative and sovereignty of the state. This was particularly the case when a price reduction was unaccompanied by an increase in output to offset the reduction in government revenues. Moreover, a unilateral change in price was construed as a change in the terms of the relationship between the state and the companies, with no opportunity for input in the decision by the former. OPEC's creation was thus in response to common opposition on the part of host governments to the oil companies' announced price reduction.

The founding of OPEC and its consequent attempts to have the oil companies cancel the price reduction illustrate the point made earlier, that OPEC was allowed to function so long as the objectives of OPEC and of member governments were identical. As soon as the interests of the state were perceived as not being served by OPEC, however, that government found it necessary to dissociate itself from OPEC's decisions. This was demonstrated, for example, by Iraq's refusal in 1964 to agree to the terms negotiated by OPEC with respect to the expensing of royalties within the context of certain price adjustments.

The point here is that OPEC was created to function as a collection of sovereign governments, each with its own set of economic and political considerations and objectives. Based on OPEC-member actions over the last two decades, it is safe to say that these considerations and priorities are not subject to compromise should there be a contradiction between the national interests of a government and the joint interests of member countries. In fact, OPEC has been a convenient vehicle only to the extent that there is a uniformity of interests among member countries. Given this history of OPEC's conception and of member countries' relationship to it, as well as the principle of equality of benefits, OPEC's behavior is readily explained. As stated earlier, these principles also applied in pre-OPEC days, as demonstrated by the profit-sharing arrangements of the 1950s and Iraq's actions in 1956 and 1958 when it followed Saudi Arabia in applying reductions in selling allowances and discounts.

But what of OPEC as an organization and of its achievements? The record of events prior to 1971 overwhelmingly supports the contention that OPEC as an organization had but a marginal impact on the international oil industry. It is this marginality that led OPEC to be described as a labor union engaged in negotiations with an employer (the oil companies) to improve the earnings of its members. Even this analogy breaks down, however, because OPEC never used the ultimate tool of negotiation, that is, stoppage of production. The organization became important as a bargaining unit only when the oil companies agreed in 1971 to confer upon it the legitimacy of collective bargaining on the issue of pricing of crude oil. But here again, OPEC was a follower and not a leader. Leadership had been provided in the previous year by the new government of Libya, when it achieved what seemed beyond the capability of one government—higher oil prices and tax rates. The Libyan breakthrough, which set in motion the events leading to the Tehran Agreement, was by all accounts a turning point in government-company relationships. The misfortune of that important event is that it should rather have taken place in 1967, following the closing of the Suez Canal, and, moreover, that it should instead have been undertaken by OPEC. But OPEC the organization was not equipped to act with such foresight; only member governments were. If individual governments were unaware in 1967 of an exploitable opportunity or were unwilling to exploit it, then OPEC the organization could not be relied upon to take the initiative.

The major significance of the Libyan success does not derive from the fact that a producing government succeeded in raising prices and taxes, nor from the fact that it led, ultimately, to the Tehran Agreement. Both accomplishments were certainly important. Of greater consequence, however, is that the Libyan success altered the traditional perception of the relationships of host governments vis-à-vis companies, which was that the host governments were powerless in face of the oil companies, who were themselves backed by influential governments. In retrospect, it is this attitude that crippled oil-producing countries' ability to act in their own interests from the time of the 1951 Iranian nationalization of its oil sector to the 1970 Libyan success. (It should be pointed out here, however, that one of the primary factors that defeated the effect of the Iranian nationalization was the readiness of neighboring producing countries to make up for the lost Iranian oil by cheerfully accepting substantial increases in their output. They actually had no choice but to be cheerful, in view of the fact that they had no authority with respect to capacity and output.)

The changes that have occurred on the oil scene since the Libyan government made petroleum history have been numerous and radical. Some of these changes are easily understood, while others still defy conventional explanation.

By 1983 OPEC crude-oil prices were sixteen times higher than they were when OPEC came into existence (in real terms these prices were only six times higher). In addition, most OPEC governments now have majority if not complete ownership of their oil-producing operations, a condition that was nonexistent when OPEC came into being. These are important and lasting gains, so much so that many students of international economics contend that these gains were made at the expense of the industrial countries that are members of the OECD (Organization of Economic Co-operation and Development). Such an assumption, however, is not only false but reflects an insensitivity to actual developments.

It is true that on the face of it the distribution of the economic rent has changed dramatically, in that the OPEC countries' share in the rent has increased in both nominal and real terms. But to say that this improvement has occurred to the detriment of the OECD countries is a superficial judgment that indicates a lack of familiarity with the evolution of the concession agreements. One could more accurately state that through such gains OPEC countries were able to put an end to the unrestricted transfer of their resources, a process that was carried out with the knowledge, support, and active help of the governments of the OECD countries. This transfer of real resources from the OPEC countries to the OECD countries, which started long before OPEC and OECD were created, contributed considerably to the enormous economic growth that has characterized the history of the industrialized countries since the end of World War II. Oil served not only as the vehicle for the transfer of wealth, but, thanks to the tight control of oil by the few major companies, it also served as an instrument to attain foreign policy objectives of some of the majors' home governments. This is not a question of semantics but, rather, of reading the record as it was written by the governments of the major oil-importing countries, especially that of the United States.

It is important, in the author's opinion, to recall how two prominent students of the oil scene (Drs. George Stocking and Nadim Al-Pachachi) described the pattern of power relations that existed between the oil companies and the oil-producing countries until the early 1970s. Commenting on the main features of the concession arrangements, Stocking wrote that "never in modern times have governments granted so much to so few for so long" (Stocking 1970, 130). But did these governments really grant the concessions of their own volition? The record is clear on this point and it is not necessary to review it in depth. The asymmetry of relations between governments and companies that resulted in the long and sustained transfer of resources to the OECD countries was driven home by Al-Pachachi when he stated that in 1935 Iraq's oil department was composed of a director, who did not have a high school diploma, and one junior clerk. And as late as 1951 when Iraq negotiated its profit-sharing agreement with Iraq Petroleum Company, no one on the Iraqi side had heard of posted prices, not to mention technical and economic studies (Al-Pachachi 1968, 2).

It has also been argued that the enormous increase in the prices of crude oil were of such magnitude that OPEC-member countries can now be classified as belonging to the group of rich countries. To be sure, some countries such as Kuwait and the United Arab Emirtes have the highest per-capita income in the world. But it is well known that this exceptional condition reflects no more than unspendable accumulated assets in foreign money and capital markets. All OPEC countries, including even the richest, are underdeveloped and belong to that group known as developing countries. Suffice it to say that in 1979 the OPEC countries contained 7.7 percent of the world population and had 4.2 percent of its gross national product (GNP).

Leaving these differing interpretations aside, a central question is how to account for OPEC's successes in so few years. A frequent explanation is that OPEC the organization tended to follow suit in instances where a member government initiated action that proved successful. Once success was attained by a member government, other OPEC governments imitated these actions on the premise that benefits extended to one government should be extended to other governments. In such a situation OPEC therefore provided the framework for a collective action whose outcome in most cases was a foregone conclusion.

The pivotal role of individual governments and the importance of their actions in relation to OPEC can be seen also when such governments failed to share the same motives or perceptions of conditions or events. Thus, when an individual action was not copied by other governments, OPEC the organization has often not played any role. This has been the case particularly when acts by certain governments have been interpreted as being purely political or were drastic in scope and consequence. An illustration of a politically motivated action was the nationalization by Libya of the interests of British Petroleum Company in 1971. The 1972 Iraq nationalization of the operations of Iraq Petroleum Companies is another example of an action that other countries and hence OPEC chose not to follow. And the embargo measures and production cutbacks that were instituted in 1973 and that were not followed by the non-Arab members of OPEC are further instances in which certain OPEC countries had no reason and/or no incentive to adopt the same measures. In summary, during the last two decades of its existence OPEC has tended to follow policy initiatives taken by individual member governments. It has been the ability of the member governments to establish the practice of a generalized system of benefits that has tended to confer upon OPEC its successes.

OPEC AND THE INTERNATIONAL CONTEXT

In addition to appreciating the impact of individual government action on the behavior of OPEC, it is important to note that OPEC found itself reacting crisis-management style to certain changes in the international political economy that it could have anticipated.

OPEC, for instance, was a passive observer during the late 1960s when the international monetary system was undergoing the structural changes that brought about its eventual demise in 1971. One would have thought that since the price of crude oil was quoted in U.S. dollars that OPEC would pay close attention to what was happening to the dollar. But in the absence of member initiative in this area, OPEC failed to exert an independent course of action. When the dollar was devalued in 1971 it was obvious that the prices that had been negotiated under the framework of the Tehran Agreement would have to be renegotiated to reflect the new foreign-exchange relations. Here again it was a case of rectifying fiscal loss that affected all countries simultaneously.

Another aspect of the international economy that OPEC neglected to appreciate was the structural change in the balance between supply and demand for oil. As is discussed in detail in chapter 2, the late 1960s and early 1970s witnessed the emergence of a new phenomenon—the rise in the demand for crude oil at higher rates than had been attained in previous decades. This fact was reflected first in the elimination of excess capacity in the oil industry and second in an upward pressure on the prices of oil traded in the open market. Again, confronted with these changes, neither OPEC nor any of its member countries paid any serious attention to the shifting market forces.

It is possible to attribute the passivity of OPEC and its members to the changing world conditions to the fact that control over oil output was in the hands of the oil companies. However, this explanation loses strength when applied to the period following the 1973 changes, when the setting of prices and output levels ceased to be the prerogative of the oil companies. But herein lies the paradox, as well as the reason, for OPEC's behavior. From a purely analytical viewpoint, OPEC the organization should have replaced the oil companies in monitoring market conditions, trends, and forecasts of demand. This function would have been logical for OPEC, since no one member country had the technical capacity to perform these activities. The reason why OPEC failed to act in this area appears rooted in the way OPEC was organized. To perform the global function of monitorng would have entailed granting more powers to OPEC than its members were willing to delegate to it. In other words, the fear of infringing on the rights of member governments may have contributed to this failure. As a result, OPEC and its members were unprepared to deal with some of the crucial issues and problems that arose in the aftermath of the 1974–75 world recession and more recent changes in the demand for energy in general and oil in particular. Neither OPEC nor any of its member governments has thus been equipped to deal with problems such as the erosion in the value of the dollar, worldwide inflation, the secular decline in demand for energy, the emergence of the power of the importing countries, or the continued sluggishness of the world economy—to name only a few areas in which OPEC has remained a bystander. Again one is compelled to fall back on the nature of the power relations between OPEC and its member governments to account for these seemingly inexplicable shortcomings. Such relations were made clear in the aftermath of the Iranian Revolution when market prices kept outpacing those of OPEC. All OPEC could do under the circumstances was to react to market prices by continually raising its prices in the hope of closing the gap. Again, however, many member countries found it in their interest not to adhere to the prices set by them collectively; instead they charged prices that were somewhere between official prices and market prices.

OPEC AND OECD

Historically all of the oil-producing companies that operated in the OPEC region were based in the industrialized countries, and most of the major multinational companies have been American-owned. British, French, Dutch, and, to a lesser extent, German, Japanese, and Italian interests have also been represented in the OPEC region.

The pattern of relations between these companies and their home governments has always been close. In the United States oil companies were regarded as instruments of U.S. foreign policy. Other countries have also viewed their oil companies as national assets whose interests have tended to coincide with national interests. As late as 1973 the oil companies had to verify with the OECD governments the extent of price increases that they could negotiate with OPEC negotiators. So long as the assets of the oil-producing companies in the OPEC region were controlled by the companies themselves, the OECD governments could be assured of the security of supply and the stability of prices. (This structure of relations served the industrial world well when American economic assistance for the World War II–damaged economies of Western Europe and Japan assured the flow of oil to these economies at low prices. To the extent that the oil companies aided the postwar reconstruction, their contribution was invaluable.)

When, in 1973–74, the authority for making output and price decisions passed from the few oil companies that were bound by joint production arrangements to the hands of sovereign governments, a new set of conditions was created, which made it necessary for the governments of consuming countries to respond. In other words, the role of insulating the consumers from the producers, which the companies had performed so well, had to yield to new arrangements.

The new conditions made it clear that the degree of mutuality of interests or economic interdependence between countries was strong. Oil was no longer a small component of a country's imports. Nor was the payment for oil an insignificant part of the payments flows among these countries. The financial systems in the importing countries had to be adaptive and resilient in order to absorb the financial flows from the oil-exporting countries. In addition, the economies of the oil-importing countries had to be flexible enough to capture new trading opportunities in the markets of the oil-exporting countries.

In order to cope with some of the consequences of the new oil regime, the OECD countries decided to create their own organization, the International Energy Agency (IEA). The IEA was given a number of functions, including the monitoring of oil stockpiles and the implementation of oil-sharing arrangements in case of emergency interruption of oil flows. Although the IEA can be described as a countervailing force to that of OPEC, it is not an oligopsony facing an oligopolistic OPEC in the marketplace, because the IEA was not given any power to negotiate prices or to purchase oil from the exporting countries on behalf of the importing countries. Oil-purchase negotiations were left in the hands of multinational oil companies, and of national oil companies of importing countries when such entities were sanctioned by these countries.

Regardless of the arrangements—mixed in most cases except in the United States, which has no national oil company—the new regime of oil production and pricing brought the governments of oil-producing countries and those of the OECD in direct contact on a variety of issues.

One of the more important ongoing goals of oil-producing countries, which has had direct impact on the pattern of economic relations between exporters and importers, has been the commitment of oil-producing countries to accelerate economic growth and diversification. In this regard, in striving to attain their long-term economic objectives, oil-producing governments have contended that the transfer of technology from the OECD countries is vital.

Reduced to its essential element, the issue of technology transfer refers to the need of the oil-producing countries for hastened economic development in order to ensure that their economies will be capable of sustained economic growth once their oil wealth has been depleted. Income from oil, in other words, is regarded as the vehicle to transform one form of an income-producing asset into another. A key element in this process is thus the accelerated transfer of technology from the main oil-importing industrialized countries to the developing oil-producing countries. Regardless of the merit of the position of the OPEC countries, the former group of countries are expected to play an active role in the transfer process, if oil is to continue to flow at the levels desired by the oil-importing countries.

It can be argued, of course, that the question of technology transfer wholly belongs to the private sector in the OECD countries. Such an argument, however, overlooks the fact that the OECD governments have always intervened in the process of technology transfer from one country to another in a variety of economic, military, and political contexts. This is particularly true for nuclear and computer technology. It is well known, for example, that it was under pressure from the U.S. government that the French subsidiary of International Business Machines opted not to provide the French government with technology that was deemed necessary for the advancement of President de Gaulle's program of a French nuclear striking force. A more recent example (1982) was the decision by the U.S. government to embargo the export of natural-gas pipeline technology by American firms based in the United States and abroad to the Soviet Union. The point is that governments of consuming countries can, if they wish, accelerate, decelerate, or prohibit the supply of technology. To deny them the crucial role that they can play in this process is to disregard a primary ingredient in the pattern of relations between importing and exporting countries. If the consuming governments found it expedient not only to organize themselves in the IEA but to enact legislation enabling them to regulate the energy markets, and furthermore, to enter into dialogue with OPEC, it seems only natural that they should participate in the transfer of technology. Technology, in other words, like indexation, taxes, supply of oil, and import control, cannot be separated from the rest of the package, which also includes the access of petroleum-based products to the market of the consuming countries, downstream investment, freedom of investment, protection of the purchasing power of funds already invested, and joint contribution for the benefit of the developing countries of the world. All these issues are of immediate concern to oil-producing countries.

An issue that has occupied much of the attention of policy makers and observers is that of the role of the dollar as the unit of account and store of value. In both these functions, owing to inflation and depreciation of the dollar, oil-exporting countries are being subjected to forces that are eroding the purchasing power of current income and dollar-denominated assets. Regardless of the methodology used to compute the erosion in purchasing power, the result of the exercise is the same, the only difference being the magnitude of the loss. It is this loss that has instigated demands that oil prices be expressed in currencies other than the dollar, or that prices be adjusted to reflect the loss in the value of the dollar. In both cases the issue is not really problematical, as the decision rests technically in the hands of the oil-producing countries.

In terms of the relationship of the role of the dollar to the question of the accumulated reserves, it appears that the existence of these reserves has created an external constraint on the decision-making process in some of the oil-exporting countries. The fear of these countries that they will sustain losses if they move from one currency to another has tended to restrict their freedom of action. Yet it is this fear that can be used as a bargaining instrument for the protection of the real value of these countries' assets. Recent political developments between Iran and the United States have added another dimension to the significance and the vulnerability of these assets. By freezing Iranian assets in American banks, the U.S. government in 1980 served notice to all asset holders that their access to their own assets is not always assured. Under existing conditions this means that oil-producing countries are faced with another external constraint on their freedom to make decisions.

OPEC AND OTHER THIRD WORLD COUNTRIES

One of the more significant aspects of OPEC's success in the 1970s was that it had major implications for relations between OPEC and other Third World countries on the one hand and between the Third World countries and industrialized countries on the other. For the first time in four centuries a group of developing countries reassumed control over a natural resource of strategic importance to the industrialized countries. It was feared at the time by industrialized nations that other countries might attempt to emulate OPEC and assume control over other raw materials and minerals of major importance to the industrialized countries. Some countries, to be sure, attempted to raise export taxes on their raw materials, but no action had effects comparable to what OPEC was able to accomplish.

OPEC's success was a mixed blessing to developing countries. The increase in the price of crude oil raised the cost of imported oil to all oil-importing countries. Suggestions that a two-tier price system be adopted were brushed aside for a variety of reasons. In addition, suggestions that OPEC petrofunds be channeled to Third World countries were not accepted on the grounds that capital and money markets in the industrialized countries provided more secure and more profitable opportunities to portfolio managers. Finally agreed upon was the creation of an OPEC mechanism to provide concessional loans to Third World countries to be used either for project financing or balance-of-payments financing. Several countries, primarily those with balance-of-payments surpluses, like Saudi Arabia, Kuwait, United Arab Emirates, and Iraq, established their own national funds for external development. The primary purpose of these funds was to extend grants or loans on concessional terms on a bilateral basis to other developing countries.

In addition to these financial flows, trade between OPEC countries and other Third World countries expanded noticeably. Another indicator of the increased collaboration between OPEC countries and other Third World nations was their joint participation in the establishment of what came to be known as the New International Economic Order (NIEO). OPEC countries played a leading role in boosting the efforts of Third World countries to introduce structural changes into the international economic system. These attempts found their strong expression in the convening in 1975 of the Conference on International Economic Cooperation (CIEC), known as the North-South Dialogue, which lasted eighteen months.

Nevertheless, these efforts by OPEC to use its newly acquired leverage to change aspects of the international economic system lacked coherence and focus, in that they were undertaken in response to the demands of the moment. Here again the apparent lack of unified, long-term policy objectives proved fatal.

CONFLICTS WITHIN OPEC

Given the divergent political and economic conditions and objectives among member countries and the prerogative that states should continue to be independent agents, conflicts within OPEC were inevitable.

Prior to 1971–73 conflicts eminated from the concession system itself, in that each government attempted to have its oil company maximize output in order to maximize revenue. But, as mentioned earlier, an increase in output in one country had to be at the expense of output in other countries. The phenomenal growth of Libyan output within only a few years from the time of its discovery is a case in point. Libyan oil had to be funneled through the integrated channels of oil companies that had oil interest in other OPEC countries. The latter, meanwhile, had to contend with a lower rate of growth in order to allow Libyan oil to be absorbed into the corporate operations. Yet this particular conflict was resolved within the corporate structure, which tended to insulate one government from another. As OPEC countries took over more functions and decision-making powers from the oil companies, and as member governments became the price setter within the OPEC structure, sources of frictions and conflicts multiplied.

Thus, while all OPEC-member governments applauded the October 1973 increase in the price of crude oil, when the second increase occurred in December 1973 (this one led by the Iranian government), some OPEC countries, especially Saudi Arabia, expressed their displeasure with it, although no counter action was taken. However, in 1976, 1980, and 1981, when Saudi Arabia again disagreed with other member governments' assessment of market conditions, the Saudi government resorted to varying tactics in order to have its position prevail. In 1976 the Saudi government forced the adoption of a two-tier price system in which the largest producer in the group charged the lower price. And in 1980 and 1981 it expanded its output considerably to the point of capturing market shares from its competitors, hence forcing them to accept its assessment of market forces.

On the issue of the call for repeal of the price cut—the reason for OPEC's founding in 1960—OPEC initially had no policy as to how an oil company's price decision might be reversed. The oil companies, given the nature of the concession agreement and the buyer conditions relatively prevailing in the market, could afford to ignore OPEC and its call for a price recision. The companies went so far as to refuse to recognize OPEC, therefore refusing also to negotiate with it. Several years would elapse after the creation of OPEC before the oil companies would agree—through a complicated arrangement—to negotiate with OPEC on a nonpricing issue.

The nonprice issue on which the companies agreed to negotiate was that of royalty expensing. OPEC's position was that royalty payment should be treated by the companies as an expense item rather than as part of the tax payment to government. The negotiations lasted from 1962 to 1964, and ended anticlimatically because the companies insisted that the terms of the agreement could not be extended to Iraq, which had a standing dispute with the companies. Interestingly, member countries that had no dispute with the companies approved the terms of the agreement, leaving Iraq to settle its own dispute with the companies at a later date. Although the fiscal benefits that resulted from the royalty-expensing agreement were insignificant, the manner in which the agreement was adopted was significant: in its first negotiating exercise, OPEC was found willing to abandon a participating country in accepting the terms of the agreement. Thus, the principle of collective bargaining that carried OPEC through the negotiations did not prevail in the implementation; individual member-government interests assumed precedence over collective interests.

More important than the royalty agreement in OPEC's early years was the issue of output administration. During this time, member countries found themselves having to contend with excess capacity, which tended to exert a downward pressure on prices. There was also the fear on the part of Venezuela that continued expansion of low-cost Middle East oil would capture markets that had traditionally been supplied with Venezuelan oil. Venezuela took the position within OPEC that producing countries should devise a formula that would regulate output to meet projected demand, a scheme similar to the one adopted by the Texas Railroad Commission, which regulated output from producing fields in the United States. As is noted in chapter 4, the proposed scheme was discussed extensively, only to be shelved on the premise that its implementation would compromise the sovereignty of the state.

In the late 1960s and early 1970s, as time elapsed and the forces of demand began to exert an upward pressure on prices, the Venezuelan idea for regulating output was ultimately rendered unnecessary; it was no longer a question of whether OPEC was producing too much but of whether it was producing enough.

OPEC's inability to agree to regulate output due to intra-OPEC conflicts was again brought to the fore in 1982, when the continued worldwide decline in the demand for oil motivated OPEC to place a ceiling on the total output of oil.

However, the ceiling was discarded by some members who again openly asserted their right to determine the level of their own output.

OPEC: NEW INFLUENCES AND REALITIES

The decade of the 1970s can be termed a watershed in the history of the international oil industry, due to certain important changes and events. These include the emergence of oil supply/demand imbalance in favor of the producers; the success of OPEC in engaging the oil companies in collective negotiations, which led to the conclusion of the Tehran Agreement; the nationalization of the oil concessions in Iraq; the conclusion of the Participation Agreement; the oil-price revolution of 1973–74; the emergence of the United States as the world's largest oil importer; and the eventual transfer of controlling power over the oil industry from the oil companies to the oil-producing countries. More importantly, these changes brought the role of governments in planning their nations' energy futures into sharp focus, forcing the world to recognize that important structural changes in the demand for and sources of energy would have to occur because of the fact that oil is a finite resource. The 1970s also demonstrated that the assumed harmony among the producing countries was exaggerated and that OPEC does not speak with one voice, even on matters of pricing of crude oil.

Where do we go from here and what role, if any, will OPEC the organization play? Also, how will the role of the individual countries be expressed in the 1980s? Specifically, four sets of influences can be anticipated. The first and most important influence will be the continued exercise of the prerogatives of sovereignty—and, indeed, a strengthening of this force with time. It is important to remember that OPEC was formed to protect prices from falling, at a time of continued capacity and production expansion and with crude-oil prices low. In a market where marginal quantities are assuming an ever-increasing role in price determination, or in which the demand for oil is static, there is no reason to expect that sovereignty will not assume a more powerful place in the decision-making process. This development will be aided by the fact that the national oil companies will be selling to an ever-expanding number of buyers.

A second influence will be the policy objectives of industrialization and conservation in all OPEC-member countries. Both of these national objectives are bound to affect OPEC countries' output policies.

A third influence on the behavior of producing countries can be called the disutility of portfolio. It is ironic that, for certain countries, producing oil beyond their needs will tend to create a self-dampening influence on their future freedom of action. This fact was harshly driven home in November 1979 when the U.S. government froze assets held by the Iranian government in American banks.

The fourth influence that will tend to shape future policy is the extent to which member countries are willing and able to work with other developing countries in order to introduce changes into the international economic system.

These issues and influences are addressed in more depth in succeeding chapters. The next chapter turns first, however, to the pricing behavior of OPEC.

CHAPTER 2

Oil-Price Behavior under OPEC

Between 1971 and 1982, the Organization of Petroleum Exporting Countries exerted a major influence on the international oil industry and, consequently, on the economies of the industrial nations and other oil-importing countries. Because of the range and magnitude of oil consumption as an energy source and as a raw material, the pricing behavior of OPEC has become a prominent concern for all oil-importing countries. Prices that OPEC-member countries charge for their oil constitute a major cost component in a large number of products. The fact that many industrial nations have been attempting to formulate more realistic energy policies underscores the importance of understanding OPEC pricing behavior and its evolution over the last decade. Before analyzing such behavior, however, a few observations are in order.

The history of the international oil industry before OPEC can be described in terms of various agreements among the major oil companies (Exxon Corporation, Mobil Oil Corporation, Texaco, Standard Oil Company of California (Socal), Gulf Oil Corporation, British Petroleum Company (BP), and Shell Petroleum Company). These agreements were aimed at price fixing, market sharing, cross hauling, and other elements of economic behavior that had the effect of limiting competition in favor of an international oil cartel. The major oil companies were the dominant force in international oil in terms of concentration ratio, size of the firms, and assets. Their joint control of the operating companies in oil-producing countries enabled them to regulate production and set oil prices throughout the world, from the inception of the industry until the early 1980s.

The management of the world oil industry by the few major oil firms was described as an international petroleum cartel in a report prepared in 1952 by the Federal Trade Commission (FTC) for the U.S. Senate Select Committee on Small Businesses and released under the title, *International Petroleum Cartel*. The findings in the FTC report were supported more than twenty years later when the Subcommittee on Multinational Corporations of the U.S. Senate Committee on Foreign Relations released its hearings and reports on *The International Petroleum Cartel, The Iranian Consortium, and U.S. National Security* (1974) and *Multinational Oil Corporations and U.S. Foreign Policy* (1975—henceforth, *MNC* report).

These observations illustrate that the term *cartel* which has also been used to describe OPEC's behavior, is not new. OPEC, as is discussed in chapter 4, is not a cartel. However, it was conceived as a force counter to that of the oil companies and, therefore, by its very nature, had the effect of limiting the free play of market forces. It should be emphasized, however, as the reports just cited amply demonstrate, that a free market in international oil never existed in the first place. What happened was that the control over the pricing of crude oil began to move on a small scale from the seven major oil companies to the OPEC countries, first in 1971 and more significantly in 1973.

The character of the concession agreements governing the relationship between the oil companies and the governments of the oil-producing countries inevitably gave rise to conflicts. Such conflicts frequently centered on the size of the area under concession, the duration and exclusive aspect of the concessions, pricing and output policies, government revenues, cost-accounting methods, the surrender of rights of taxation, fixity of legal terms, settlement of disputes, and the sovereignty of a foreign-oil enclave within a sovereign state.[1] In order to ascertain the significance of these conflicts and the impact of the shift of control over pricing from the oil companies to OPEC, it is useful, before dealing with OPEC pricing policies, to analyze the pricing practices of the oil companies prior to 1971.

HISTORICAL BACKGROUND BEFORE 1971

Long before OPEC was formed, the international oil industry was dominated by seven vertically integrated major companies (the majors), which controlled over 90 percent of the world oil production outside the United States and the Soviet Union in addition to most transportation, refining, and marketing facilities. The American majors also controlled a sizable part of the American oil industry. As early as 1928, the dominant majors (Exxon, BP, and Shell) entered into cartel arrangements to eliminate competitive pricing by fixing market shares, controlling output growth from various sources, exchanging oil to lessen cross hauling, agreeing whether to exclude competitors or admit them into the cartel system, and ultimately agreeing to sell crude oil and products at a fixed price regardless of source or production cost. Prices at the U.S. Gulf (of Mexico) Coast terminals, as published in *Platt's Oilgram*, constituted the basis for price quotations throughout the world.

In order to integrate the American oil output with the cartel's policy to regulate world output to maintain prices, the industry persuaded oil-producing states to adopt a series of regulations controlling oil production by prorating the estimated demand for crude oil among all producing fields and wells. Demand was estimated on the basis of current prices so that additional production would not undermine the existing price structure. The Connally Hot Oil Act, enacted in the U.S. in 1935, enforced state regulations by prohibiting interstate sales of crude oil produced in violation of state restrictions. Thus, the prorating mechanism that stabilized U.S. crude prices also served to stabilize prices throughout the world, since U.S. Gulf Coast prices were the prices at which oil was sold on the international market. It should be noted here that because of this control system, consumers in Iraq were charged prices based upon quotations at the U.S. Gulf Coast, despite that (1) the crude oil was produced in Iraq, (2) it was produced at low cost, (3) it was refined in a nearby refinery, and (4) the products were marketed by a local company.

The majors, whose goal was an orderly development of oil production through market allocation and price stabilization, were able to solidify their control through the utilization of two important strategies. The first was the joint ownership of oil-producing companies in the Middle East and Venezuela. This technique went far toward helping the majors to coordinate and direct output to meet corporate oil requirements and avoid excessive output. Second, in order to allow new oil to enter the world market through the majors' integrated channels, long-term contracts were concluded between certain majors. The provisions of these contracts, which specified where crude oil was to be marketed and the terms of its sale, had the effect of tightening the joint control of the majors over the international oil industry (Alnasrawi 1975, 370–72).

As the Second World War was coming to an end, it became clear that the United States would no longer continue to be a major exporter of oil and that the Middle East would be called upon to meet the rising needs of the world. But in order to forestall unregulated growth of that region's output, a treaty between the governments of the United States and the United Kingdom was concluded in 1944. This Anglo-American Oil Agreement had, broadly speaking, two major objectives: (1) to enable U.S. oil companies to have more access to Middle East oil, and (2) to recommend how supply could be correlated with demand so as to further the orderly conduct of the international petroleum trade.

A study prepared for the U.S. Senate Committee on Foreign Relations concluded that the eventual takeover of oil-price control by the majors was attributed to the ineffectiveness of the Anglo-American Oil Agreement: "Given the fact that there was more Middle East oil than there were markets for it, it was obvious that production allocations were going to be made. . . . The problem, therefore, was not whether but who would control that international allocation mechanism. As it turned out, the failure of the Anglo-American Oil Agreement delegated this global function to the major international oil companies" (*MNC* report, 42–43).

Although the short-lived Iranian nationalization of 1951 presented a temporary challenge to the majors' authority, by 1954 the majors had almost total control over the oil produced in Iran, Iraq, Kuwait, and Saudi Arabia. As a consequence, the majors held enormous power over the political and economic destinies of these countries. However, this control was being tested by new forces, including the entry of newcomers offering better terms to host governments, the reentry of Soviet oil into the world market, and the emergence in producing countries of oil technocrats who questioned some of the operational principles and practices of the oil companies.

In the United States an oil-import quota system was introduced in 1957 on a voluntary basis and was made mandatory in 1959 to preserve the American output control system (prorationing) and to ensure that domestic prices were kept above foreign crude prices. But the U.S. import quota system forced the newcomers to sell their low-cost oil—developed for their refineries in the U.S. in the first place—at less than the majors' posted prices. This, in turn led the majors to reduce posted prices from $2.08 per barrel to $1.90 in February 1959 and again to $1.80 in August 1960. These unilateral reductions had the effect of reducing the per-barrel revenue from 82¢ to 75¢, or a drop of 9 percent. The August 1960 price cut, as mentioned in chapter 1 prompted the creation of OPEC the following month.[2]

But although the pricing issue instigated OPEC's formation, and successive OPEC conferences adopted resolutions calling for the restoration of prices to their pre-August 1960 level, OPEC's achievement in this vitally important area was dismal, and by 1963 OPEC itself shelved the issue. Instead, OPEC concentrated on the issue of royalty expensing. Briefly put, royalty under the concession agreements was fixed at 12.5 percent of the posted price of crude oil and was credited by the companies against their income tax liability to the producing countries. Thus, under the fifty-fifty profit-sharing system, a company's tax liability would be one-half the posted price minus production cost, less royalty. Royalty expensing, on the other hand, would change a company's tax liability to one-half the posted price minus cost, including royalty. Thus, the expensing of the royalty would increase company tax liability and government revenue by an amount equal to one-half of the royalty.[3]

The agreement on the expensing of royalty, plus the abandonment of the price issue, left OPEC with no issue to test its collective bargaining power until 1971, when the Tehran price agreement was negotiated by OPEC and the oil companies operating in member countries.[4]

The Tehran Agreement, and the other agreements it generated, represent a landmark in OPEC's history and in the evolution of its pricing behavior. Because of its importance the Tehran Agreement is dealt with in some detail in the following section.

COMPANIES, GOVERNMENTS, AND THE TEHRAN PRICE AGREEMENT

The home governments of the majors have always played a role in securing privileged positions for their companies in oil-producing countries. The history of the struggle to control Iraq's oil in the early part of this century is a case in point.[5] And as late as 1952 when the U.S. Department of Justice attempted to prosecute major oil companies for their violation of antitrust laws, the U.S. State Department intervened on behalf of the companies on the grounds that "the institution of these proceedings against the company cartel would not help the achievement of the foreign policy aims of the United States in the Middle East and has the possibility of seriously impairing their attainment" (quoted in U.S. Congress, Senate Committee on Foreign Relations 1974, 5).

In the earlier-mentioned *MNC* report, which assessed the relationship between the U.S. foreign policy and the major oil companies it was noted that the system of oil allocation—between oil-producing countries—was administered by the multinational oil corporations with the assistance of the U.S. government. The system was premised on two assumptions: (1) that the companies were instruments of U.S. foreign policy and (2) that the interests of the companies were basically identical with the U.S. national interests. The report identifies U.S. foreign policy objectives as: (1) the provision of a steady oil supply to Europe and Japan at reasonable prices for post–World War II reconstruction and sustained economic growth, (2) that stable governments be maintained in pro-Western oil-producing countries, and (3) that American multinational oil corporations be a dominant force in world oil trade. The report further states that these three policy goals were largely attained during the 1950s and 1960s (*MNC* report, 2). Given that the companies were instruments of U.S. foreign policy, it was not only logical but imperative that oil would become an instrument of economic policy for the oil-producing countries. But before oil could be used as a catalyst for economic change, these countries had to have control over this resource—in other words, they had to have the ability, individually or collectively, to determine the level of output and prices. Thus, the attainment of economic sovereignty over oil became crucial if these countries were to develop and diversify their economies which, to this point, had remained nearsightedly dependent on one depletable resource.

An initial attempt at gaining some control over the determination of output and prices was made in 1970 when the Libyan government ordered a series of output cutbacks for conservation purposes. This was followed by a negotiated price agreement that raised prices and tax rates. These two measures were the first successful attempts by a government of an oil-producing country to assert its sovereignty over this vital economic resource since the Iranian nationalization twenty years earlier.

The Libyan success seemed to trigger a number of irreversible developments that hastened the transfer of economic control from the companies to the governments. First, in order to avoid a repetition of the Libyan experience, the companies decided on their own initiative to raise prices and tax rates for other countries before resorting to negotiations. Second, the Libyan experience proved that, in the presence of certain market conditions and the appropriate combination of economic variables, negotiations with oil companies could be conducted according to a well-defined timetable, rather than have them be protracted over several years, as was the habit of the oil companies. Third, like any oligopoly, the Libyan government found it easier to target for negotiations the smaller oligopolist (oil company) and the one that was dependent on Libyan oil. Once their ranks were broken, the larger oligopolists had no choice but to follow suit and agree to the same terms. Fourth, and most importantly, OPEC-member countries found it possible to reach an agreement among themselves on a group of demands to be negotiated collectively with the oil companies.

The stage was set for the celebrated Tehran negotiations. These negotiations which were OPEC's first major experiment in collective bargaining, also marked the first time that the oil companies agreed to negotiate with OPEC as an intergovernmental organization in an effort to modify concession agreements and raise prices. The joint strategy that was adopted by the companies was encouraged in the U.S. by the State Department and facilitated by the Department of Justice's issuance of a Business Review letter that provided the companies with antitrust clearance. The negotiations between OPEC and the oil companies culminated in the Tehran Agreement of February 1971, but not before a special OPEC conference had threatened to legislate the terms of the proposed agreement and to impose an embargo on companies that refused to comply with the legislation. The financial terms of the five-year agreement provided for: (1) a stabilization of the income tax rate at a rate of 55 percent; (2) a uniform increase of 33¢ per barrel in the posted prices of crude oils exported from Gulf terminals; (3) another uniform increase of 2¢ per barrel for freight disparity; (4) further uniform increases of 5¢ per barrel effective June 1, 1971, and on January 1 of 1973, 1974, and 1975; (5) an increase of 2.5 percent in posted prices effective June 1, 1971, and on January 1 of 1973, 1974, and

1975; (6) elimination of existing OPEC allowances; and (7) adoption of a new system for the adjustment of gravity differentials. In terms of government revenue, these terms amounted to a gain of 30¢ per barrel in 1971, rising by another 20¢ per barrel in 1975.[6]

It should be noted that the Tehran Agreement covered oil exports from Gulf terminals only. Exports from Mediterranean terminals in Iraq, Saudi Arabia, and Libya were subject to another round of negotiations that were concluded in April in the case of Libya and in June in the case of Saudi Arabia and Iraq. Algeria and Venezuela chose to legislate their own price changes, while Indonesia followed its own path outside the framework of the Tehran Agreement. The Tehran Agreement paved the way for these other negotiations. But as soon as the Tehran and other price agreements were concluded, negotiators had to deal with oil prices again in light of the international monetary crisis that culminated in the collapse of the international monetary system and the end of the convertibility of the dollar into gold.

The de facto devaluation of the dollar prompted OPEC to ask for an upward adjustment in crude-oil prices to compensate for loss in the dollar's purchasing power vis-à-vis other major currencies. An agreement, Geneva I, was reached, according to which these prices were raised by 8.5 percent to reflect the official devaluation of the dollar in terms of gold. The devaluation of the dollar, in turn, was undertaken within the context of realignment of a number of currencies under the provisions of the Smithsonian Agreement of December 1971.

The force of the provisions of the Smithsonian Agreement proved short-lived, however. In February 1973 the United States devalued the dollar once again by 10 percent in terms of gold (the official gold price was raised from $38.00 per ounce to $42.22 per ounce). Once again another set of negotiations was launched, resulting in another agreement, Geneva II, which adjusted OPEC crude-oil prices upward to reflect the dollar's second devaluation (OPEC 1973a, 1975). Several points can be made with respect to the impact of collective bargaining in the Tehran Agreement and the other agreements that soon followed.

First, the entire experience supports the contention that OPEC's collective successes tended to stem from individual member-countries' successes. The Libyan success in raising crude-oil prices and tax rates made it inevitable that other countries would receive similar fiscal treatment. The vehicle of collective negotiations proved to be the easiest and safest way to ensure that all countries would receive similar fiscal benefits. In other words, from the viewpoint of the oil companies, individual country negotiations might have resulted in spiraling and escalating rounds of new fiscal demands that would have had to be constantly negotiated.

In addition to emphasizing the value of collective negotiations, the 1971 agreements had other implications for OPEC pricing behavior in subsequent years. For instance, the agreements introduced the principle of compensation for dollar depreciation and devaluation, a principle invoked by OPEC in the late 1970s. The agreements also initiated the principle of compensation for inflation. Although the rate of compensation was relatively modest and was not related to any price index, it nevertheless served to recognize the relevence of oil-revenue purchasing power in real terms. Again this principle was to assume some importance in policy formulation by OPEC at a later date.

It is curious that the central question of how crude-oil prices were arrived at by the negotiators was unanswered in the Tehran Agreement. What, then, was the rationale for the 33¢ per-barrel increase? In the early stages of the bargaining, the OPEC negotiators did actually have a rationale for demanding a price increase. Their position was that crude prices should reflect the rise in product prices in the main consuming countries; in other words the increase in product prices, reflecting changing conditions of demand, should in turn be reflected in higher prices of crude oil. In the absence of such an increase the notional profit split between the companies and the host governments would change in favor of the former. This last point deserves elaboration.

Under the fifty-fifty profit-sharing system, the governments, as stated earlier, were to receive one-half of the difference between production cost and posted prices. Implied in this "partnership" was the stability of product prices. Since the demand for crude oil is derived demand, its price has to reflect the prices of the refined products. This was essentially the argument used as the rationale for the price reductions of 1959 and 1960. What the OPEC negotiators wanted in the early rounds of the negotiations was a catch-up increase in crude-oil prices that would reflect these changes in demand conditions. To support this position they maintained that such an increment in crude prices should not be passed on to the consumers, because the prices had already been raised to them. The rationale of linking crude prices to product prices was abandoned by OPEC early in the talks. But once this rationale was discarded, OPEC had no other rationale to replace it. Hence, haggling had to be viewed as the central determinant in the negotiations.

Although the negotiating parties may not have realized it, the Tehran Agreement was the outcome of negotiations between two oligopolies attempting to maximize benefits or minimize cost. This pattern of bilateral negotiations was repeated in the two years following to adjust posted prices upward to reflect the depreciated value of the dollar, the currency in which crude oil is priced and government revenue is computed. The Tehran Agreement was not a long-lasting accord because its provisions could not withstand the ensuing significant changes in the international oil industry and the world economy. These changes, which had been gathering force for some time, anticipated the 1973 oil-price revolution.

THE PRICE REVOLUTION OF 1973

The average annual growth rate of energy consumption had, up to 1973, been higher than that of the consuming countries' gross national products (5.1 percent versus 4.7 percent for the period 1965–73), and the growth rate of oil was much higher than that of other energy sources (7.7 percent versus 3.2 percent for the same period) (Exxon 1977; 1980). It is clear from these growth rates that oil was used not only to satisfy the expanding world energy demand but to displace other forms of energy—mainly coal—and as nonenergy input. It is important to note that between 1957 and 1970 government per-barrel revenue in the Middle East stood at 86¢. During the same period, however, prices of overall exports increased by 22 percent in the United States, by 14 percent in Canada, 17 percent in the United Kingdom, 14 percent in France, 21 percent in Germany, 7 percent in Italy, and 4 percent in Japan. Thus, while these countries' oil-import prices declined in real terms, OPEC-member prices of imported goods from these countries rose substantially.

The extent of the decline can be seen in an index compiled by *Petroleum Intelligence Weekly*. According to this index—which took into consideration changes in currency values in relation to the U.S. dollar—the landed price of oil was much lower in Germany, Italy, the Netherlands, and Japan in 1970 than it was in 1957. And in terms of dollars, the selling price of Middle East oil underwent a long and sustained decline of 32 percent from 1957 to 1970. Even with subsequent tax-price increases (due to the Tehran and related agreements), the 1972 Middle East oil prices were as much as 20 percent below the 1957 level in terms of most consuming countries' own currency outlays.[7] Given these relationships and the high rate of return on investment in the oil industry, one is compelled to conclude that there has been a sustained and massive transfer of wealth from the oil-producing countries to the developed countries, owing to the structure of the international oil industry and the international economy. The net effect of these institutional arrangements was to force these countries to pay higher prices for goods whose production was greatly helped by the constantly declining price of oil.

In conjunction with the forces that led to an increase not only in demand for OPEC oil but of OPEC's share in oil trade and in consumption there was a new awareness on the part of producing countries that certain measures to limit output for the purpose of conservation were necessary. Libya in 1970 and Kuwait in 1972 decided that in the long-term interest of their economies, oil output should be stabilized or even reduced. But such conservation measures tended to tax the production capacities of other producing countries. Nor was this situation helped when Iraq nationalized the Iraq Petroleum Company in 1972. Libya's conservation measures were especially important for the emerging supply/demand imbalance that was caused by the increase in the demand for Libyan oil, whose particularly high quality made it more desirable by the industrialized countries that had become increasingly concerned about the quality of the environment.

The supply/demand picture that was emerging, in which a buyer's market was becoming a seller's market, seemed at the time to be permanent rather than transitory. In addition to these market forces, OPEC-member countries were closely observing the spiraling world-wide inflation that had the effect of eroding the per-barrel income from oil.

As these forces of change were unfolding, a number of oil-producing countries began to question in rapid succession the wisdom of having locked crude-oil prices into a five-year agreement with the oil companies. It was not long before the belief prevailed among member countries that crude-oil prices should be raised.

The question before member countries in 1973 was whether prices should be set unilaterally by OPEC—a practice that had been in effect in Venezuela, Indonesia, and Algeria—or whether a negotiated revision of the Tehran Agreement should be undertaken. The members decided to negotiate and to try to gain acceptance for a rise in posted prices by $2.00 per barrel over the $3.11 per barrel as of October 1, 1973. The new posted price of about $5.00 per barrel was arrived at by simply adding to the prevailing posted price an amount equal to the increase in company profit per barrel between 1970–71 and September 1973, which OPEC had estimated to be $2.20 per barrel.[8] The suspension of negotiations, on October 11, 1973, prompted OPEC governments on October 16 to unilaterally raise posted prices by $2.00 per barrel (see table 1). The next day, Arab oil producers decided to reduce output and impose an embargo on oil exports to the United States and the Netherlands, in retaliation for their support of Israel during the October War. The cutback measures reduced the November output of Arab countries by some 20 percent from the September output and created a shortage that forced market prices to skyrocket. As a result, the Nigerian government was able to sell its royalty oil at $20.00 a barrel and the National Iranian Oil Company sold its oil in the open market at $17.00 a barrel when the posted price of the same oil was $5.00 a barrel. This change in supply conditions encouraged the Iranian government to lead a drive at OPEC's December 1973 meeting to raise the posted price to $11.65 per barrel, thereby providing $7.00 of per-barrel revenue for the government.[9]

By January 1, 1974, the situation was such that the government revenue take on the Saudi Arabian Light marker crude (34° gravity) oil was set at $7.00 per barrel. Given a royalty rate of 12.5 percent and an income tax rate of 55 percent, the posted price for the market crude was set at $11.65 per barrel (table 1). The cost to the companies equaled the government take plus production cost, or a total of $7.10 per barrel (assuming a production of 10¢ per barrel). Then, effective January 1, 1974, the Kuwaiti government reached a new participation agreement with the oil companies that raised its equity share in the oil concession to 60 percent.

According to this new agreement, the tax-paid cost on the companies' 40 percent share of the oil (equity oil) was the $7.10 per barrel mentioned earlier, but on the oil the companies exported in excess of their 40 percent equity share the companies were to pay 94 percent of the posted price ($10.96 per barrel buy-back price). The buy-back price was the price to be charged by Kuwait to third parties.

The Kuwaiti model, which was followed by the other producing countries in the Gulf, created an interesting anomaly in the market: it enabled the majors to undercut government sales to third parties, since the cost of the equity oil to the majors was about $4.00 per barrel less than the price at which governments were willing to sell their participation crude. This situation was clearly untenable. In order to correct it, a series of actions were undertaken to eliminate the gap between the prices of participation oil and equity oil. These actions culminated in an increase in the royalty rate from 12.5 percent to 20 percent and an increase in the income tax rate from 55 percent to 85 percent—accompanied by a reduction of 40¢ per barrel in posted prices, a reduction in the buy-back price to 93 percent, and a freeze on prices for the first nine months of 1975. Thus, by January 1, 1975, the relationships were as follows: the posted price was $11.25; the buy-back price was $10.45; the average government take was $10.12; and average tax-paid cost was $10.25, giving the majors an advantage of 21¢ per barrel over competitors. Posted prices remained at these levels until October 1, 1975, when they were raised by 10 percent and again frozen at those levels until January 1, 1977, when the new two-tier price system was created. The two-tier price system lasted for only six months, at which time OPEC-member countries agreed on a price reunification. The system proved, however, to be the forerunner of a variety of price combinations ranging from a multitier price system to the absence of any system. These varied pricing systems are dealt with in the following section.

Table 1. Evolution of Crude-Oil Posted or Tax-Reference Prices
and Official Selling Prices for Arabian Light 34° at
Ras Tanura, Saudi Arabia, 1948–82 (U.S. Dollars per Barrel)

Year and Month	Posted or Tax-Reference Prices	Official Selling Prices
1948 April	2.18	—[a]
July	2.03	—
1949 April	1.84	—
October	1.71	—
1953 February	1.93	—
1957 June	2.08	—
1959 February	1.90	—
1960 August	1.80	—
1971 February	2.18	—
June	2.29	—
1972 January	2.48	—
1973 January	2.60	—
April	2.74	—
June	2.90	—
July	2.96	—
August	3.07	—
October 1	3.01	—
October 16	5.12	—
November 1	5.18	—
December 1	5.04	—

TWO-TIER AND MULTI-TIER PRICING

The October/December 1973 price increases were set in the midst of rapidly changing economic and political conditions that helped OPEC countries appropriate the power to establish prices. In order to systematize postings, the oil-producing countries selected Arabian Light crude (34° gravity) as the benchmark for all other posted prices in the Gulf region. Once the price of the marker (or the base) crude was set, other posted prices were determined according to the oil's gravity, sulfur content, and geographical location (these three elements are known as the OPEC differentials).

The decision to assume control over prices meant that OPEC would have to devise a rationale for its decisions to change prices in spite of the built-in forces of conflict among member nations. The difficulty involved in arriving at a con-

Table 1. *Continued*

Year and Month	Posted or Tax-Reference Prices	Official Selling Prices
1974 January	11.65	—
November	11.25	10.46
1975 October	12.38	11.51
1977 January	13.00	12.09
July	13.67	12.70
1979 January	14.34	13.34
April	15.46	14.55
June	19.36	18.00
November	25.81	24.00
1980 January	27.96	26.00
April	30.11	28.00
August	32.26	30.00
November	34.41	32.00
1981 January	34.41	32.00
1982 January	34.00	34.00

Sources: OPEC, *Annual Statistical Bulletin*, 1980, pp. 135–37; U.N. Economic Commission for Europe, *The Price of Oil in Western Europe*; Neil H. Jacoby, *Multinational Oil* (New York: Macmillan Co., 1974).
Note: Posted price for Arabian Light has been used by OPEC-member countries as the benchmark price for the crude-oil price structure. The official selling price charged by any member country—including Saudi Arabia—may or may not coincide with the benchmark price.
ªDash denotes no official or government selling prices.

sistent and generally satisfactory rationale is evidenced by the fact that the arguments for price setting have changed considerably over the years.

The first price change of October 1973 was rationalized by the fact that the market prices were higher than posted prices. In order to restore the market-posted price relationship that prevailed at the time of the Tehran Agreement, posted prices were raised above market prices by 40 percent.

The December 1973 price increase was similarly rationalized on the basis of market prices, but this time OPEC decided to fix the exporting governments' per-barrel revenue before determining the posted price needed to yield that particular revenue given the prevailing royalty and tax rates. Fixing government revenue first to arrive at posted prices meant the abandonment of the 1.4/1.0 ratio between posted prices and market prices.[10] As these changes demonstrate, OPEC was groping for a generally acceptable pricing policy when it acquired control over its oil.

In June 1974 the first serious split among member countries occurred. Continued worldwide inflation had prompted most of the OPEC countries to advocate an upward revision of posted prices to protect the purchasing power of government revenue, but Saudi Arabia argued that the January 1, 1974, price hike had been made possible by politically motivated production cutbacks and that the continuation of such prices tended to undermine the economies of the industrial and developing countries. Furthermore, the Saudis threatened that if other member countries carried out the proposed increases both in posted prices (from $11.65 to $12.67 per barrel of the marker crude) and in taxes (from 55 percent to 87 percent), the Saudi government would unilaterally reduce prices and back up this move by immediately putting an extra three million barrels a day of exports on the market. Had the price and tax proposals been adopted, the net effect would have been to raise OPEC-member-governments' revenue and the cost of oil by $4.00 per barrel.[11] Rather than adopting such an increase, OPEC agreed to raise the royalty rate by 2 percent (from 12.5 percent), yielding an increment in revenue of 10¢ a barrel. The influence of Saudi Arabia in oil price negotiations was clearly felt by other member countries; Saudi Arabia not only forced them to abandon the proposed increases, but it chose to disassociate itself from the 2 percent increase in royalty rate.

It will be recalled that OPEC had already abandoned the relationship between posted and market prices as a policy guide for setting posted prices. OPEC instead adopted the method of fixing government per-barrel revenue ($7.00 as of January 1, 1974), then setting posted prices at the levels required to yield that revenue. Then, in 1974, the adoption of participation agreements created a situation in which the same oil was sold at different prices, thereby raising the weighted average revenue to $9.32 per barrel.

OPEC's inability to raise prices in the first three quarters of 1974 was mitigated by the 10¢ per-barrel increase in revenue (to $9.42), made effective as of July 1. Although posted prices remained frozen for the balance of 1974, the OPEC countries (except Saudi Arabia) decided that for the fourth quarter of that year the weighted average of government take (revenue from equity oil and participation oil) would be increased by 3.5 percent (amounting to 33¢ per barrel, or from $9.42 to $9.74 per barrel) to compensate for inflation in the industrialized countries. This increase was implemented by raising the royalty rate to 16.67 percent (from 14.5 percent in the companies' equity oil (40 percent of production) and by increasing the tax rate from 55 percent to 65.75 percent.[12] These two increments raised government take (and company tax-paid cost) on equity oil by $1.15 per barrel (from $7.11 to $8.26), but the weighted average increase of both government take and company cost was raised by 33¢ per barrel.

As mentioned earlier in this chapter, the participation agreements created a situation in which the majors enjoyed a significant advantage over their competitors, who were mainly the oil-producing countries' national oil companies. This situation arose because the national oil companies had to sell their participation oil at a price set at 93 percent of the posted prices. The majors, on the other hand, had the advantage of averaging their cost, because they had to pay $7.00 per barrel in royalty and taxes on 40 percent of their output (in other words, equity oil) and 93 percent of the posted price on what they bought back of the participation oil from the government—the "buy-back" price. The weighted average of the tax-paid cost for the majors was $9.52 per barrel, compared to a buy-back price of $11.05 per barrel. To close this loophole and to reduce excessive company profits, OPEC adopted certain measures that lowered the posted price to $11.25 (from $11.65 per barrel) and raised both the tax rate to 85 percent and royalty to 20 percent on equity crude. The net effect of these measures, which became effective on January 1, 1975, was to raise the average take of governments to $10.12 per barrel (from $9.75) and to provide competitive relief to independent oil companies. These decisions were accompanied by another decision to freeze posted prices through September 1975.[13]

This $10.12 per-barrel government take had four features: (1) it provided a single pricing system for OPEC, since Saudi Arabia was one of the formulators of this system; (2) it provided relief to the nonmajors by limiting the majors' margin to 22¢ per barrel ($10.12 minus the $9.80 government take on equity oil); (3) it assumed a production cost of 10¢ per barrel; and (4) it contained no agreement among member countries on market prices, that is, direct sales. This final point was especially important for Saudi Arabia, which refused to commit itself not to make direct sales at prices below the buy-back price.[14] It is essential to note that the $10.12 government-revenue-plus-production cost became the actual price of oil, replacing posted prices for all practical purposes.

Although OPEC had already decided to freeze prices through September 1975, it was clear that this position was far from stable. OPEC reaffirmed its price decision in June of 1975 but warned that, in view of increasing inflation, the depreciation of the dollar, and the consequent erosion of the real value of the oil revenues of member countries, it had decided to readjust its crude prices as of October 1, 1975.[15]

In September of the same year OPEC decided to raise the price of the marker crude by 10 percent, to $11.51 per barrel (from $10.46). Although most member countries were in favor of an even-higher price, the influence of Saudi Arabia once again limited the increase. Because it was of the opinion that a price rise was unnecessary in view of the apparent excess capacity and the worldwide economic recession, the Saudi oil minister Ahmad Z. Yamani threatened that if

OPEC were to raise prices by 15 percent or 20 percent, his government would leave its own prices frozen and would let its output rise to the limit of its capacity.[16]

The readoption of the new marker price of $11.51 per barrel signaled yet another change in OPEC's pricing behavior, in that the earlier practice of using the average government take as the operative price figure for computing the marker crude posted price had been discarded. It should be noted, as well, that the same OPEC resolution that increased prices by 10 percent also froze the new price through June 1976.[17]

The price increase of 1975 came at a time of reduced demand for oil because of the severe economic recession in industrial countries. This reduced demand led, in turn, to an absolute decline in OPEC crude-oil output, from 30.8 million barrels per day (MBD) in 1974 to 27.2 MBD in 1975, the first major slowdown in oil output since OPEC's formation. Since there was no system or mechanism to allocate the reduction, its impact tended to be distributed unevenly among the member countries. While 90 percent of the decline in output was absorbed by Saudi Arabia, Iran, Venezuela, and Nigeria, Iraq, on the other hand, was able to register a close to 20 percent increase in its output.[18] In the face of declining demand and in the absence of joint production control, it was inevitable that certain countries found themselves reducing their selling prices relative to the price of the marker crude in order to protect their shares of the market.[19]

In June of 1976, having awaited the results of the Conference on International Economic Cooperation, the majority of OPEC countries opted once again for an upward revision of the price of the marker crude, which had been fixed in September 1975 at $11.51 per barrel. They based their argument for a 20 percent price increase on the inflation-caused erosion in purchasing power of the oil dollar. OPEC's own studies at the time revealed that the prices of goods imported by the OPEC countries increased by 20 percent between October 1, 1975, and June 30, 1976. Once again, however, the Saudi government insisted that no increase was necessary, and backed its argument by a threat. The argument was that a price increase would serve to slow down economic recovery in industrial countries and that stable prices in the face of rising demand for oil would discourage member countries from resorting to price and nonprice competition. Moreover, stable prices were considered by the Saudis as a means of restoring cohesion to OPEC so that it would be in a stronger position to take the initiative in world economic forums. In the end, the Saudi threat—that it would refuse to go along with any price increase, therefore forcing OPEC to find a new marker crude to replace Arabian Light—caused the majority of OPEC members to abandon their position and agree to freeze prices for the remainder of 1976. Had the Saudis been forced to follow through with their threat, the net effect of such a move would have been the collapse of the OPEC pricing system, since Arabian Light was (and is) the largest-volume crude moving in world trade.[20] Thus, the powerful influence of Saudi Arabia was once again used to force a price freeze on other governments, who reluctantly acquiesced in order to preserve the unity of OPEC.

Nevertheless, public criticism of the Saudi position on prices by other members of OPEC reflected an inherent conflict of political and economic interests among the diverse nations constituting OPEC.[21] Although OPEC was and continues to be a useful instrument for limiting price competition, it should always be remembered that individual members have at different times resorted to the concept of sovereignty and/or national interest to justify their independent behavior in the face of the declared OPEC policy. For example, the Saudi government has always rejected the idea of having its oil prices set by other OPEC countries. It has also maintained that other countries such as Iraq and Libya demonstrated independence from OPEC pricing policy by cutting their prices, thereby damaging the interests of Saudi Arabia.[22] The Saudis' claim was based on the evident decline in the oil output both of OPEC between 1974 and 1975 (by 11.5 percent) and of Saudi Arabia (by 16.5 percent, as contrasted to Iraq's output, which actually increased (by 17 percent).

The oil-price conflict found its clearest expression in the OPEC meeting of December 1976, when member countries failed to agree on a uniform price increase to be effective January 1, 1977. Discord resulted from Saudi Arabia's continuing stance that prices be kept frozen at the October 1975 level. Opponents of this position cited continued rising import prices as a strong argument in favor of raising oil prices.[23]

In the end, the question before OPEC was not whether prices should be increased but rather by how much. At one end of the spectrum Iraq supported an upward price adjustment to compensate for the loss in purchasing power of oil revenue that had been sustained by producing countries since the October 1973 price increase. According to the Iraqi government, the loss amounted to about 40 percent. (More recently, since the time of the last price increase of October 1975, OPEC's own Economic Commission Board has estimated that the rate of imported inflation for OPEC countries from October 1975 to December 1976 was 26 percent.) At the other end of the spectrum, the Saudi government contended that a sharp increase in the price of oil was unwarranted because it could harm the economic recovery of the industrial countries.[24] As to the rate of inflation, the Saudi government asserted that according to International Monetary Fund (IMF) data, the rise in the index of the industrial countries' export prices from October 1975 to December 1976 was only between 4 percent and 8 percent (depending on the currency used for calculation). The variance between the estimates of OPEC and the IMF is attributed by OPEC to the fact that the IMF indices are predominantly a function of inter-OECD trade, thus suggesting a high degree of price discrimination against OPEC countries. Another explanation is that OPEC indices of import inflation are based on price statistics as supplied by each member country, as opposed to the more generalized export price indices published by the IMF.

These differing assessments were manifested in the various price increase proposals, which ranged from 26 percent (proposed by Iraq) to a freeze (proposed by Saudi Arabia). Most member countries advocated increases of 10 percent or 15 percent. Although the Saudi position did not prevail this time (only one country, the United Arab Emirates, supported the Saudis), OPEC was unable to reach agreement on a uniform price increase. Instead, both Saudi Arabia and the United Arab Emirates decided to increase their price by 5 percent for the year 1977, while the remaining eleven members opted for a price rise of 10 percent for the first half of 1977 and another 5 percent for the second half of the year. Consequently, for the first time since pricing of crude oil became one of OPEC's functions, a two-tier pricing system was officially introduced. The two-tier system meant that for the eleven countries the price of theoretical Arabian Light marker crude was to be raised from $11.51 per barrel to $12.70 per barrel on January 1, 1977, and then to $13.30 per barrel on July 1, 1977. For Saudi Arabia and the United Arab Emirates the price of the same Arabian Light was set at $12.09 per barrel for the whole year. The gap between the upper tier and the lower tier amounted to 61¢ a barrel during the first half of 1977 and $1.21 per barrel during the second half. In an attempt to make its price prevail and force a downward adjustment by other countries, the Saudi government decided to lift the ceiling of 8.5 MBD on its output; however, a majority of OPEC members were willing to reduce their own production in order to counteract the Saudi decision and to maintain the 10 percent price increase.[25]

Although the Saudi pricing decision was backed by a decision to expand output, one should not overlook a number of limits that continue to be imposed on the freedom of that government. First, although Saudi Arabia has remained the largest oil-producing country, its share of OPEC's total output was less than one-third at that time. Second, other OPEC members made it clear that any significant increase in the Saudi output would be construed as an act of aggression against OPEC. Third, the world demand was such that all OPEC oil was needed (even though oil buyers gravitate first toward the lower-priced oil, then move on to the higher-priced oil to meet their needs, the lower-priced Saudi oil did not constitute a true threat to other OPEC members). Fourth, there were certain markets where, at that price differential, the Saudi oil could not displace the higher-priced oil because of quality and/or geographical location; this was especially true for the African crude oils. Fifth, the Saudi government has always been of the opinion that the preservation and survival of OPEC is of utmost importance for its own political and economic interest, particularly because the International Energy Agency was perceived by Saudi Arabia as an instrument of confrontation to break up OPEC.[26] Sixth, given the nature of Arab politics, other OPEC members doubted that the Saudis would use their oil "weapon" to damage the interest of other Arab countries. This point was underlined by the Iraqi oil minister, Tayeh Abdul-Karim, when he said: "We believe that Saudi Arabia will not be able to maintain an isolated stand on prices and production. Oil and energy are hot issues in the Arab world, and Arab public opinion will not allow any one Arab oil-producing country to undermine the price structure and violate OPEC solidarity."[27] Seventh, the severe weather conditions during the 1976–77 winter led to a surge in product prices, enabling refiners to outpace the 5 percent Saudi Arabian crude price hike and, in many cases, even the 10 percent boosts of the OPEC majority.[28] As a result, the upper-tier price countries outside the Middle East—except for Ecuador—registered an increase in output over that of the fourth quarter of 1976 and even a higher increase over the first quarter of 1976. The upper-tier price countries in the Middle East registered sizable reductions in their output relative to the 1976 fourth quarter, but—except for Kuwait and Qatar—showed major increases in production relative to that of the first quarter of 1976. The lower-tier price countries—Saudi Arabia and United Arab Emirates—were able to increase their output by less than 1 percent over the 1976 fourth quarter, although they had made substantial gains over the first quarter of 1976.[29] It should be noted in this connection that in the first quarter of 1977 OPEC registered a decline in output from the previous quarter of 6.5 percent (10.3 percent in the Middle East), but showed an increase of 11.6 percent over the first quarter of 1976. The decline in the early part of 1977 was caused by the downturn in the high stocks that had been accumulated during the latter part of 1976 in anticipation of the year-end price increase.[30] Eighth, all the major oil companies operating in the low-tier price countries had (and have) interests in other OPEC countries, a factor that had the effect of restraining these companies from giving an overwhelming preference to the lower-priced oil.[31] A related point is that the Saudi position tended to favor the American majors (which lift about 80 percent of that country's oil) as well as the United States, for which Saudi Arabia is a major supplier. Japan and Western Europe are more dependent on the other OPEC countries for their oil. Such divergence is bound to influence the behavior of the oil companies in attempting to lessen price discrimination and thus also reduce the instability of the two-tier price system. Ninth, member countries realized that their power to set prices might be eroded if they allowed the two-tier price to continue for an extended time period. This awareness explains the attempts, initiated soon after the introduction of the two-tier system, to narrow the gap between the two prices in order to restore both a unified price system and the unity of OPEC itself.[32]

As stated earlier, the two-tier system proved to be a temporary solution. In July 1977, Saudi Arabia and the United Arab Emirates agreed to increase the price of the marker crude (Arabian Light) by 5 percent, thus bringing the price into parity with other member countries. This joint action was taken in response to the decision of the majority not to implement their resolution of December 1976 that posted prices be raised by 5 percent effective July 1, 1977.[33]

The reinstated unity among member countries continued until the December 1977 OPEC Conference, when the question of a price readjustment was again considered; however, again, member countries were unable to reach a consensus. The lack of agreement meant a de facto price freeze for 1978, an outcome the Saudi government had been determined to achieve.[34]

The ability of Saudi Arabia to maintain its price leadership soon had to yield, however, owing to changes brought about by the Iranian Revolution. The impact of the Iranian Revolution on OPEC's pricing behavior is dealt with in the section following.

THE IRANIAN REVOLUTION
AND THE SECOND PRICE SHOCK

The restored price unity of 1977 brought with it the recognition that Saudi Arabia had assumed the price leadership role in OPEC. This leadership implied two things. First, the government of Saudi Arabia could, if it wished, expand output to maintain price stability. In other words what OPEC had failed to do (that is, achieve management of output, precisely because of the Saudi refusal to sanction such a scheme) was carried out by Saudi Arabia on its own terms. On this point Saudi Arabia remained faithful to its long-standing position that output level is determined by its government alone. Second, the Saudi government believed that given the dependency of the oil-producing countries on demand conditions in the industrialized countries, OPEC should follow a policy of price stability and price predictability; in other words, OPEC should fine tune its price structure so as to be sensitive not only to current economic conditions in the North (industrialized countries) but also to the long-term implications of higher OPEC prices. Demand elasticity for oil, the Saudis argued, could not be expected to remain low regardless of the price increase. After a certain price level either demand would decline or substitutes would be developed, or both conditions would result.

Having succeeded in restoring a common price, $12.70 per barrel of Arabian

Light in July 1977, OPEC, under the leadership of Saudi Arabia, moved in the direction of price stability. The July 1977 price of $12.70 was allowed to continue throughout 1978. And when OPEC agreed that market conditions would justify an increase in the price of crude oil in 1979, it was decided that this increase should be introduced in four stages to yield an average increase of 10 percent for the year. These increments were to be staggered quarterly as follows: 5 percent in the first quarter; 3.81 percent for the second quarter; 2.30 percent in the third quarter; and 2.70 percent for the last quarter. The projected price by the end of 1979 was to be $14.54, as compared with $12.70 by the end of 1978.[35]

It was hoped by OPEC that this new method of staggered quarterly increases would be a stabilizing influence in a market that had been characterized by great uncertainty. By announcing a year in advance the scheduled price increases, OPEC sought to remove from the oil market much of the anticipatory buying that tended to precede every OPEC price-setting meeting. The success of the new pricing initiative was predicated on the assumption that there would be no major disruption in the supply pattern of crude oil; in other words, it was assumed that all producing countries would maintain their respective shares of the market and that total output in 1979 would be sufficient to meet the projected demand for OPEC oil.

Yet no sooner had 1979 been ushered in than both the international oil industry and OPEC pricing behavior were exposed to a serious shock, the direct result of the Iranian Revolution, which brought to power a new regime under the leadership of Ayatollah Khomeini.

When the Iranian Revolution was pending, an early market effect was the reduction in oil output as a result of strikes by Iranian oil workers. Although output was restored, its level was not allowed to match the average output for the first three quarters of 1978. The magnitude of the reduction in Iranian oil output was reflected in the decline in Iran's share of OPEC's total oil export, from 17 percent in 1977 to 16.3 percent in 1978, to 8.9 percent in 1979, and to 3.4 percent in 1980. Between 1977 and 1980 Iran's total exports of oil and refined products declined from a level of close to 5 MBD in 1977 to less than 1 MBD in 1980. It is within the context of these changing market conditions that OPEC's new pricing method was introduced. Obviously, the removal from the market of 3 MBD to 4 MBD of oil and products represented a major shock to a supply/demand pattern already under strain, and the behavior of the market in the last quarter of 1978 and in the two years succeeding reflected the new conditions. The immediate shortage that gave rise to panic buying and to the expectation that the shortage might persist resulted in the widening of the gap between OPEC official prices and the spot-market prices.

For the years 1975 through 1977 and for the first three quarters of 1978 the gap between these two prices was insignificant, ranging from 4¢ per barrel to

39¢ per barrel. Most of the time the difference was close to the lower end of the range. In the first quarter of 1978 the spot-market price was actually 4¢ below the official price. The two prices coincided in the second quarter. In the third quarter the spot-market price was 9¢ above the official price, but in the fourth quarter the difference had jumped to 80¢ per barrel. From 80¢ per barrel, the difference (or the premium) surged to a level of almost $16 per barrel in the last quarter of 1979.[36]

In addition to the disappearance of a major segment of the Iranian oil from the world oil market, the member countries of the IEA were increasing their purchases of crude oil for their strategic stockpile programs, a situation that intensified the already-heavy demand for crude oil. The fact that the United States was moving toward the last phases of its own crude-oil price deregulation program helped to strengthen the upward pressure on the world price structure.

It is clear from these observations that the new OPEC price initiative was doomed to fail from the moment it became effective in January 1979. The upward pressure on the OPEC price structure and the widening gap between spot-market and official prices underlined the fact that the OPEC price levels could not clear the market. Nor were member countries in a position to expand output fast enough to dampen the high price expectations in the market, although OPEC was able by the end of the year to produce enough oil to offset the loss of Iranian oil to the market. In other words OPEC, having unified prices, found itself unable to administer prices. This loss of price leadership left OPEC with no option but to follow price developments in the spot market and attempt to adjust its prices accordingly. But to follow market trends meant in effect that different OPEC countries would assess the market differently, which meant that there could be no agreement as to what prices could be charged. Thus, in the early months of 1979 the OPEC countries decided that while retaining the official prices, they would be allowed the freedom to impose temporary surcharges and premiums to reflect market conditions. For all intents and purposes, this decision meant that the OPEC official price would be considered a floor price, with the ceiling determined by individual member countries. Thus, OPEC found itself inadvertently introducing a multitier price system for its member countries' crude oil.

OPEC prices, however, continued to lag behind market prices, which meant that member countries were forfeiting substantial profits to other buyers and sellers in the market. In order to close this gap and to restrain the price spiral, OPEC agreed to introduce yet another initiative in the pricing system. This initiative was aimed at accelerating the staggered increases for the year 1979 by bringing them all forward and making them effective for the second quarter of 1979. In others words the $14.54 per-barrel price that was supposed to go into effect on October 1, 1979 was made effective as of April 1, 1979 (Al-Chalabi 1980, 87–90).

The new price, however, did not pick up the slack between the official OPEC price and spot-market prices. The chaotic conditions in the market, as reflected in the wide disparity between official and market prices and in the myriad prices charged by OPEC-member countries, prompted OPEC to reevaluate the price structure, with the result that yet another initiative was introduced. The initiative, which became effective on July 1, 1979, stipulated that member countries would be free to charge any price they deemed necessary provided such a price did not exceed $23.50 per barrel. This was the first time in OPEC's history that a pricing ceiling was introduced that could not be exceeded by a member country's own price. With the introduction of the ceiling, Saudi Arabia charged the lowest price, $18.00 per barrel for its light crude of 34° API (American Petroleum Institute). One of the anomalies of this system was the pricing behavior of various producers with respect to the same quality crude; thus, other countries in the same exporting region as Saudi Arabia were charging $20.00–$21.00 per barrel for the same light crude. This pricing differential between Saudi Arabia and other producing countries allowed buyers of Saudi oil a significant price advantage over their competitors and resulted in wide profit margins for their operations.

Although the $23.50 ceiling was regarded by OPEC-member countries as a step toward another price reunification it, like the two-tier system, proved to be a feeble attempt in the face of market conditions that continued to induce member countries to adjust oil prices upward periodically. It was the African group of OPEC-member countries that decided to exceed the ceiling in the fourth quarter of 1979. Other OPEC countries soon followed suit and upped their prices. Saudi Arabia, however, continued to charge $18.00 per barrel. It was not long before the gap in the price between Saudi Arabian crude and that of the same-quality crude of other countries had widened to $5.50 per barrel, as compared to $2.00 earlier in the year. It was clear to all member countries that such disparities could not be allowed to persist. An attempt to restore price unity was made but without success: Saudi Arabia decided to raise its price from $18.00 to $24.00 per barrel just prior to the December 1979 OPEC pricing conference, but this move seemed to backfire, in that it was construed as confirming the belief that the differential between market and official prices would persist as a reflection of tight market conditions. These divergent assessments of market conditions within OPEC made agreement impossible. The ineffective attempt to exert price leadership by OPEC was thus officially abandoned and each member was to set its own prices. OPEC's failure to agree on a price or a price structure meant, in effect, that member countries elected to call upon the market forces to arbitrate their differences. In other words if the tight market conditions of 1979 carried over into 1980, prices could be expected to continue their upward trend, whereas if market conditions changed in 1980 and demand for oil declined then the upward price trend might be arrested or even reversed.[37]

As stated, the increase in the price of the Arabian Light to $24 per barrel failed to bring stability to the price structure because OPEC-member countries opted to follow the Saudi Arabian example by raising their prices by a similar magnitude. And with this round of price increases, member countries found themselves in the same relative position they had been in prior to the Saudi price increase. The new price increases, which brought the price of Iranian Light to $30 per barrel—or $6 per barrel above the comparable Arabian Light—then prompted the Saudi government in January 1980 to raise its price by another $2, to $26 per barrel (table 1).

It should be noted here that as profit maximizers, member countries may be seen to have acted rationally during that time, so long as they did not concern themselves with the long-run consequences of their actions. And given the widespread perception that market conditions warranted these price changes, it was not surprising that the incentive to stabilize prices was weak.

The perceptions that the market was willing to absorb higher prices was demonstrated again in April 1980, when the Saudis decided to raise Arabian Light by another $2 per barrel, to $28 per barrel. As might have been expected, as soon as this change was announced other countries likewise raised their prices by the same amount. Again, the relative positions of prices remained unchanged.[38]

While OPEC-member countries were elevating their prices, changes in underlying market conditions were occurring that resulted in a narrowing of the gap between official and spot prices, so much so that the gap that had amounted to about $16 per barrel in the fourth quarter of 1979 almost disappeared during the second quarter of 1980. The economic sluggishiness that had begun to make itself felt in the industrialized economies led to a marked decline in the demand for crude oil. On the supply side, the government of Saudi Arabia continued to adhere to its policy of a high level of output even in the face of changing demand conditions. These two forces combined resulted in a substantial decline in the spot-market price for crude oil. The altered demand condition and the relative weakness of the market prompted OPEC-member countries to attempt to narrow the spread in their prices in the hope that some kind of price reunification might accrue. As a step in this direction it was agreed in June 1980 to resurrect the concept of price ceiling. Saudi Arabia would continue (for the time being) to charge $28 for its Arabian Light, while other Gulf producers would charge $32 for the same-quality crude (called Theoretical Marker in order to differentiate it from the Official Marker that has traditionally been Arabian Light). And in order to strengthen its position within OPEC for future price bargaining, Saudi Arabia decided, in spite of the changing demand, to continue to keep its output higher than its traditional ceiling of 8.5 MBD.

In September 1980 another move was made to meet the Saudi demand that prices be reunified around the Official Marker. OPEC-member countries agreed to raise the price of the Official Marker to $30 per barrel, while maintaining the price of the Theoretical Marker at its previous $32 per barrel.[39] This change in the relative position in prices in favor of Saudi Arabia was unaccompanied, however, by a reduction in the Saudi output to its traditional ceiling of 8.5 MBD.

No sooner was this agreement concluded than a major disruption in supply conditions occurred due to the Iraq-Iran war, which erupted in September 1980 and caused the destruction of the major parts of the oil-exporting capacity of these two countries. The change in the supply pattern itself was reflected in the Saudi decision to raise its output to 10 MBD in an attempt to make up for the decline in oil exports from Iraq and Iran. Other countries such as Kuwait, Libya, and the United Arab Emirates, which had reduced output during the year in an effort to absorb some of the decline in demand, found themselves reversing these earlier decisions in the face of the consequences of the Iraq-Iran war. By the end of 1980 it had become obvious that the loss of exports due to the Gulf war was offset by increases from other sources and that prices would not repeat the 1979 spiral that was triggered by the Iranian Revolution.

This unforeseen change in the supply side of the market was evinced by the emergence of another gap between the spot and official price. This induced OPEC to allow member countries to raise prices to reflect the changed supply conditions. Thus, in December of 1980 it was agreed to raise the price of the Official Marker to $32 per barrel, while allowing countries in the Gulf to charge up to $36 per barrel for the Theoretical Marker, with an additional $5 per barrel for the African crudes (table 1).[40]

The adoption of the new system coincided with the realization that the removal from the market of oil exports from Iraq and Iran failed to reverse the downward pressure on prices caused by the decline in demand for oil. This realization and the displacement of other member countries' crude with Saudi oil forced a number of member countries to reexamine the price structure.

The reexamination that took place under conditions of an oil glut in 1981 resulted in a decision to freeze the price structure for the duration of the year. The next step was another reunification of the Official Marker and Theoretical

Marker prices. This was done by allowing the Official Marker price to rise by $2, to $34 per barrel, and by, in turn, reducing the Theoretical Marker price to $34 per barrel.

The preceding review tends to support the contention that OPEC was not in a position to determine crude-oil prices. During the first decade of OPEC's existence, prices were set by the oil companies. For a brief period, 1971–73, prices were set according to the provisions of the Tehran Agreement. When the price-setting power shifted to the governments after 1973, OPEC as an organization continued to be without price-setting prerogatives. Instead, member governments became the primary price setters.

Having surveyed the pricing behavior of crude oil throughout the life of OPEC, the task of the next chapter is to analyze the forces that tended to determine these prices.

CHAPTER 3

Crude-Oil Price Determination before and after the Emergence of OPEC

This chapter analyzes the various forces responsible for the determination of crude-oil prices under the OPEC regime, against the background of post–World War II pricing policies. First, a word of explanation about OPEC price differentials.

OPEC-member countries produce a variety of crude oils with a wide range of quality. To allow for the different qualities, price differential systems were adopted by the oil industry in 1950, with the lighter crude commanding a higher price than the heavier crude. Another source of differential in crude-oil prices is the locational advantage (geographic proximity to consuming countries) of a particular crude. A third source of differential is the sulphur content of the oil: the lower the sulphur content, the higher the price, since the cost of refining tends to be lower for low-sulphur crudes. These quality and locational differences are referred to as OPEC differentials or, simply, differentials. For the purposes of this volume, the convention of using Arabian Light of 34° as the OPEC marker crude is adopted throughout. Under normal conditions, price deviations of other crudes tend to reflect quality and locational advantages (or differentials). The pattern of relations between the price of Arabian Light and other crudes is dealt with fully as the analysis proceeds.

Any discussion of price determination under OPEC is greatly aided by a knowledge of crude-oil price determination in the decades prior to the emergence of OPEC. The first part of the chapter addresses this period.

PRICE DETERMINATION BEFORE OPEC

In December 1950 the first posting of export prices for Middle East oil was made public by oil-exporting companies. This public posting, in the form of a schedule showing price quotations for various crudes exported from the Gulf and Mediterranean terminals, was a new development necessitated by the then-emerging pattern of profit sharing between oil-producing governments and oil companies. The publication of posted prices was significant also in that it was another step toward the ultimate delinking of Middle East prices from the posted prices in the U.S. Gulf of Mexico (U.S. Gulf). In the period before 1950 the prices of Middle East crude oil—both at the source and at delivery—were identical to those in the U.S. Gulf, although the cost of production varied widely. In other words, the cost of oil to the consumer equaled the price of oil at the U.S. Gulf plus the cost of transportation from the U.S. Gulf—regardless of the actual source of supply, the actual cost of production, and the actual cost of transportation.

This U.S. Gulf pricing formula, which remained in effect until 1941, inevitably resulted in price discrimination in favor of or against various buyers, depending on the distances of points of delivery in relation to points of supply. If the consumer, for instance, were located close to the basing point, that is, U.S. Gulf, the consumer would not be discriminated against since he paid the prevailing price plus actual freight cost. If the consumer, however, were located outside the basing point region and in another oil-producing region, say the Middle East, then this consumer would be discriminated against by an amount equal to the difference in the transportation charges between the U.S. Gulf and the exporting point in the Middle East, not to mention the cost of production differentials.

The oil consumer in, for example, Iraq is a good case in point. According to the provisions of a 1931 agreement between the Iraqi government and the oil companies, Iraq was to be supplied with oil products for local consumption at prices to be "increased or decreased by the amount of any variation in world prices as expressed by the published prices for cargo lots . . . f.o.b. [free on board] United States ports in the Gulf of Mexico" (Federal Trade Commission 1952, 95). This system had the effect of discriminating against the Iraqi consumers not only because of the phantom freight, which was considerable by itself since Iraq was an oil-producing country, but also because the Iraqi consumer was charged a price based on the much-higher United States cost of production relative to the production cost in Iraq.

The successful functioning of the single-point system of pricing in the oil industry[1] may be explained by several factors. To begin with crude oil is a commodity that can be and is standardized. The main economic characteristic of crude oils is their gravity, which indicates their gasoline-yielding proportion. Given that gasoline is the major refined product, the gravity of crude oil is of primary economic importance. Since a barrel of any grade of crude has a measurable value that is equivalent in some volume to every other grade, and since the crude grades are close substitutes to the refiners, the quality differences of the crude grades have become reducible to price terms (Bain 1944, 37–38). Another factor that helped in the functioning of the system was the distances between consumption and production centers, a fact that made transportation costs an important element in the delivered price (Melmaid 1962, 283–98).

The continued functioning of the single-point system could have continued if the dominant position of the United States had remained unchallenged, but such was not the case, because the Middle East emerged as another major production center.

A "New" Production Center

One of the effects of the basing point system was to allow the high-cost producer to stay in the industry,[2] a fact that weakened the incentive to reduce production costs (Stocking 1950, 159–80). With the basing point system adhered to by the world oil industry (except for Mexico, Rumania, and the Soviet Union), this method of pricing had the effect of retarding the expansion of the low-cost production of Middle East oil. This in turn deprived the Middle East, as well as adjacent markets, of the benefits of this oil.

However, as the capacity of the Middle East oil industry expanded, an outlet for the increased output had to be found either in the adjacent markets or in markets closer to the United States. But in order to penetrate new markets, Middle East oil producers either had to reduce prices below the U.S. Gulf levels, and perhaps invite retaliation, or engage in freight absorption but retain the U.S. Gulf price formula. The latter approach was resorted to by the Middle East oil producers in order to expand their markets in the direction of the United States. To achieve this they had to forfeit phantom freight on sales made in their vicinity (Smithies 1949, 308–18). They selected this pricing strategy for several reasons.

First, as pointed out in chapter 2, the corporate structure of the oil industry was such that all of the international majors in the Middle East (with the exception of British Petroleum and Standard Oil of California) also had major interests in the Western Hemisphere oil industry. Thus it was possible for the industry to accommodate the expanding capacity of the Middle East by operating that source of oil as a nonbasing point, quoting as its free on board prices those of the U.S. Gulf (Smithies 1949, 308–18).

Second, the military operations of World War II in the Mediterranean forced a shift in the geographical distribution of the oil exports (Federal Trade Commission 1952, 355). This shift resulted in the reduction of Middle East exports to Western Europe on the one hand and the increase in these exports to other Eastern Hemisphere markets on the other hand, causing the latter market to become more dependent on the Middle East for its oil. The largescale military operations in the Eastern Hemisphere that stepped up the demand for Middle East oil, together with a dependence on the Middle East to meet this demand, prompted the British government (as the major buyer of Middle East oil) to question the validity of basing the price of its oil supplies on the prevailing prices in the U.S. Gulf. The investigation led the British Auditor General to report the following:

> *In the course of their inquiries the committee found that in many cases the price of bunker oils charged or proposed to be charged to the Ministry of Transport at ports in the Indian Ocean and the Middle East included an element described as an origin differential. This differential (which did not represent actual costs incurred by suppliers . . .) was a means of equating c.i.f. [cost, insurance, and freight] prices whatever the point of production. The general result was that when the source of supply was more distant than the Gulf the application of the differential would operate to the disadvantage of the supplier and, when it was nearer to his advantage. . . . We could no longer accept this origin differential automatically as a proper element in bunker prices in overseas ports mainly because owing to the vital necessity for getting the utmost possible service out of tanker tonnage, it was a matter of policy and principle to draw supplies from the nearest available source. It was no longer a matter of commercial competition. It was a matter of imposed policy that every ton of oil that could be drawn from a near source had to be taken from that source and none other. (quoted in Federal Trade Commission 1952, 356)*

To solve these problems a solution was arrived at whereby the British government would pay the same price for the oil bought in the Middle East as for oil of comparable quality at the U.S. Gulf, plus the actual freight costs from the Middle East to the final destination. The British Auditor General stated in this connection: "In view of the difficulty of arriving at production costs and in the knowledge that f.o.b. prices in the Gulf of Mexico were controlled by the United States government at levels given a fair return, the committee accepted f.o.b. prices for Persian Gulf production centers approximating the f.o.b. prices in the Gulf of Mexico" (quoted in Federal Trade Commission 1952, 356). Obviously, this new arrangement reflected the fact that the Middle East was becoming an important production center with its own new basing point, making its own f.o.b. sales in adjacent as well as other markets. (It should be noted that although the establishment of the Middle East as a new basing point has met some of the demands of the British government by eliminating the phantom freight, Great Britain has not, however, severed its link with U.S. Gulf.)

The change in the pricing formula in effect resulted in yielding identical net-back prices instead of delivered prices. While the prewar U.S. Gulf-plus formula had the effect of equalizing the delivered prices to any buyer, with the sellers receiving unequal net-backs depending on the location of their sources of supply vis-à-vis the buyers, the new formula worked to equalize the net-backs irrespective of the location of the buyer.

Postwar Developments

A number of developments in the world market in the postwar period dictated a series of changes in the oil-price structure.

First, the United States was rapidly reversing its role from that of a major oil exporter to that of a major oil importer, with most of its imports drawn from the nearby Caribbean sources. By 1949 U.S. oil imports from the Caribbean region had reached 0.6 MBD (U.S. Department of Energy 1978, 23).

Second, there was a considerable increase in the demand for oil and its products because of postwar reconstruction, the expansion of the industrial sectors in many countries, the mechanization of agriculture, the relatively high demand for oil for military purposes in peacetime, and the increase in the number of automobiles.

Third, the Middle East capacity continued to expand. In 1940 the region's average production was 0.3 MBD, or only 4.8 percent of the world total production. This figure rose to 0.7 MBD in 1946 (10.1 percent of world total production) and to 1.8 MBD (18.4 percent of world total production) in 1950.

As the Middle East capacity expanded, more markets had to be found to absorb the area's supply within the existing price structure. This was accomplished when delivered prices for the oil exports from the Middle East and the Caribbean were equalized at an equidistant point in the mid-Mediterranean (southern France).[3] But in order for the Middle East oil exporter to push his oil beyond the equidistant point and in the direction of his competitor, the exporter had to reduce his freight charges on his shipments to any point beyond the mid-Mediterranean (Smithies 1949, 312). In other words, while the equality of the f.o.b. prices in both regions could be maintained for the sales made up to the point of equalized delivered prices, the Middle East oil exporter's f.o.b. prices for shipments beyond that point would be less than the U.S. Gulf f.o.b. prices. To make adjustments for the new situation a change in the pricing formula that would position the Middle East oil deeper into the territory of its competitor was necessary.

By mid-1948, the United Kingdom became the point at which the delivered prices from the Middle East and the United States were equalized with the Middle East f.o.b. price, which was set at $2.22 per barrel of light crude (Federal Trade Commission 1952, 362). This new price formula was arrived at as follows: to the U.S. crude price was added the U.S. Maritime Commission freight rates from the U.S. Gulf to the United Kingdom, from which was then deducted the U.S. Maritime freight from Abadan, Iran to the United Kingdom.[4] The resulting figure became the crude-oil price f.o.b. Middle East exporting terminals.

The calculation of this new price ($2.22) was made in the following manner.[5]

Iranian Crude Price Formula
(Per-barrel Price for 36° API)

Items in Price	Amount ($)	Cumulative Totals
1. Posted well-head price, West-Texas sour crude as published in *National Petroleum News*.	2.44	
2. Charges to U.S. Gulf (Interstate Commerce Commission [ICC] rates for gathering, pipeline, evaporation, allowance, and terminal loading, plus one-cent marketing charge).	+0.31	$2.75 f.o.b. U.S. Gulf price for West-Texas sour crude.
3. U.S. Maritime Commission freight— United States to Southampton, United Kingdom	+1.02	$3.77 delivered United Kingdom for West-Texas sour crude
4. U.S. Maritime Commission freight— Abadan, Iran to Southampton, United Kingdom	−1.55	
5. Free on board Abadan price for Iranian crude	2.22	

Note: Until 1951 the Eastern Mediterranean terminals were the only outlet for the Iraqi oil. However, the prices at the Gulf served as the basis for the calculation of the prices at these terminals. In other words, the price at the Eastern Mediterranean was equal to the price at the Gulf, plus the freight cost from the Gulf to the Eastern Mediterranean.

With this new formula, the equality of the f.o.b. prices maintained during World War II was replaced by a differential to compensate for the locational disadvantage of the Middle East oil and to help its exporters displace the Caribbean oil from its remaining markets in the Eastern Hemisphere.

The equalization of prices at the United Kingdom was followed by another reduction in the Middle East oil prices, whereby the equalization point was moved westward to New York. Several forces propelled the companies to reduce Middle East prices. First, the realization that the United States had become a major oil importer opened up new opportunities for the relatively low-cost Middle East oil to replace Caribbean oil in the American market. Second, restrictions adopted by the companies themselves on their own marketing freedom made it imperative that the American market be penetrated. This was particularly true in the case of Gulf, Mobil, and Exxon, which had agreed under different restrictive corporate arrangements to market their oil in Western Europe and the United States.

When Middle East oil began to be imported in large quantities in 1948 in the United States, it became obvious that the European buyer was being subjected to price discrimination relative to the American buyer; in other words, Middle East oil had to be sold at lower f.o.b. prices to American importers. But such discrimination drew an objection from the U.S. Economic Cooperation Administration (ECA), which was financing the oil imports of the European countries under the provisions of the Marshall Plan.[6] These pressures motivated the companies to reduce Middle East prices as early as May 1948. These reductions continued in effect until October 1949, when the price was set at $1.75 per barrel of Arabian Light instead of $2.22 (the previous year's price that had been arrived at when the United Kingdom was selected as the equalization point).

The new price with New York as the equalization point was formulated similarly to the earlier price, but this time American prices and freight costs were computed from the Middle East to New York. New York had become the new watershed where oils from the Caribbean basin and the Middle East were supposed to compete.

While the reductions in the Middle East oil prices created a gap with respect to the prices for American oil of similar qualities, other factors tended to further widen the spread. These factors included the removal of price controls in the postwar period and the imposition in the 1950s of the oil-import quota system in the United States. Thus in 1948 the ratio of the price of Arabian Light to that of East Texas Light was 84 percent. By the end of 1949 the ratio had declined to 66 percent. And by the time OPEC was created the ratio had dropped to 55 percent.

Oligopoly in the Crude-Oil Market

The ability of the oil industry to set prices under a single-basing point system and its ability to adjust prices downward to allow for Middle East oil to compete in various markets derives from the oligopolistic structure of the industry. As late as 1959 over 90 percent of Middle East oil was controlled by seven sellers, the major multinational oil firms. This high concentration ratio was reinforced by the fact that some of the same oil firms controlled significant segments of the oil industry in the United States and the Caribbean. Another aspect of the structure of the oil industry was the special role played by the American government in enabling the U.S. oil industry to regulate oil output and therefore crude oil prices in the U.S. market.

As early as the mid-1930s the oil industry persuaded the U.S. Congress to establish the Interstate Oil Compact Commission, which authorized individual states to regulate oil output within their borders. The provisions of this act were strengthened when Congress enacted in 1935 the Connally Hot Oil Act, prohibiting producers not in compliance with state prorationing regulation from selling oil in interstate commerce. Both pieces of legislation had the effect of enforcing output restrictions with the result that prices were raised above the competitive levels (Mead 1979, 212–28). Having removed much of the uncertainty associated with supply, as indicated by monthly demand forecasts provided by the U.S. Department of the Interior, and having entered into joint ownership and marketing arrangements, the major oil companies found themselves in the position to regulate output and export from another region such as the Middle East.

The development of Middle East oil and the setting of its prices were done in a manner that preserved the stability of the price structure and prevented an outbreak of ruinous price and supply wars among the oil-producing companies. The stability of the prices of Middle East oil in the decade prior to the creation of OPEC may be seen from the price data in table 1. The price quotations in the table illustrate that with minor changes, mostly downward, Middle East oil prices remained stable for more than two decades before being raised as a result of the 1971 Tehran Agreement.

In addition to the fact that few sellers were producing a homogeneous product, the stability of Middle East oil prices was enhanced by two other considerations. First, the heavy investment in the vertically integrated oil industry could have suffered seriously had the sellers engaged in any serious price competition. Second, given the prolific nature of Middle East oil fields, the sellers found themselves faced with a declining marginal cost that made it unnecessary to raise prices. These conditions made it especially conducive for the sellers to develop a pattern of relationships among themselves to secure concurrent or collusive price action.

The nature of the commodity made the collusion all the more imperative. Crude oil, as mentioned above, is a homogeneous commodity, a fact that makes the industry more conducive to cutthroat competition once price reduction is initiated and responded to. In order to forestall the disastrous consequences of this kind of competition, the industry had to resort either to monopolistic competition through product differentiation, or to perfect oligopoly through price leadership, or to forming a monopoly (Boulding 1966, 664). The first alternative, that of product differentiation, is impractical, since the oil industry consists mainly of a small number of large producers selling mostly to their own refineries. The alternative to product differentiation in an industry such as this narrows down to adopting a collusive price action, which could take any of the following forms (Bain 1944, 281–83):

1. A cartel or formal agreement to set uniform or related prices plus an output quota for each member of the cartel and market territories; moreover, the industry profit is divided according to some formula.

2. A collusive agreement covering selling price, while leaving other matters open to competition.

3. The convention or custom of price leadership, with one of the sellers setting the price that the rivals will follow; nonprice competition is left open.

4. Adoption by the oligopolists of a common formula for computing prices that results in identical or similar prices.

5. Adoption by the oligopolists of conservative price policies, whereby prices are changed only in response to major shifts in costs and the habit is followed of just matching their rivals' price change.

Thus, collusive action can take many forms, ranging from pooling of resources, distributing output quotas, setting prices, and dividing markets and profits to the "spontaneous coordination" of business policies, which does not presuppose direct contact (Fellner 1950, 54–62).

As to the oil industry in the Middle East, the behavior of the sellers throughout the 1950s shows that the collusive action took the form of price leadership. However, the leadership was not always exercised by any one seller.[7] Thus, in December 1950 came the first public posting of export prices for the Middle East crude oil, when Mobil issued a schedule showing price quotations for the Arabian, Qatari, and Iraqi oil.[8] As stated at the beginning of this chapter, the publication of the posted prices was made necessary because of the profit sharing that was developing between the oil companies and the host governments.

Iraqi crude oil was the only oil offered for sale at the Eastern Mediterranean terminals until December 1950 and was priced at $2.41 per barrel of 36° API. In that month a new pipeline was inaugurated to bring the Arabian oil to the Eastern Mediterranean for the first time. This created a new situation, because the sellers had to post a price for the Arabian oil. Mobil decided to set the price of the Arabian oil on a par with the Iraqi oil, at $2.41 per barrel. California-Texas Oil Corporation (Caltex), a marketing company owned by Texaco and Socal, set the price of the Arabian oil at $2.45 per barrel, while Exxon decided to set the price at $2.55 per barrel. But since the sellers of the Iraqi oil—BP, Compagnie Française des Pétroles (CFP), and Shell—did not change their postings, and since in a market such as this only one price should rule if the oligopolists are not to lose their business to their competitors, Caltex and Exxon decided to revise their price quotations by reducing the price of the Arabian oil to $2.41 per barrel effective December 2, 1950.[9]

On May 28, 1951, BP raised the prices of its oils in the Gulf region by 13¢ per barrel. This price increase was copied by Shell on May 30 and by Gulf and Socal on June 4.[10] (In April 1951 Mobil had raised the price of its crude oil at the Eastern Mediterranean by 16.5¢ per barrel [from $2.41 to $2.58]. But since no other rival followed Mobil's lead, Mobil decided to reinstate the old price.)[11] On February 5, 1953, Exxon led in reducing the prices of the Iraq and Arabian oils at the East Mediterranean by 12¢ per barrel. This action was then imitated by the other sellers.[12]

In mid-1953 a series of price changes occurred that reflected how different market evaluations by various sellers resulted in different prices, which had to be adjusted to reestablish a uniform price if the sellers were to protect their positions. On July 10, 1953, Gulf boosted the price of its oil by 25¢ per barrel, an increase that was matched a week later by BP, Shell, and Exxon. This move raised the price of crude oil to $2.00 per barrel. However, the sellers behaved differently with regard to price changes in the Eastern Mediterranean. While BP raised its price by 25¢ per barrel (from $2.29 to $2.54), Exxon raised the price by 10¢ only (to $2.39 per barrel), and Caltex and Shell by 15¢ (to $2.44 per barrel).[13] But these price differences could not last for long; hence, following the lead of Exxon, Caltex revised its price increase from 15¢ to 10¢. BP, Shell, and Mobil responded immediately by revising their price changes to 10¢ only, thus settling the Eastern Mediterranean price of crude oil at $2.39 per barrel.[14] During the same week two further adjustments took place. First, the increase in the Gulf prices was revised from 25¢ to 22¢—a move initiated by Caltex and followed by the other sellers.[15] Second, this new revision was applied to all the crude oils offered for sale in the Gulf, with the exception of Iraq crude oil. While the price of crude oil of 36° API was set at $1.97 per barrel, Iraq crude oil of the same quality was set at $1.92 per barrel. This 5¢ differential was explained by the locational disadvantage of Fao, the loading port for Iraqi oil at the Gulf.[16]

The next price change was initiated by Exxon on February 2, 1956, when it increased the price of Iraqi oil at the Eastern Mediterranean by 7¢ (to $2.46 per barrel) and reduced the price at the Gulf by 5¢ (to $1.87 per barrel). BP, although following Exxon with regard to the price of Iraqi oil at the Gulf, raised the price at the Mediterranean by 10¢. When the other sellers decided to follow Exxon's lead at both points, however, BP decided to revise its price increase at the Mediterranean to 7¢.[17]

Exxon took the lead again on December 18, 1956, when it decided to raise the price at the Eastern Mediterranean by 23¢ (to $2.69 per barrel). It was not until March 18, 1957, that Mobil responded by raising its price by the same amount, a move that was then imitated by BP and CFP.[18] This was the only instance when there was a considerable time lag in the rivals' responses during the period under consideration. The reason for the delay lies in the historical context of events of that period. During the 1956 Suez crisis the pipelines that brought Iraqi oil to the Mediterranean were blown up; hence BP and CFP were deprived of their oil supplies in that area. Exxon, on the other hand, continued uninterruptedly to draw its supplies from Saudi Arabia. When the pumping capacity of the Iraq Petroleum Company's pipelines was partially restored in March 1957, with some of the supplies of BP and CFP appearing again at the Mediterranean, a price change was in order.

The next round of price changes was initiated by BP when it decided, on May 28, 1957, to raise the price of Iraq oil in the Gulf by 13¢ per barrel (to $2.00),[19] an increase that was then matched by the other sellers.

Three months later, on September 8, 1957, BP reversed its position and decided to lower the price of the Iraqi oil at the Mediterranean by 10¢ per barrel (to $2.59). This reduction was copied by the other sellers.[20]

This price cut was followed by another one on January 3, 1958 when Exxon lowered the price of the Iraqi oil at the Mediterranean by 10¢ a barrel, thus bringing it down to $2.49 per barrel, only 3¢ above its pre-Suez level. The other sellers then followed suit.[21]

On February 13, 1959, another round of price cuts was initiated by BP when it reduced the prices of all its Middle East oils by 18¢ a barrel.[22] All other sellers in the area followed BP's lead and posted the same prices.[23]

The last series of price changes in the period prior to OPEC, which occurred in August 1960, again demonstrate what can happen in a market of diverse sellers with equally divergent analyses of the market forces.

On August 9, 1960, Exxon cut the prices of its oils by an amount ranging from 4¢ to 14¢ per barrel. The Iraqi oil at the Mediterranean was priced at $2.17 per barrel, a cut of 14¢. At the Gulf, Exxon decided to reduce the price of Iraqi oil by 12¢, to $1.70 per barrel. The response to Exxon's move was uneven: Shell followed Exxon's example by setting the same prices for its oils at both exporting regions. BP, on the other hand, pegged its Mediterranean price at $2.21 per barrel, while Mobil went to $2.19 per barrel and CFP to $2.23 per barrel. As to the prices in the Gulf region, BP and CFP decided to set the price of their oil at $1.74, while Mobil followed Exxon's lead by setting its price at $1.70 per barrel.[24] Clearly this situation could not prevail, since it had the potential for a ruinous competitive price cutting. Such danger was alleviated when Shell decided to revise its price changes to the levels set by BP. This, in turn, forced Exxon to abandon its earlier postings and align its prices with those set by BP. Other sellers followed suit (table 1).[25]

It can be seen from this review that the leadership in initiating price changes was practiced by different sellers at different times. This rotation of leadership was possible because each of the major sellers controlled a considerable share of the market. Moreover, the prices during this period were being reduced in order to allow Middle East oil to expand its share of the energy market. Another force was also operating to encourage price reductions, however; this was the challenge posed by the new entrants in international oil—the independents, or the newcomers.

The Independents: Entry and Impact

Any attempt to explain the behavior of the price of crude oil during the period under consideration would be incomplete without a discussion of the role of independents. In considering oil output and prices, both in the OPEC region and world wide, it should be remembered that during the first half of the twentieth century the bulk of oil output outside the United States and the Soviet Union was produced by the seven largest vertically integrated multinational oil companies, which, as late as 1953, were responsible for 87 percent of all the oil produced outside those two countries. In addition, almost all of OPEC oil was produced by these seven companies. By 1963 these majors were responsible for 86 percent of the oil produced in the OPEC region, but by 1970 their share had declined to 77 percent of the total output. The balance between OPEC's total output and that of the seven majors was produced by a number of oil enterprises that came to be known as the independent oil companies, or sometimes the newcomers.

Several factors made it either feasible or imperative for the new entrants to venture into the international oil industry. One such factor was the need to secure sources of crude oil to meet refinery requirements in consumption centers. Such backward integration was necessary if the refinery operations in the home countries were to be free from the supply decisions of the major international oil companies. Another consideration was the change from coal to oil as the major energy source in many European countries. This shift from indigenous to foreign energy sources gave oil a national security dimension and, in turn, encouraged national oil companies to enter into the international oil industry to secure oil for national markets. In other words, it was felt that national economies should not be totally dependent on the fortunes and behavior of the seven major oil companies. A third consideration was the desire of the oil-producing countries to grant concessions to oil companies other than the majors. If the independents were forthcoming with better terms, so much the better. In order to secure concession agreements from oil-producing countries, the independents did in fact offer better terms to the host governments. These new concessions involved the relinquishment of areas covered by the original concession holders or, as in the case of the neutral zone between Kuwait and Saudi Arabia, areas not covered by the original agreements. (Libya, on the other hand, enacted petroleum legislation confining concessions to well-defined areas so as to encourage the entry of a relatively large number of oil firms.) Still another factor encouraging the entrance of new companies was the emergence of national oil companies in the oil-producing countries themselves. These companies were organized to produce oil in the areas that companies had had to relinquish or, as in the case of Iraq, areas that were taken over from the original concession holders. The rapid increase in the world demand for oil further spurred the newcomers. This phenomenon permitted the introduction of newly discovered oil, such as the Libyan oil, into the international oil market by the newcomers.

The U.S. government itself played an important role in encouraging the independents to enter the international oil industry. Thus when the Iranian government of Dr. Muhammad Mossadegh was overthrown in 1953, the U.S. government played a major role in restructuring the concession agreement. Prior to the nationalization act of 1951, British Petroleum was the only major oil company operating in Iran, but according to the provisions of the Consortium Oil Agreement of 1954, the share of BP was reduced to 40 percent, with the remaining 60 percent going to other companies, including a number of small newcomers. The emergence of the United States in the postwar period as the major world superpower facilitated American oil firms' entrance into the international oil industry, since the political barriers to entry that had been imposed by European governments were removed. Another aspect of U.S. government policy that stimulated newcomers' entry was the decision to allow foreign tax payments to be credited against a firm's tax liability to the U.S. government, instead of its being deducted as a cost element.

Although such incentives were important, another and equally important force encouraged firms to move into international oil. This was the profitability of investing in the oil industry in the OPEC region, especially in the Middle

East. In this connection, the average ratio of gross income to total net assets of the oil-producing companies in the Middle East was 111 percent for the period 1948–60, and the average ratio of net income to total net assets was 67 percent for the same period. The corresponding rates of return in Venezuela for the same period were computed to be 49 percent and 21 percent, respectively. By contrast, the ratio of net income to net assets on similar investment during this time in the United States was computed to be only 10.8 percent.[26]

These data emphasize that Middle East oil deposits provided a strong pull for newcomers to enter the industry. Such entry provided no serious threat to the price-setting power of the larger corporations, so long as demand conditions were buoyant enough to absorb all the oil produced by the majors and independents. Such was the case until 1957, when the U.S. government decided to restrict foreign-oil imports in order to protect the domestic oil industry from the lower-cost foreign oil. The oil-import quota system that was made mandatory in 1959 forced the independents to compete more aggressively with the majors in markets outside the United States.

In addition to the oil offered by the independents, there was Soviet oil that was reintroduced to world markets outside Eastern Europe in 1953. In its drive to recapture its pre–World War II share of the world market, the Soviet Union resorted to trade agreements and other inducements, especially in its trade with developing countries. The U.S.S.R. found receptive buyers in Western Europe, as well as in other parts of the world. This was not surprising, since oil-importing countries were interested in conserving their foreign-exchange earnings, expanding their own exports, and increasing their bargaining position vis-à-vis their traditional suppliers, the major oil companies.

The combined effect of U.S. oil policies, which restricted oil imports, and of the Soviet Union's policy, which promoted oil exports, exerted a downward pressure on crude-oil prices. This pressure manifested itself in the granting of discounts off the posted prices to nonaffiliated refiners. But as the pressure continued, the marketing affiliates of the majors found themselves at a competitive disadvantage in relation to third-party buyers. In order to preserve their own positions in consuming centers, the majors started to lower the prices charged to their own affiliates. Since the oil companies, both majors and nonmajors, were paying taxes to host governments on the basis of posted prices, the posted prices became also tax-reference prices, so long as they were different from the actual market prices charged by the sellers.

The extent of the reduction of the prices of crude oil due to the increase in the supply of oil can be appreciated from the following price data compiled by Neil Jacoby. According to Jacoby, prices of crude oil delivered to Western Europe rose by 22 percent between 1953 and 1957, from $3.08 to $3.75 per barrel. But with changing market conditions in the latter 1950s, the average price had dropped by 40 percent between 1957 and 1965, from $3.75 to $2.27 per barrel. Even as late as 1972 the price was $2.95 per barrel, or lower than it had been two decades earlier, despite the general inflation and the price rise of the early 1970s.[27]

The decline in the delivered prices of oil sold to Japan was even more dramatic than that in Western Europe. The average delivered price to the Japanese market peaked at $3.48 per barrel in 1957. By 1970 the price of oil had declined by 48 percent, to $1.80 per barrel—and that decline occurred in the face of a rapidly growing Japanese demand.[28]

It should be noted that the revenue of the oil-producing countries was insulated from the market-price decline so long as the posted prices remained unchanged. But to keep the prices static meant that the oil companies had to absorb the entire reduction in the price. It was possible to maintain this situation if the companies thought the conditions of excess supply were temporary. The persistence of buyers' market conditions during the 1950s and most of the 1960s, however, led the companies to consider a reduction in posted prices. Such reduction had the effect of shifting one-half of the price cut to the governments, since the revenue of the latter was based on the difference between the cost of production and the posted prices.

Thus, in February 1959, the companies decided to lower posted prices from $2.08 per barrel for Arabian Light to $1.90 per barrel, to be followed by another reduction to $1.80 per barrel in August 1960. This last price cut provided the oil-producing countries with the impetus to create OPEC. And with the creation of OPEC, posted prices remained frozen throughout the 1960s.

To summarize, Middle East oil prices prior to the formation of OPEC were determined by the interaction of several influences, all of which tended to increase the monopoly elements of the industry. In the first place, oil resources were developed by a few large multinational, vertically integrated firms. These firms were engaged in joint-ownership contractual arrangements that enabled them to regulate Middle East oil output to meet primarily the needs of their own operations in the final consumer markets throughout the world. The small number of these firms, their interdependence, and the standardized nature of the product provided the necessary conditions for oligopolistic pricing and monopoly profits. This was enforced by three factors. First, the phenomenal rise in the demand for oil in the postwar period provided expanded markets for the increased output of the oil companies without their having to resort to price competition. In addition, the fact that marginal cost was so low relative to the price enabled the companies to engage in price reductions without having to be concerned about the profitability of their investment at this phase of the industry. The third factor was the role of government both in the United States and in the oil-producing countries. The U.S. government, by providing the necessary output-regulating mechanisms in the United States, enabled the industry to charge monopolistic prices without having to be concerned about the consequences of entry in the industry. And by relating Middle East prices to the American prices, the oil industry was in a position to set what amounted to price ceilings for Middle East oil prices. While the American prices provided a ceiling, the floor was set by the governments of oil-producing countries. This was a direct consequence of profit-sharing agreements adopted in the early 1950s that continued in effect until the early 1970s. The respective governments' interests in seeing the companies avoid price reduction is clear, since any such reduction would result in a reduction in these governments' per-barrel revenue.

Inspite of the institutional rigidities in the system and the monopolistic aspects of the industry, the control of the majors was being eroded in the 1950s, owing to the emergence of new forces in the international oil markets, including the entry of new oil firms in the international oil market; the reentry of Soviet oil in the world market; the American oil import-quota system; and the rising importance of national oil companies in both oil-importing and oil-exporting countries. These agents of change resulted in larger quantities of oil being offered on the world market outside and beyond the control of the major oil companies. This rise in supply and in the number of buyers and sellers had the effect of reducing the price-setting powers of the established oligopolists, which in turn led to a series of reductions in the price of crude oil. Initially, the companies absorbed these cuts when they chose not to reduce posted prices, but eventually, in 1959 and 1960, the companies reduced the posted prices.

PRICE ADMINISTRATION UNDER OPEC, 1960–71

From 1960 (when OPEC was formed) to 1971, (when the Tehran Agreement was concluded), the basic determinants of crude-oil prices remained the same. In other words, OPEC during this period failed to alter the structure of relations responsible for establishing these prices. As might have been anticipated, the first resolution of the newly created OPEC declared that crude-oil prices should be restored to the pre-August-1960 levels, and a request to this effect was issued to the companies involved. OPEC, however, failed to articulate why the prices should be restored to their pre-August level or to any level, for that matter. It also neglected to consider a plan of action should the companies fail to respond to its demand. Thus, in the absence of either a price-change rationale or a potential threat of sanctions, the oil companies found no compelling reason to change their position. And so the first plea of OPEC's founding members was ignored.

A call for negotiations two years later on the issue of prices was turned down again by the companies on the grounds that price determination was solely the prerogative of the oil companies. It was not until 1971 that the companies finally consented to negotiate with OPEC-member countries for the purpose of determining crude-oil prices. In the interim, from 1960 to 1971, OPEC was able to claim for itself some measure of success, in that it succeeded in halting the downward pressure on crude-oil prices. The fact that OPEC-member countries' import prices continued to increase the freezing of crude-oil nominal prices assured, in effect, a continued decline in the real prices of crude oil. The decline in the real price of crude oil for the period 1947 to 1970 was estimated to be 65 percent.[29]

In this context, although posted prices remained frozen during the 1960s, realized or actual market prices (that is, prices charged to independent buyers) continued to fall. But since government per-barrel revenue was related to posted prices, these prices became, in effect, tax-reference prices. With both the posted prices and government receipt fixed, OPEC-member countries found themselves fixed-price sellers, as it were, of oil to the oil companies operating in their territories. The fear of these governments that the continued downward pressure on market prices might eventually result in a formal reduction in posted prices and, consequently, a reduction in their income prompted them to consider output regulation policies.

The idea of securing some kind of agreement to regulate total output was considered seriously by OPEC as a policy instrument to stabilize prices. The several attempts made by OPEC-member countries during the 1960s to reach an agreement on a framework for adopting production policy were, however, unsuccessful. OPEC's failure in this regard is not surprising, in light of the fact that member governments had no control over the volume of output in their respective countries, so long as the concession agreements were the operative instruments for the exploitation of oil resources. In other words it was necessary for member governments to nationalize the operations of the oil companies before they could contemplate a successful production program. Moreover, the tendency throughout the 1960s was for member countries to deal with their concession holders on an individual rather than a collective basis.

Yet during this decade OPEC and its member countries developed a number of principles or long-run policy objectives, each of which contained elements that had some determining force in setting prices. These elements were articulated in the Declaratory Statement of Petroleum Policy, which was adopted by OPEC in 1968 and laid the grounds for many of the changes that have occurred since. The major aspects of this important policy statement are discussed in the paragraphs following.[30]

The 1968 OPEC policy statement originated as an alternative to the adoption of a uniform petroleum law governing the petroleum policies of all member countries. The statement was adopted at a time when the countries of the Third World were striving to assert their inalienable right to exercise sovereignty over their natural resources. Such reaffirmation of these rights found its expression in numerous United Nations (U.N.) resolutions, culminating in the 1966 U.N. Resolution on Permanent Sovereignty Over Natural Resources. The 1968 OPEC statement adopted the principles of direct exploitation of oil resources by the government; participation in the ownership of the operating companies; relinquishment of areas not developed by the companies; and conservation. It furthermore affirmed that posted prices should be determined by the governments and that these prices should be linked to the prices of imported goods in order to prevent erosion in oil-revenue purchasing power.

These principles, while providing guidelines that OPEC-member countries could agree upon, allowed these countries complete freedom in the pursuit of their national interests.

PRICE ADMINISTRATION IN THE AFTERMATH OF 1973

The 1968 OPEC policy statement provided a framework for many of the decisions taken by OPEC and/or its member countries in the areas of participation, price determination, conservation, mode of development, relinquishment, and contract renegotiation. The principle on prices that is of particular relevance here contained three main elements. These were that

1. Posted prices should be determined by the government.

2. These prices should move in such a manner as to prevent any deterioration in their relationship to the prices of manufactured goods traded internationally.

3. These prices should be consistent with each other among various member countries, subject to location and quality differentials.[31]

This price principle introduced several concepts that tended to govern OPEC price determination, including, first, the concept of price indexation. Price indexation maintained that since oil constitutes not only a major part of a member country's GNP but the bulk of its exports as well as the major—if not the only—source of foreign exchange earnings, changes in posted prices should be undertaken periodically in order to mitigate against the rise in import prices. Second, the concept of the economic sovereignty of governments over oil (and thus over posted prices) was reaffirmed. And third, the concept of similar pricing was introduced in order to avoid price competition among producing countries. The drastic change in the status of oil-producing countries that took place in the early 1970s amounted to the functional equivalent of nationalization: The rapidity with which changes occurred in the structure of the international oil industry, beginning with the Tehran Agreement and followed by the two Geneva agreements, the Participation Agreement, the output cut and export embargo measures, the unilateral determination of prices, and, in three months' time, the doubling and redoubling of prices, meant that the producing countries, the consuming countries, and the oil companies faced a whole new situation in which the pattern of power relations was being rearranged in favor of the producing countries.

The new era transformed the producing countries from tax collectors to output setters and price setters. The elaborate system of vertical integration that had been built up over a half century by the oil companies suddenly found one of its important and least competitive phases under the control of host governments. But this power shift was not accompanied by a new OPEC-created mechanism to regulate output from various supply sources, to replace the mechanism that the oil companies had developed and put to use in the oil-producing countries during the era of the concession system. In the end, in spite of the oil-producing governments' new roles and in spite of the prerogatives of sovereignty, the OPEC countries were few in number, and fewer of them controlled most of the reserves and the output. In other words, the basic fact of the industry, with its high concentration ratio and oligopolistic nature, remained the same, the exception being, of course, that the oligopolists now were states instead of companies.

Understanding the difference between the nature of oligopolist states and oligopolist companies is central to comprehending price determination. Under the concession system, members of the oligopoly were essentially private enterprises whose sole interest was to maximize profits. Given the potential threat of nationalization prior to the end of the concession period, the profit maximizer was interested in producing as much as possible without regard to the principle of conserving a depletable resource.

But to say OPEC-member countries constitute an oligopoly is of limited usefulness, in that the observed behavior of the oligopolist in a private-sector setting does not conform to that of OPEC-member governments. This is so because a government's concerns and interests transcend the mere equalization of marginal cost and marginal revenue or the vertical distance between the average cost and average revenue curves. More specifically, a government in an oil-producing country and, unlike its corporate predecessor, is very interested in the issue of economic development and diversification and all that this entails. A government is also concerned with integrating the oil sector with other sectors of the economy as well as with developing oil and natural-gas-based industries. A government is interested, furthermore, in using oil exports as a vehicle for technology and for other imports. Moreover, a government is interested in the welfare of future generations—hence the desire to stretch oil reserves over as many years as possible. Finally, external and internal economic and political considerations also influence the decisions of governments with respect to output and prices.

With these considerations in mind, the question remains of how to explain the level and direction of OPEC prices. The section following sheds some light on this matter.

OIL PRICE DETERMINATION
AND ECONOMIC DEVELOPMENT

A pool of oil is a capital asset, much like a printing press or a building or any other reproducible capital asset. The only difference is that the natural resource is not reproducible and draws its market value, ultimately, from the prospect of extraction and sale (Solow 1974, 2).

The nonreproducibility and therefore the exhaustibility of oil resources have always been driving forces behind many of the policies, including pricing policies of oil-producing countries. The realization of the limited life span of oil reserves has played a decisive role in government's attempts to conserve their resource while also achieving an acceptable rate of economic growth and diversification. The replacement or the transformation of one asset into another has consistently been a major policy determinant.

In 1950, long before OPEC was created, the government of Iraq, for instance, adopted the policy of linking oil to economic development by creating a special development board to oversee all revenue from oil (which was earmarked for the expressed objective of economic development and diversification).

When OPEC adopted its policy statement in 1968, it recognized this tie between oil and development when it stated that hydrocarbon resources are limited and exhaustible and that their proper exploitation determines the present and future conditions of economic development of member countries. Again, in 1975, the Solemn Declaration of Sovereigns and Heads of State of OPEC Member Countries stressed that the exploitation of the depletable oil resources in their countries must be based, first and foremost, upon the best interests of their peoples and that oil, which is the major source of their income, constitutes a vital element in their development.[32] This connection between oil prices and economic development was articulated as follows:

> *Oil exporting countries must view oil prices in terms of the material collateral they get in lieu of the finite resource they deplete. They maximize their gains when they have the greatest access to wealth (best represented by high economic growth for their economies) with a minimum depletion of oil reserves.*
>
> *In the long term, this means that a production and depletion policy would be judged efficient to the extent that it succeeds in serving the purpose of bringing the economy of the producing country to the highest possible level of economic development sustainable without further need for oil revenues at the time when petroleum is no longer available for export. Nominally, this means the highest unit price which earns the foreign exchange necessary for fixed capital formation. (Al-Chalabi and Al-Janabi 1980, 339)*

Given the nature of oil as a finite natural resource, its linkage to economic development, as well as its importance to the economies of the oil-importing countries, one cannot speak of oil-price determination in the conventional sense. Instead one must focus on those elements that determine the level of price and, consequently, the economic rent derived by OPEC-member countries.

First, because oil is a fixed, exhaustible commodity, a certain payment must naturally be made by the user to the owner of this fixed quantity; this payment is separate from both the actual cost of extraction and the monopoly-profit elements mentioned earlier.

Second, while oil is depletable, some of its products happen also to be indispensable for certain uses; in other words, there are no oil substitutes whose changing prices may exert a restraining effect on the price of oil. Moreover, the technical costs of producing oil substitutes are much higher than the current prices of oil (estimated production costs of most alternative energy sources have multiplied several times since 1973).

Third, the cost of producing oil outside the OPEC countries—the North Sea, for example—is high enough to make it a determining element of the price of OPEC oil.[33]

Fourth, the concept of indexation has always been a significant element in OPEC's pricing policy. The argument, simply, is that the world markets are dominated by few producers who determine prices noncompetitively. Economic development in OPEC countries calls for the importation of a wide array of commodities, food, raw materials, manufactured goods, capital goods, and so forth. The prices of these imports have risen over time, while between 1950 and 1970 the price of oil was either reduced by the majors or was kept stable.

This relative loss in the purchasing power of oil revenue was accelerated by the sharp price inflation that still continues to rule the world markets.

Fifth, oil output at pre-1973 prices was more than sufficient to meet the financial needs of at least some member countries. Hence, the price of oil was regarded by these countries as an instrument to control increases in the rate of demand.[34]

Sixth, within OPEC, as discussed later in this book, there is no general agreement as to what criteria should be used to determine prices. This is not surprising, in view of the differences among member countries as to political orientation, pragmatism, economic development, population size, individual petroleum experience, and oil production and reserves. For example, in a country like Saudi Arabia, which has a relatively small population but a high reserve/output ratio, the tendency has been to maximize revenue by raising output. On the other hand, in a country like Iran, whose population is much larger than that of Saudi Arabia but whose reserve/output ratio is much smaller, the tendency has been to push for higher prices to maximize revenue.

Seventh, some member countries maintained that if OPEC prices were related to import prices, then OPEC should set its prices so as not to aggravate the rate of inflation in the industrial countries.[35] The counter argument has been that inflation was neither caused by nor sustained by the level of oil prices, and that inflation itself led OPEC to take action in setting prices in the first place. Supporters of the second position have insisted that the disparity between oil price increases and import price increases is so great as to deny a direct relationship (Sarkis 1977, 24–30).

Eighth, since the bulk of OPEC oil is exported to the industrialized countries, it follows that the main consuming countries are in a position to influence both demand and supply through public policy and consequently, oil prices. For example, they can engage (and have already engaged) in a vigorous policy of conservation, of accelerated development of alternative energy sources of energy, and of stockpiling. By adjusting their tax policies with respect to oil import or consumption, they can exert a major influence on demand and therefore on the prices that OPEC can charge.

To recapitulate, any explanation of price determination under OPEC should be sought outside conventional economic theory models. Concepts such as cartel and oligopoly are not applicable to OPEC pricing in light of OPEC's observed behavior over the last decade. Many elements have contributed to price determination to a different degree at different times. Although OPEC has never articulated any coherent pricing policies, certain pricing elements have emerged over the years that can be construed as constituting a policy. These are outlined next.

At the core of OPEC pricing policy has always been the desire to protect the purchasing power of its revenue. To attain this objective, OPEC based its position, up to 1973, on the following arguments: that oil is an exhaustible resource whose owners should be compensated for its use; that the purchasing power of the oil dollar should be protected from inflation and major currency fluctuations; and that, since oil constitutes a major sector of member countries' economies and the major source—potentially, the only source—of their foreign exchange earnings, its price should not be allowed to be unilaterally determined by the oil companies. In other words, since national economic development plans are dependent on the revenue from oil, the determination of oil revenue and prices should not remain in the hands of oil companies exclusively.

The worldwide inflation and currency upheavals of the 1970s and the emergence of the United States as the chief oil importer in the world aggravated an already tight supply situation and drove market prices above posted prices, motivating OPEC to renegotiate the terms of the Tehran Agreement of 1971 to reflect the new market conditions. The failure to reach a new agreement in 1973 prompted the producing countries to raise prices unilaterally, thereby causing a historic shift in the controlling power over price determination. While OPEC is an important price-determining force, it shares this power with the consuming countries, whose demand determines the level of oil output. OPEC countries also share the price-determining power with other oil-producing countries outside the OPEC region. The behavior of the oil companies with access to varying supply sources is also a significant pricing influence.

One reason for the inadequacy of conventional economic analysis in explaining OPEC pricing policy is that political forces and objectives have played and will continue to play an important role in determining oil prices. Another reason relates to the structure of OPEC itself. OPEC, by its members' design, is an intergovernmental agency with no powers or authority to enforce decisions. Although member countries share common interests, they continue to retain for themselves the final say with respect to the price and output level of their own oil.

Finally, it should be remembered that it has been only since 1973 that OPEC acquired control over prices. Given the multitude of political and economic forces that affect the behavior of member countries, it may well take OPEC some time to devise a rational oil-pricing policy, if ever.

CHAPTER 4

OPEC and the
Management of Oil Output

A principal objective of the oil-producing countries has been to exert some control over decisions relating to the volume of oil output. This was particularly true during the 1960s, when both prices and government revenue per unit of output were frozen. In order for the government to increase revenue, total output and export thus had to be expanded.

In attempting to expand output, governments had to contend with several major structural considerations, none of which was under their control. In the first place, the provisions of the concession agreements left the determination of the output level for any one country in the hands of an operating company in that country, a company that was in turn jointly owned by several multinational oil companies. These operating companies were formed for the sole purpose of extracting oil and delivering it at export points to their parent companies. The parent companies had to determine their output needs from any one country in light of their requirements from all other producing regions in the world.

Second, while it is true that the majors could increase output from any one country at any time, they could not do so in all the countries at the same time without creating an oil glut in the market.

Third, while the majors did control oil production in all member countries, newcomers in the market could acquire oil concessions outside the OPEC region. This meant that even when some of the same majors were partners in a newly acquired non-OPEC oil-producing area, oil from such areas had to find its way in the international market, and in turn had to be sold at the expense of the established oil-producing countries.

The fourth consideration was the discovery of oil within the national economic boundaries of some of the major oil-importing countries, such as the finding of North Sea oil and the Alaskan oil fields.

Fifth, the reintroduction in 1953 of Soviet oil to the world oil market affected the ability of the controlling oil companies to regulate output.

The sixth and final consideration was the mechanism used by the companies in trying to meet their global oil requirements from their extensive and geographically diverse oil fields. This mechanism served several objecives: It answered the global oil needs of each of the multinational oil companies from a number of concession areas; it reconciled the competitive objectives of the various oligopolists; it served the objective of regulating output from different countries in order to allow for the entry of oil from new producing areas in the world; it acted as a bargaining instrument with governments whose demands were considered detrimental to the common commercial objective of the companies; and it constituted a planning tool utilized by companies in making capital-investment decisions in different countries.

Given the importance of the mechanism for regulating output both before OPEC's creation and for most of the period since, the mechanism is described here in some detail. The discussion begins with a brief outline of the output control arrangement in the United States, since these arrangements constituted the basis upon which the world oil industry evolved.

THE OIL OUTPUT
PRORATIONING IN THE UNITED STATES

In the late twenties and early thirties a number of factors contributed to the oversupply of crude oil, among which were the decline in demand for crude oil because of the Great Depression in the United States and the discovery of the East Texas fields. These changes led to a marked fall in the prices of oil. In order to compensate for their losses, numerous oil producers aggravated the situation by stepping up the rate of production. This in turn created a chaotic supply situation accompanied by waste to such a degree that widespread interest developed in regulating crude-oil production.[1]

By 1935 most of the oil-producing states had adopted some instruments for conserving natural resources and protecting the interests of property holders in oil fields. These instruments took the form of prorationing measures that sought to regulate production by fixing a maximum rate of production based on some objective criterion. Though prorationing does not prevent the drilling of new areas or new wells, it endeavors to protect the correlative rights of each producer from a common reservoir to an equitable share in the total market for crude oil produced in that reservoir.[2]

The control of crude-oil production by each state in the U.S. would not have been effective without the contribution of the federal government in four areas. First, in 1935, the U.S. Congress passed the Interstate Compact to Conserve Oil and Gas, which authorized the states to cooperatively develop conservation programs. Second, the earlier-mentioned Connally Hot Oil Act of 1935 prohibited the transportation in interstate commerce of any oil produced in violation of a state's conservation laws. This act provided the states with a powerful means to enforce their conservation programs. Third was the enactment, beginning in 1932, of tariffs and similar measures designed to control the flow of foreign oil. Fourth was the publication beginning in 1930 by the U.S. Bureau of Mines of the monthly expected demand for oil (McLean and Haigh 1954, 109–10).

The basic features of the states' programs were intended to prevent production in excess of a field's maximum efficient rate of production, as well as to ensure the allocation of a field's production among various property holders, plus the adjustment of production to market demand (McLean and Haigh 1954, 109–10). This last feature was the heart of the prorationing policy and provided the foundation on which the whole price structure was built. It required that the expected total demand for the state's crude oil, as projected by the Bureau of Mines, be allocated among the oil-producing wells in the state, leaving it to producers to operate their wells for as many days during the month as deemed economical.

In Texas the eighty-eight thousand prorated wells were allowed in 1960 (the year of OPEC's formation) to produce only about 1.4 MBD, or an average of 16 BD each. This represented just over one-quarter of the average maximum rate at which these wells could produce efficiently.[3]

Given the fact that oil importers were required to submit in advance an estimate of their expected imports (since 1959 these imports have been restricted to about 9 percent to 10 percent of the local demand), it is not difficult to see how these conservation and prorationing measures have removed the power to control the supply of oil from the domain of private decision-making units to the public authorities.

Thus, if the expected demand exceeded the state-authorized total supply plus the import quotas, the allowable production from each well was permitted to increase. If, on the other hand, the demand fell short of domestic supply plus imports, a cut in the allowable production had to be made. In either case, the authorities were in a position to regulate the volume of output in such a way as to avoid both excess supply and excess demand and consequently, any short-run price fluctuations that might result. This meant that the price required to clear the market in a certain state of demand was not only stabilized but was also required to leave a profit margin to the producer with the highest production cost.

While authorities in the United States were playing a major role in determining the volume of the crude-oil output and were reconciling the conflicting interests that arose from the correlative rights of ownership on the one hand and the diverging interests of the oil-producing states on the other, corresponding conflicts and differences in the OPEC region were left to the oil companies to handle. Specifically, there were two sets of conflicting interests; the first was between the oil-producing countries and the second between the oil companies themselves.

As to the first, it was natural that each oil-producing country would have preferred that as much oil be lifted and marketed as possible, since the oil revenue, given the price, was a function of the output. But because the rate of output was determined not by the government but by the operating oil company in that country, and because the major international oil companies jointly owned these operating companies in more than one oil-producing country, it was left to these major companies to balance the conflicting interests of these countries. Given that these major companies were also the sellers of the oil they produced, it follows that it was in their interest to regulate the oil supply in such a way as to maximize profits by maintaining price stability. Thus, these companies were playing, in effect, a role similar to that played by federal authorities in the United States with regard to regulating the crude-oil supply.

It is clear that this supply-regulating power of the international majors would have been greatly impaired and the orderly development of oil resources would not have been possible had the majors been unable to resolve their own conflicting interests and recognize their common interests as a group.

That the majors were able to achieve unity was demonstrated by the success of these companies in limiting the development of the production of the lower-cost oil of the Middle East in order not to disturb the prevailing stability. Hence the oil drawn from sources as far apart as Iraq and Venezuela was settled by the majors in a pattern that tended to be determined by the respective market shares of these companies in consuming countries. This in turn helped to determine an acceptable level of production in each oil-producing country. The collective interest of the majors passed one of its severest tests when the Iranian government of Dr. Muhammad Mossadegh failed to sell its nationalized oil during the time that its dispute with one of the majors (BP) remained unsettled.[4]

In addition to the forces of stability that tended to dominate the international oil industry from the time of the inception of the prorationing system in the United States, output regulation in the OPEC region prior to the formation of OPEC was strengthened by a number of corporate arrangements unique to the OPEC region.

A key feature of the international oil industry in the OPEC region was the creation of operating companies. Companies such as Kuwait Oil Company (KPC), or Iraq Petroleum Company (IPC), and the Arabian American Oil

Company (Aramco) were owned jointly by a number of the major oil companies. While these operating companies were independent legal entities, their investment and output patterns had to be determined, as mentioned earlier, by the parent companies in response to the regional and worldwide interests of the latter.

Thus IPC, for instance, was owned by five companies, all of whom owned interest in Iran's oil concession; two held interests in Aramco; one held interest in KOC; and all five owned the operating companies in Qatar and the United Arab Emirates.

It is clear from this pattern of ownership that even without formal collusion, the companies' common knowledge of each partner's oil requirements had the effect of enabling the parent companies to regulate output for the entire group.

Not only did common knowledge of the requirements of various partners aid in planning a company's lifting requirements, but the instrument of joint ownership had other important implications for determining the pattern of investment and the level of future output.

The manner in which output and investment decisions were made for IPC is a good illustration of these implications. By agreement, the owners of IPC were entitled to receive oil at cost in proportion to their ownership shares in IPC. Those partners in need of more oil were required to buy it from other partners at a price higher than the cost of production but lower than the posted price. Moreover, investment plans for IPC were made for five-year intervals to start five years prior to the beginning of the investment period. (Thus, investment for the period 1957–61, for example, had to be planned in 1952.) In addition to these built-in rigidities, there was also the so-called five-sevenths rule, according to which the total amount of oil to be produced was computed by adding up the amounts nominated by various partners and then reducing it if the highest single nomination exceeded five-sevenths of the sum of the two lowest nominations (Penrose 1968, 157–59). The intent of such a rule was to limit the amount of oil that could be lifted from Iraq. Obviously, such rules made it extremely difficult for the government of Iraq to hope for an increase in output, considering the fact that the producing company was locked into a ten-year operating procedure that deprived it of flexibility. Yet the companies that owned IPC had alternative sources of oil in other OPEC regions, which helped them to regulate their total supply with relative ease.

Another feature that contributed to the regulation of output was the long-term contracts for the sale and purchase of oil concluded between some of the major oil companies. These contracts were negotiated to last for long periods of time and to cover substantial quantities of oil priced on a cost-plus basis. The contracts were also restrictive with respect to markets where buyers could dispose of their purchased oil. It is relevant to mention here that since the oil was priced on a cost-plus basis, these contracts served as a useful means of disclosure in terms of production-cost elements. Some of these contracts (such as between BP and Exxon or BP and Mobil) were so similar in detail that the competitors were made privy to the production plans and the cost of production of their rivals. Moreover, by giving BP the choice of delivering the contracted oil from either Kuwait or Iran, Exxon and Mobil were given access to the production data of another competitor, Gulf, which (with BP) owned the Kuwaiti concession. And since Gulf had its own long-term contract to sell oil to Shell, the other companies involved—BP, Exxon, and Mobil—found themselves having access to Shell's production and market plans (Federal Trade Commission 1952, ch. 6).

The significance of the disclosure clauses in these contracts can be seen in at least two areas. First, any seller contemplating a move to alter the current price was in a better position to predict his rivals' reaction than if he had no such information. Second, this disclosure, plus the joint ownership of the producing companies, provided the sellers with the motive to adopt a uniform or similar production-cost accounting system, which, in turn enabled similar assessment of output programs.

To recapitulate, the international oil industry in the OPEC region had absolute control over the determination of output volumes from the producing fields in member-country national territories. The nature of the concession system, the creation of jointly owned operating companies, and the long-term contracts concluded by the major oil companies that owned the operating companies in member countries tended to strengthen the position of the majors in regulating output from their widely scattered sources of supply from the Middle East, North Africa, the Far East, and Venezuela. Yet, the position of the multinational oil companies could not remain unchallenged. The strength of the oil companies derives, in the last analysis, from the stability of the forces underlying the international economic system.

The creation of OPEC proved, after a time lag, to be a potent force in the world political economy. The pages following are devoted to the study of the management of oil output under OPEC.

OUTPUT DETERMINATION UNDER OPEC

The creation of OPEC in 1960 did not initially alter the manner in which output was determined. This observation should not be construed, however, to mean that there were no efforts to influence the level of output by one country or the other. While some countries did succeed in having their output increased, other countries failed to persuade the oil companies to agree to a higher output. Several examples illustrate this point.

Iraq throughout the 1950s had a long-standing dispute with the oil companies over a number of commercial matters. The change in the political system that was brought about by the 1958 revolution accelerated the pace of the dispute between the two parties, with Iraq attempting to change some of the practices by the companies with respect to the level of oil output. The failure to reach a settlement on the issues of the dispute led the government of Iraq to enact in 1961 the celebrated Law Number 80 (entitled Defining the Exploitation Areas for the Oil Companies), which confined the companies to only one-half of 1 percent of the concession area. In other words, the government of Iraq appropriated to itself all the acreage that had not been exploited by the IPC.

The dispute with the oil companies continued throughout the 1960s, with Iraq's oil output failing to increase at the same rate as that of other countries. Thus, between 1960 and 1970, the annual rate of growth for Iraq's oil output was 4.7 percent, compared with an annual rate of growth of 13 percent for the region as a whole. The dispute between Iraq and the companies helped the companies to introduce the Libyan oil to the world market, as well as to boost oil output in Iran, Saudi Arabia, and Kuwait at rates that were higher than would otherwise have been the case.

The level of output in Iran was also a subject of contention between the Iranian government and the oil companies. The dispute was different from that in Iraq, in that the point of disagreement was the rate of output growth itself. The Iranian government had demanded that oil production be boosted to a level that would generate enough revenue to meet the projected needs of Iran's development plan. From the vantage point of the oil companies, the problem was that Iran was only one of a number of countries that the companies had to accommodate, while from Iran's viewpoint, oil was the only source of revenue for its development needs.

Opposition to Iran's demands came also from other oil-producing countries in the region, which concluded, and correctly so, that any abnormal increase in Iran's output would have to be at the expense of their own output growth. Although Iran made its demand for higher output in 1966, six years after OPEC's creation, no effort was made by OPEC to intervene.

Iran's demands for higher output and higher revenue were related not only to Iran's economic planning objectives but also to its desire to become the regional strong power. While the demands were legitimate from the Iranian government's viewpoint, accession by the oil companies to the demands would have undermined the elaborate structure of output allocation that the companies had devised to serve their collective interests (*MNC* report 1975, 107). The dispute intensified to the point that the governments of the major oil companies were drawn into it. While the British and French governments supported their own companies' stance that Iran's demand for higher output should be met, the U.S. government took the position adopted by the American companies that Iran's output should increase at the same rate as that of other countries in the region. The differing corporate positions expressed here reflected the companies' varying access to the oil resources of the region as well as their evaluation of the importance of each source of supply. Thus, the major American companies that owned Aramco and had interests in Iran's oil tended to be wary of jeopardizing their interest in Saudi Arbia. The French company, on the other hand, which had access to a larger amount of oil from Iraq but was restricted by its partners' decision, was very interested in increasing its oil lifting from Iran.

The Iranian demands for higher output were met for a two-year period, 1966 and 1967, with output increased for these years by close to 13 percent and 22 percent, respectively, as compared with output growth rates of 12 percent and 6 percent, respectively, for the entire Middle East. However, the long-term growth rates of Iranian oil output and of the Middle East region as a whole were not that divergent. Thus, for the period 1957–73, the average annual growth rate of exports from Iran was 11.8 percent, compared with an 11.1 percent average annual growth rate for the countries of the Middle East where members of the Iranian consortium had oil concessions (*MNC* report 1975, 103).

While the Iranian government was attempting to persuade the companies to relate their output to Iran's needs for revenue, the Saudi oil minister, Ahmed Z. Yamani, claimed that his government "had never interfered with the export plans of the companies operating in Saudi Arabia."[5] The Iranian government, however, in demanding still higher output in 1968, asserted that decisions regarding the volume of output could not be made by the companies unilaterally. The government stated its position as follows: "We, as the owners of this oil and the masters of this land, must have a say in the production of this wealth because the needs of this country are clear. It is clear to what purpose the country's revenues are being spent. No firm, no company, no organization can tell us, merely because it has an agreement with us, that we will produce and export so much of your national wealth. . . ."[6] In support of its demand for higher output, Iran resorted not only to its previous arguments of economic development and a larger need for defense following the withdrawal in the early 1960s of the British forces from the Gulf, but it contended that its case was far more valid than that of its neighbors and fellow members of OPEC who, so Iran claimed, were indulging in wasteful consumption and in the accumulation of foreign exchange in foreign banks. In stating its belief that dealing with the companies directly was more effective than dealing with them collectively through OPEC, Iran thus laid bare its own assessment of OPEC.

Compounding the problem for both OPEC and Iran's neighboring Arab countries was Iran's decision to appeal directly and publicly to the consuming countries, stating that its case was not only valid but that Iran was more deserving of a special treatment. Certain Arab oil observers responded by telling the government of Iran that it had the right, of course, to demand higher output but this did not have to be done at the expense of fellow OPEC-member countries, especially when the main reason for OPEC's existence was to help member countries to coordinate policies. The Iranian government was furthermore told that the path to higher revenue would be better served by demanding higher per-barrel revenue rather than higher output. Moreover, in an observation that proved prophetic, the Shah of Iran was told that his argument that Iran had a stable, pro-Western government was an exaggeration, since circumstances could easily change whereby a different government would come to power and nationalize the Iranian oil industry.[7]

From the viewpoint of policy coordination through OPEC, the Consortium Oil Agreement of 1954 had the effects of delaying the day when collective decision making and collective bargaining by member countries could occur. Had Iran, for instance, attempted to attain its objectives through OPEC, it conceivably could have accelerated the pace of collective bargaining for member countries. But to do that would have put up for public debate Iran's strategic and political objectives for the Gulf region. Iran, given its objectives at the time, was not about to ask an intergovernmental organization such as OPEC to help it obtain the revenue it sought from the oil companies.

The ability of the oil companies to accommodate the Iranian demand for higher output as recently as the late 1960s was rather remarkable in view of a number of considerations. First, the companies that owned equity shares in the Iranian Consortium and who also owned shares in other concessions must have had to "perform a political balancing act in order to keep their concessions" (*MNC* report 1975, 96). This was particularly important for the American majors that owned Aramco, since:

> *For the four Aramco parents, the most important allocation was between Iran and Saudi Arabia. Although the companies successfully avoided any fixed production commitments, Iran nevertheless won an agreement from the Consortium in 1954 to match the average annual growth rate for the Middle East. Thereafter, it became a fact of life that Aramco had to give Saudi Arabia equal treatment. The 1951 Iranian nationalization of BP allowed Aramco to make Saudi Arabia*

the largest Middle East producer. Although Saudi Arabia kept that distinction over the years, the Aramco parents nevertheless held their Arabian production in line with the Iranian Consortium's. (MNC report 1976, 96)

Second, the balancing of competing claims by the two major oil-producing countries must have required elaborate corporate cooperation and highly sophisticated planning by the oil companies. Regardless of whether or not there were cartel arrangements, the nature of production planning by these companies required coordination that was tantamount to one planning mechanism for all the participants in the various concessions.

Third, in their attempt to keep their concessions, the companies found themselves adhering to the principle of the most-favored nation; in other words, an increase in the output of one country had to be matched by a similar though not identical increase in the output of another country. It was an important consideration for governments that benefits be accorded all of them (Hartshorn 1978, 4–6).

Fourth, in adopting an allocation mechanism that proved workable, the companies demonstrated that production planning in various sovereign states was not only feasible but necessary. Concepts and prerogatives of sovereignty did not seem to have been an obstacle to production planning and country quotas. This observation raises the question of why it was possible for the oil companies to engage in production allocation within the OPEC region, yet such an allocation proved unattainable by the governments of member countries in the aftermath of their assuming control over their oil sectors.

OPEC'S PRODUCTION PLANS AND QUOTAS

While the price reduction of 1960 provided the stimulus for the creation of OPEC, the underlying rationale for the price cuts was the excess oil-producing capacity in the major oil-exporting countries. Specifically, the continued expansion of capacity and output in the Middle East and the displacement of Venezuelan oil from its traditional markets prompted Venezuela to examine the feasibility of production planning. But in order to engage in such an undertaking, Venezuela needed the cooperation of other oil-exporting countries. It was this attempt to encourage the oil-exporting countries to cooperate for the purpose of production planning that gave rise to the creation of OPEC (Rouhani 1971, 75–77).

Venezuela's argument was simple and straightforward: The only way to forestall a downward pressure on prices would be to engage in production programming. Without such a program, the oil companies would be free to install productive capacity that would increase output and eventually exert pressure on prices. The pacesetting example of the oil-producing states in the United States was cited at the time as a rational act whose lesson should not be lost to the oil-producing countries. Venezuela's attempt to press upon the Middle East oil-producing countries that one cannot expect to arrest the price decline without addressing the question of the level of output was successful enough to lead these countries to agree to the creation of OPEC (Rouhani 1971, 211–14). Indeed, OPEC's first resolution recognized the linkage between production planning and price when it stated that member countries "shall study and formulate a system to ensure the stabilization of prices by, among other means, the regulation of production" (OPEC, *Resolutions Adopted, Resolution 1*, September 1960).

Although, as stated, OPEC was formed at a time when an excess capacity output caused downward pressure on prices, the attention of most of the members countries was focused not on the relationship between prices and output but on price alone. In fact, only a few months after OPEC had adopted its production-related resolution, the government of Iran disclaimed (in December 1960) interest in regulating output, asserting that the idea of production programming was impractical and that Iran would insist to receive "at least one half of each year's growth in total Middle East production, and be restored as fast as possible to its historical position as No. 1 Middle East oil producer which it had lost during the 1951–54 shutdown" (Seymour 1980, 40).

Not only did the Iranian government find it more beneficial from the perspective of its own national interests not to subscribe to prorationing as expounded by Venezuela, but other governments in the Middle East were either unable or unwilling to support the concept. Iraq, for instance, decided to boycott the deliberations of OPEC for more than two years, owing to Iraq's political dispute with Kuwait; Iraq was placed in the difficult position of having to settle a disagreement with its operating company before it could agree to any plan for programming. In addition, both Kuwait and Saudi Arabia were unwilling to look at production planning as a viable policy vehicle for price stabilization (Seymour 1980, 41).

The failure of the OPEC founding members to regard prorationing as a serious policy may be explained under the circumstances by at least two factors. First, the governments of the oil-producing countries in the Middle East lacked the technical personnel necessary for an undertaking such as production programming. Second, by the time OPEC was founded, oil-exporting countries were more interested in expanding output and penetrating new markets than in having their output regulated. Middle East governments were interested in expanding output and export as the route to increasing revenue. Having convinced themselves that a price increase was unattainable, they found themselves pressing the oil companies to increase output.

Another consideration, of course, was the fact that the Middle East governments could not engage in any production prorationing without the consent of the oil companies or without coercing them to cooperate in implementing such a program. And, naturally, the companies were opposed to any interference in their production plans. The failure of the Venezuelan initiative for prorationing left OPEC to concentrate on the pricing issue. Topics such as pricing and revenue per barrel of output provided more common ground for agreement and therefore common policy objectives.

Having decided to focus on improving per-barrel revenue, OPEC-member countries did not address the question of production programming until 1965. It has been postulated by Ian Seymour that an informal agreement was reached between Venezuela and the Middle East producing countries to the effect that the latter should attempt to raise their revenue per unit of output to the level of Venezuela's. This was thought to be a sufficient condition for the elimination of the cost advantage that the Middle East had over Venezuela. Once these differentials were eliminated, Venezuela and the producing countries in the Middle East addressed the issue of production programming more formally (Seymour 1980, 41), as described in the next section.

THE 1965 JOINT PRODUCTION PROGRAM

The 1965 attempt by OPEC to adopt a production program was motivated by several considerations. For one thing, it became evident, after five years of negotiations and consultations with the operating companies, that the companies were not going to raise prices. The freedom of the operating companies to install capacity, plus the entry of newcomers, added to the downward pressures on posted prices. In addition, the wide fluctuations in the annual growth rates of output in individual countries introduced a significant element of uncertainty that tended to compromise individual governments' ability to plan for economic development. Moreover, a number of governments felt that the companies, having failed to stabilize output and raise prices, should be challenged through collective action by OPEC to regulate total output.

Such collective efforts, if successful, promised to have a widespread affect on the companies. This view was reflected in the position taken by Aramco and the operating companies in Iran and Libya, which was that the governments had no right to engage in regulating output and, furthermore, that these companies would take their host governments to international arbitration to prevent such regulation (Seymour 1980, 195).

The decision by OPEC-member countries to experiment with production programming was very tentative and, as the considerations just described make clear, was related to the objective of price stability. The 1965 resolution to adopt a joint production program sought to counteract the continuing erosion of crude and product prices as a result of the unrestricted competitive use of excess producing capacity. OPEC then resolved "to adopt as a transitory measure a production plan calling for [a] rational increase in production from [the] OPEC area to meet estimated increases in world demand" (OPEC, *Resolutions Adopted, Resolution 61*, July 1965).

Although a plan for production regulation was adopted by OPEC, it was not, however, implemented, for several reasons. First, any plan that has as its objective the regulation of oil output and therefore the regulation of the most important economic sector in a number of countries must receive not only the formal support of the participants but their willingness to accept the allocations envisaged in the plan. This in turn requires that participants be prepared to compromise on the essential issue of the prerogatives of nations. In addition, a plan to regulate output could be acceptable to the participants only so long as the allocations under the plan tended to meet the oil output envisaged by participating governments. For example, one of the reasons responsible for the successful prorationing program in the United States was the willingness of Texas to become the residual producing state in the sense that oil-production requirements of other states were met first (given the oil demand forecasts), with the balance being supplied from wells within Texas. In terms of the relative position of its reserves with respect to other member countries, the country within OPEC corresponding to Texas would be Saudi Arabia. Yet while the allocation program was acceptable to Iran, since its quota under the OPEC plan coincided with its demands, this was not the case with Saudi Arabia. Kuwait and Iraq likewise received entitlements under the plan that were beneath their expectation. And Libya, which was posting high rates of output growth, declared that it would not abide by the limits imposed on its output by the OPEC production plan (Seymour 1980, 203–5).

Thus, the initial production plan, which was to last for a twelve-month period ending in June 1966, was aborted in February 1966 when Saudi Arabia announced that it was no longer bound by the OPEC program. The Saudi dissatisfaction with the plan stemmed not only from its disagreement with the allotment given to it under the OPEC plan, but also because it felt that the OPEC plan could not be expected to succeed while output from producing areas outside the OPEC region was not being controlled (Seymour 1980, 203–05). In other words, the government of Saudi Arabia did not feel that the OPEC region should play the role of the residual supplier in the world. Another factor that contributed to the failure of this first OPEC production plan was the position of the oil companies. As might be anticipated, the companies operating in the OPEC region maintained that a production plan by OPEC-member countries constituted a violation of the contractual arrangements under the concession system, which gave the companies the legal rights to produce and export whatever quantities of oil they deemed fit without government intervention. Given the lack of a consensus among the producing countries themselves and the ability of the oil companies to reward certain governments and withhold such reward from others, the first OPEC plan was bound to fail.

In addition to the basic contradictions outlined above, there was a major flaw in the production plan's purpose. The plan was intended neither to conserve oil resources over the long run nor to regulate the rate of increase in supply, but to stabilize and/or increase per-unit revenue. And if this objective could be attained by means other than regulating output, countries would naturally opt for such a means. This point of view was articulated by Ahmed Yamani, the Saudi oil minister, in 1968: "If product prices should fall to the extent where tax levels are threatened, then Saudi Arabia—which for various reasons, is now opposed to prorationing of production—will become a prime supporter of such a measure. Oil is a wasting asset and Saudi Arabia would rather keep it in the ground than have it move onto the market at distress prices."[8] The view that OPEC would perhaps have resorted to prorationing only in the event of a serious erosion of crude-oil prices has also been voiced by Fuad Rouhani, another observer of OPEC behavior (Rouhani 1971, 215).

THE 1970 PRODUCTION PROGRAM

The collapse of the 1965 production program allowed individual governments to pursue their own production and export policies in conjunction with the oil companies. The emphasis was on higher output, with the degree of success varying from country to country depending on the particular conditions of the country, as well as the nature of government-company relations. Yet in 1967 OPEC thought it necessary to reaffirm its conviction that a joint production program was an effective instrument for the pursuit of the organization's fundamental objectives of stabilizing and maintaining crude and product prices. Toward this end, OPEC instructed its economic commission to undertake a comprehensive study with a view to perfecting an economically predictable system for the program's implementation (OPEC, *Resolutions Adopted, Resolution 84*, November 1967).

This interest in production programming took another major step in June 1970 when OPEC resolved to adopt a production plan calling for "rational increases in production from the OPEC area to meet estimated increases in world demand during the period 1971–1975" (OPEC, *Resolutions Adopted,*

Resolution 112, June 1970). No sooner had this resolution been adopted than price and tax changes diverted attention from output regulation to fiscal matters. Specifically, the success of the Libyan government in negotiating with the operating companies an upward adjustment in posted prices and tax rates encouraged other OPEC-member countries to attempt to persuade the companies to accord them similar price and tax benefits. This change in policy orientation provided the stimulus for the formulation in December 1970 of a number of resolutions that led to the eventual collective bargaining that produced the celebrated Tehran Agreement of 1971. In addition to the immediate concern with posted prices and tax rates, there were other reasons for the demise of the five-year production plan that OPEC adopted in 1970.

One reason was the marked change in market conditions, which generated increased demand for crude oil relative to productive capacity. In other words, the excess capacity that characterized much of the 1960s was gradually disappearing. The disappearance of excess capacity and the increase in demand at higher rates than the industry had anticipated created an upward pressure on crude oil and product prices. The need to regulate output for the purpose of stabilizing prices, which was the reason for production programming, had vanished. The question then became whether OPEC could or should produce oil in quantities that would meet the world's spiraling demand.

Another factor was the continuing lack of commitment to the principle of production programming on the part of most countries. With the exception of Venezuela, no other member country was willing to submit to the mechanism of an OPEC-supervised production plan. The shift in emphasis from higher volume to higher prices was accelerated in the aftermath of both the 1973 price revolution and the reversion of control of the oil sector to individual member governments. But in assuming control over their oil sectors, individual governments also inherited the responsibility of determining the level of output within their own national borders. In other words, the production-control mechanism that had been administered by the major oil companies was not replaced by a similar production allocation mechanism under OPEC; national decisions took precedence over any other consideration.

The newly decentralized, uncoordinated production policies could have resulted in excess capacity in the oil market during the 1970s were it not for the impact of certain fortuitous forces. As early as 1970 major producing countries with small populations, principally Kuwait and Libya, had decided to curtail output in the interest of conservation and in order to lengthen the life span of their oil reserves. These decisions allowed other countries to expand output without fear of creating an oil glut in the world market. Another factor that tended to favor the producing countries was the relatively low elasticity of demand for oil in the short run. Although prices had been increased sharply, the economies of the consuming countries managed to adjust to the new realities, which saved the producing countries from having to compete for a shrinking market. When the 1974/75 recession resulted in a lower demand for oil, some producing countries found themselves with sufficient foreign-exchange reserves to finance their imports, while other countries, especially Saudi Arabia, allowed their output to decline dramatically to alleviate the recession-induced decline in demand. The world oil market was such that OPEC countries found themselves in a position to raise crude oil prices in the face of decreasing demand (Al-Chalabi 1980, 108).

In the second half of the 1970s, it became evident that new realities in the supply/demand balance were calling for a new assessment of the prospects of production planning. Thus, Iraq and Libya proposed several times that OPEC should consider the adoption of a "contingency plan" for production programming, although these proposals were repeatedly rejected by Saudi Arabia.[9] Yet, the appearance of what was considered to be an oil glut in the market in 1977 and 1978 prompted OPEC-member countries to arrive at a quasi-informal, unpublicized agreement to restrain output.[10]

The adoption of such an arrangement was implied in a statement made by Yamani when he said that his country had "borne the brunt of disposing of the glut in the oil market when some 1.5 MBD of oil . . . 'disappeared' from the market thanks to Saudi Arabia which implemented this policy without publicizing it."[11] The same point was confirmed by the Iraq oil minister Tayeh Abdul-Karim, when he said that OPEC had a production organization plan that intended to restrain output growth in order to eliminate an oil glut.[12]

Following the price revolution of 1973, the remainder of the 1970s witnessed the disappearance of the production-allocation mechanism that was developed and used by the major oil companies. The dispersion of the power to regulate production among the various member countries did not lead to competitive price-cutting through volume expansion. The world demand for oil was sufficiently high to allow member countries to meet their fiscal requirements through their own output plans. But as soon as world demand began to change, stresses in the system started to appear. It was not until mid-1981, however, that OPEC decided that some form of production planning was in order.

PRODUCTION PROGRAMMING IN 1981 AND 1982

OPEC's experiment with production planning in the years 1981 and 1982 was both short-lived and inconclusive. In June 1981 the majority of member countries decided, informally, to reduce their combined output by 10 percent.

Individual countries proposed cuts that ranged from 16.7 percent for Kuwait to 5 percent for Ecuador. Although this decision was noteworthy merely because it was adopted at all, it fell short, however, of its main objective, owing mainly to the decision of Saudi Arabia to dissociate itself from the plan.[13] This was significant since Saudi Arabia's output at the time was 41 percent of OPEC's total output. Saudi Arabia's decision not to participate was expected for two reasons. First, Saudi Arabia has always adhered to the position that the level of oil output is a matter of internal policy; thus it could not be allowed to be affected by OPEC. Second, the decision to reduce output was intended to eliminate the oil glut, which was attributed, among other things, to a policy decision by the government of Saudi Arabia to increase its output above historical levels in order to force prices downward.

But the agreed-upon ceilings on output proved irrelevant, because the demand conditions for oil were such that most countries found themselves producing below their assigned quotas anyway. These weak demand conditions, together with the persistence of the Saudi government in producing above its normal ceiling—10 MBD as opposed to a ceiling of 8.5 MBD—caused many countries to lose major shares of their markets to Saudi Arabia and threatened the very existence of OPEC. Faced with these conditions, a compromise was reached whereby the government of Saudi Arabia agreed to reduce its output to the traditional ceiling of 8.5 MBD and to raise its price by $2 to $34 per barrel, in exchange for a reduction in the price of the marker by other member countries from $36 to $34 per barrel.[14]

The worldwide recession continued to exert a downward pressure on demand. This fact and the fact that oil companies thought it profitable to engage in a policy of destocking, prompted OPEC to adopt another production plan with quotas assigned to member countries. The combined output of member countries was set at 18.5 MBD for the year 1982. But once again, market conditions made it difficult for member countries to reach this combined level of output. Disagreement by certain member countries as to their quotas led once more to the collapse of an attempt by OPEC to regulate output. And again, output determination was left to individual countries.[15]

To recapitulate, OPEC policies to regulate output have met with less success than those that have been intended to set crude-oil prices. While member countries have agreed to improve per-barrel revenue, there has been no such agreement concerning output. On the contrary, members have been themselves competing with each other to have the oil companies increase output and export from their areas of concession. As late as June 1970, for instance, the government of Iran maintained that it was concerned not with higher oil prices but with expanding output as the main policy instrument for higher revenue.

The production-allocation mechanism that the oil companies provided prior to 1973 was not replaced by a similar mechanism when the oil concession reverted to the governments of the oil-producing countries after the 1973 price revolution. Although several attempts at production programming were made by OPEC as early as 1965, none of these was successful. The absence of an OPEC production plan meant, of necessity, that the level of output in each member country had to be determined by the economic and political considerations of each country. It was not until 1983, as is noted in chapter 7, that OPEC-member countries finally agreed on a production plan.

OPEC AS A "CARTEL": THE FLAWED CASE

The unanimity and the speed with which OPEC-member countries raised oil prices in the last quarter of 1973, together with the collusive behavior of the Arab oil-producing governments to reduce output and ban exports to certain countries, led many economists to view OPEC as a cartel.[16] This is understandable, given the major changes that a small group of developing countries were able to introduce in the international oil industry—changes that not only led to a sharp improvement in these countries' terms of trade but that also effected the transfer of controlling power over output and future prices to these countries. In addition to OPEC's being regarded as a cartel; it was also feared that OPEC might set an example to other raw-material exporting countries to form their own cartels. This fear was voiced, for example, when bauxite exporters increased their export earnings in 1974 and 1975, an act that led one author to describe the International Bauxite Association as a new OPEC in bauxite.[17]

Yet, on both theoretical and empirical grounds OPEC cannot be described as a cartel. The problem with a cartel theory as applied to OPEC is that it is imposed on the pricing behavior of an intergovernmental organization that lacks the necessary conditions and attributes of a commodity cartel. Economic theory on the subject of commodity cartels is explicit.[18] In order for a cartel to exist in a given market, certain features are called for, including an output quota system that determines the share of each member in the total output of the industry; an agreed-upon common price or price structure; and an agreement on quantitative and/or geographic market sharing. The primary functions of a cartel are two: the first is to prevent competitive selling by the firms and the second is to prevent or at least regulate the entry of new firms in the industry. These functions are designed to serve the overall objective of profit maximization.

The degree of rigidity with which cartels observe these rules varies. Cartels may be formal and rigid, with an organization that is empowered to sell the product on behalf of the cartel members. Agricultural cooperative societies and milk boards illustrate this type of cartel, as do labor unions that negotiate on behalf of their members to fix wage rates.

Commodity cartels have had a mixed degree of acceptance. While they are part of the acceptable market behavior of Europe, they are illegal in the United States under the provisions of the Sherman Antitrust Act. Yet even in the United States one can say that the essence of cartel behavior has been recaptured in the form of holding companies and mergers, both of which are legal. The international oil industry, as well as the American oil industry, present some of the most interesting examples of cartel behavior. As early as 1928 the so-called As Is Agreement, or the Achnacarry Agreement, which was concluded by Exxon, BP, and Shell, had all the attributes of a commodity cartel. The agreement, which was negotiated in the aftermath of a costly price competition, established certain principles to govern the actions of the members of the group with respect to their present and future share of the market; the cost of oil transacted between members of the group; the size and location of production facilities to be installed; utilization of existing production facilities; and the setting of export and delivered prices.

The 1928 cartelization effort by the three major oil companies was aided by the cartelization efforts in the American oil industry. The prorationing system was administered by the Texas Railroad Commission and by the U.S. government ensured that oil output in the United States, the largest oil-producing country at the time, would be regulated to meet anticipated demand. Moreover, the international oil industry was in a position to strengthen its efforts toward cartelization through other mechanisms. One such mechanism was the basing point system of pricing, which had the advantage of setting uniform delivered prices for oil to any consumption center on the basis of the posted prices at the U.S. Gulf of Mexico, regardless of the actual production center or the cost of production. More important, however, was the ability of the oil companies to regulate oil output from diverse centers of production. This was accomplished through their joint ownership of oil-producing subsidiaries in the host countries. In other words, the oil-producing countries served as the functional equivalent of multiplant operations of the single firm.

So far as newcomers were concerned, these were kept away by the nature of the concession agreement system that operated at the time. And in those instances where newcomers actually succeeded in entering the industry, the industry had enough economic rent to accommodate the new entrants, which had only a small fraction of the market anyway.

It was in this industry structure that OPEC was created. Since neither member countries nor the oil companies allowed OPEC any serious voice in government-company relations prior to the Tehran Agreement of 1971, OPEC remained for all practical purposes of marginal importance at best. Although the Tehran Agreement introduced the principle of collective bargaining, the scope of the principle was confined to prices only. Output decisions remained in the domain of corporate prerogatives.

The next question that needs to be addressed is: Did the structural transformation in the post-1973 era change the character of OPEC from the noncartel it was to that of a cartel? To many economists, as noted earlier, the answer was yes. Yet close examination of the empirical evidence shows that OPEC simply was not a cartel. OPEC could not have been, given its own limited prerogatives on the one hand and the unlimited prerogatives of each member country vis-à-vis OPEC on the other hand. An explanation of this is in order.

To begin with, OPEC-member countries in 1973 supplied close to 53 percent of the world oil output and about 25 percent of the world consumption of energy. By 1982 the ratios had declined to 39 percent and 17 percent respectively. And as of this writing, in mid-1983, the share of OPEC oil output has declined to 29 percent of the world total. Based on these indicators, it is hard to justify pinning the cartel label on an oganization that produces less than one-third of the world output. Moreover, OPEC output, as was pointed out earlier, is not determined jointly by member countries but by the decisions of the individual countries. This is a major departure from the corporate output-regulating mechanism that prevailed in the OPEC region under the concession agreement system. Yet even if OPEC-member countries do not regulate output, they are still small in number, a fact that may give the appearance of collusive and cartellike behavior. But the small number, it should be emphasized, is not an indicator of cartel behavior. It is useful to remember in this context that any industry that departs from the purely competitive textbook model must have some elements of monopoly. Depending on these monopoly elements, as well as the nature of the product and the number of sellers, the typical market structures of monopolistic competition, ologopoly, bilateral oligopoly, cartel, and so forth usually apply. Looking at OPEC's structure, history, decision-making process, and the dominant position of member countries in OPEC's deliberations, it can be said that OPEC does not and cannot fall under any of the market structures listed here. For one thing, the ultimate objective of any business firm, regardless of its market structure, is profit maximization, and market imperfections help the firm to attain this objective. In the case of the cartel, it is important not only that prices be administered but that output be regulated and market-sharing arrangements observed in order for profits to be maximized. In the case of OPEC, none of these conditions is found. The question of market-sharing arrangements is easily dispensed with in terms of OPEC because neither OPEC as an organization, nor its member countries, nor their national oil companies have any such arrangements: marketing of oil is done by a national company working independently of any other national company.

As to the issue of output regulation, it is clear that prior to March 1983 OPEC failed to reach and observe any agreement on output programming. During the 1960s output decisions were in the hands of the oil companies. During the 1970s the rise in oil prices made such an agreement unnecessary for a number of member countries. More important, the governments of OPEC-member countries have always placed economic and political national considerations above the common economic interests of the group. It is these national interests that, in the final analysis, render fruitless any attempt to categorize an organization like OPEC. The major flaw in attempting to label OPEC stems from trying to impose the behavior of a firm—which has profit maximization as its single most important goal—on the behavior of a group of political entities, each one of which has different and numerous political, social, and economic objectives. Furthermore, each OPEC-member country has a different set of domestic and international priorities. One has only to compare the behavior of Iran with that of either Saudi Arabia or Iraq to realize how difficult it is to attempt to establish common domestic and international priorities to guide common oil-production policies.

Finally, on the issue of prices, it will be recalled that the 1973 pricing decisions provided the immediate and convenient justification for designating OPEC a cartel. The justification was stengthened by the similarity between Saudi Arabia and Texas, in that the former was the dominant force within OPEC while the latter was the dominant oil force in the United States. Any serious decline in the demand for oil would, so it was thought, be absorbed by Saudi Arabia. (if Texas did it for the benefit of all producers, why should not Saudi Arabia do it?) This conception, however, was both simplistic and uncritical. As this chapter and chapter 3 have demonstrated, the Saudis tended to expand their output at the expense of other producers to the point that they engineered an oil glut in the market.

Before leaving this issue, two points are worth reiterating. First, OPEC, for whatever reasons, has always reacted to changing market conditions; its prices have invariably been adjusted, with a time lag, after market prices have risen above posted or official prices. OPEC-member countries have allowed themselves to become residual suppliers of oil. This has meant that member countries have been willing to let the buyers determine their output for them. Had OPEC acted in the tradition of profit maximization, it would have been necessary for OPEC to regulate output and prices. Second, the behavior of the largest producer, Saudi Arabia, has not conformed to what one might expect from the leading producer. A cartel is supposed to benefit from higher prices, and the largest producer is supposed to help maximize profits for the group. But in the case of OPEC, the largest producer has not only been uninterested in raising prices but on several occasions has decided to raise output in an attempt either to prevent the prices from rising or to actually force them down.

In a nutshell, it is difficult to take seriously any attempt to apply textbook economic analysis that was developed to describe the behavior of a profit-maximizing firm to the behavior of governments that happen to own an exhaustible resource such as oil. OPEC is simply OPEC, and to attempt to force it into any of the frameworks of conventional economic analysis is a futile exercise.

CHAPTER 5

OPEC and the Industrialized Countries: The Increased Dependency

It was not until the 1973–74 crude-oil price revolution, thirteen years after OPEC's formation, that OPEC became the subject of much analysis and study, both at the professional and popular levels. So great was the impact of the price changes, together with the output cutback and embargo measures taken by the Arab members of OPEC, that the industrialized countries hoped that by examining OPEC's motives and behavior they might prevent similar occurrences in the future.

Neither the impact of the OPEC decisions on the industrialized economies nor the consequences of these decisions for industrialized and Third World economies alike should be minimized in scope or significance. As mentioned earlier, the industrialized countries' economies had developed on the basis of low-cost energy, mainly oil, that was supplied essentially by the OPEC-member countries. Not only were the industrialized countries always assured of the oil supply but they were also the beneficiaries of the supply of an essential commodity whose price was constantly moving downward, first in absolute terms, then in real terms. Moreover, both the political economy and the economy of the international industry made it possible to ensure that oil would be supplied at low cost and in almost unlimited quantities to meet the needs of the industrialized economies.

This long-term pattern of petroleum relations that intertwined with the postwar-long era of economic prosperity in industrialized countries was, so it seemed, ruptured suddenly by the price and output and embargo measures in 1973.

With no similar experience with another industry or group of countries to guide them, the first reaction of many non-OPEC countries to the collusive behavior of OPEC-member nations was, as described in chapter 4, to characterize OPEC as a cartel. The term *cartel*, despite its inapplicability to OPEC, provided an analytical framework for the interpretation of member countries' price and production behavior.[1] And on the basis of such analysis, policy considerations and recommendations were drawn. Whether or not the framework for these policies reflected the underlying economic and institutional arrangements within OPEC failed to receive the attention it deserved as the oil-crisis mentality gripped both professional economists and policy makers. Under these conditions every OPEC action was perceived to manifest a cartel like behavior, even if certain actions clearly violated the precepts of a cartel.

The reactions to the price revolution and its consequences centered on several important economic issues, which are summarized in the following paragraphs.[2]

In the first place the rise in the price of oil constituted an impediment to the macroeconomic policies of aggregate demand management in the industrialized countries; in other words, policies that were designed to combat inflation and recession were made difficult to implement.

Second, the process of recovery and growth was slowed as the oil-induced balance-of-payments deficits in industrialized countries necessitated that the external balance problem take precedence over economic growth. Another problem was related to the relative ability of the international financial system and its institutions to handle the sudden bulges in financial flows from the oil-producing countries. Given the limited absorptive capacity of some of these countries, it was inevitable that these countries would have current-account surpluses. The emergence of these financial surpluses found a haven in the money and capital markets of the industrialized countries. Although not borne out by subsequent events, it was feared at the time that these flows might overburden the intermediation capacity of the international financial system.

It was also alleged that the exponential growth of these surpluses in the years following the price changes would be of such magnitude that the process of real-resource transfer would be burdensome for the industrialized countries. In other words, it was assumed that when the accumulated financial assets were converted into real assets, the ability of the industrial economies to make the transition would be severely tested. The test would be particularly destabilizing if a sudden and/or massive transfer of real resources from the industrialized countries hampered their ability to meet the social and economic needs of their populations.

A corollary to this argument was the effect on the ability of the industrialized countries to provide developmental assistance as a result of the rise in the cost of imported oil. In trying to cope with their own deficit problems, industrialized countries were having an increasingly difficult time keeping the flow of official development assistance at historical levels. It was also assumed that the sudden increase in the price of oil, as well as the presumed continued effectiveness of

OPEC, would have other economic and political problems for the industrialized countries in terms of vulnerability to other OPEC actions and the conflicts and discord among the industrialized countries that might result from these actions. The 1973 OPEC actions, as well as those of the Arab oil producers, were considered the harbinger of further actions not only by OPEC but perhaps by other non-OPEC, non-oil-raw-material exporting countries.

The fear of further destabilization of the world economy was reflected in the industrialized countries' attitudes toward a number of unrelated policy measures. First, the continued effectiveness of OPEC in determining price and output was construed to be a source of continued vulnerability—political, economic, and strategic—to the industrialized countries. In other words, a repetition of the 1973–74 oil-policy measures either by OPEC or a subgroup in OPEC could not be ruled out. It was assumed that this dilemma could be solved only by reducing the effectiveness of OPEC.[3] Second, it was feared that the rise in the price of crude oil and the resultant deficits in industrial countries' balance of payments would provide a rationale to importing countries to enter into bilateral trade agreements with oil-exporting countries in order to reduce oil-related balance-of-payments deficits. Such policy behavior was thought particularly attractive to those industrialized countries such as Japan and Italy that did not have indigenous energy sources. Bilateral trade agreements, it was alleged, would undermine the policy of trade liberalization between industrialized countries. Given the difficulties that had plagued the international economic system prior to OPEC, it was thought that these bilateral agreements would give rise to a new surge of protectionism and economic nationalism, and perhaps to the formation of trade blocs.

Another fear voiced at the time was that OPEC's actions might set an example to other developing countries to engage in price setting, thus raising the cost of other imported raw materials to the industrialized countries. It was believed that such actions by other developing countries, though of a lesser magnitude than those of OPEC, would have similar effects on the economies of the industrialized nations and on the world at large (Bergsten 1978, 91-105).

The next several sections of this chapter examine these arguments in more detail in an effort to evaluate the extent to which OPEC has proven to be a power in the world economy.

OPEC AND THE PROBLEM OF STAGFLATION

The twin problems of inflation and economic stagnation found a ready explanation in the price behavior of OPEC. The argument ran as follows. An increase in the price of imported energy had the effect of raising the domestic price of energy throughout the economy. Even in countries where there were alternative and/or other sources, the low elasticity of demand for oil made it extremely difficult, if not impossible in some cases, to engage in either conservation or interfuel substitution. And since the cost of energy was an important element in household budgets, the increment in the final price to the energy consumer tended to exert an upward pressure on the consumer price index. Adding strength to the argument that oil-price increases were inflationary was the fact that petroleum products were (and are) used as feedstock and as raw materials in hundreds of products, thus spreading the effect of the cost increase throughout the economy. These inflationary pressures would in turn result in higher rates of unemployment as the higher prices reduced aggregate demand.

In assessing the impact of the oil-price rise on the inflation rates or GNP deflators, one is faced with the immense difficulty of isolating the impact of the cost of this particular commodity over the index to be measured. In and of themselves expenditures on energy amount to about 5 percent of total spending in the United States. The value of total OPEC exports is in the vicinity of 13 percent to 15 percent of total world exports. The relationship of imported oil to total oil consumption and to total energy consumption must also be taken into account. In other words, the impact of oil-price increases on the consumer price index is not a simple linear relationship. Moreover, it is problematic, when discussing the behavior of the consumer price index, to isolate the impact of significant commodity price changes from those of fiscal and monetary policies. Macroeconomic policies may or may not be adopted to counteract the effect of price changes. Given such inherent complexities in attempting to measure the impact of the rise in the cost of imported oil on the inflation rates, it is not surprising that such estimates have tended to vary.

Thus, according to early studies by the U.S. Bureau of Labor Statistics, the consumer price index in the United States had increased by 12.2 percent in the fourth quarter of 1974 over the fourth quarter of 1973. The cost of directly purchased energy during that period accounted for 11.4 percent of the rise, while other items contributed the other 88.6 percent of the increase (U.S., President 1975, 48); thus the rise in the price of energy added about 1.4 percent to the inflation rate during that period.

The impact of the rise in the price of oil on the inflation rates in other industrialized countries was much higher than that in the United States. The cost of imported oil represents a much higher component of total imports in these countries than in the United States. Taking all the industrialized countries together, it was estimated that for the OECD countries, price increases resulting from higher energy cost may have accounted for about one-fourth of the overall increase in the consumer price index ("Inflation and Stagflation" 1974,

683–98). It should be stressed that the inflation problem was aggravated and not created by the rise in the cost of energy. Inflationary pressures in industrialized countries became a policy problem as far back as 1965. These pressures became an important preoccupation of macroeconomic policy makers in the early 1970s when inflation rose precipitously. This acceleration may be seen in the rise of the consumer price index between 1970 and the third quarter of 1973 (prior to the oil-price increase), when the consumer price index rose by 16 percent in the United States, 27 percent in Japan, 19 percent in Germany, 24 percent in Italy, and 28 percent in the United Kingdom. (U.S., President 1975, 359).

Similarly, it can be argued that economic stagnation is rooted in forces other than the increase in the cost of oil or other forms of energy. Indeed, in the late 1960s and before the rise in the cost of energy, industrial countries followed economic policies that were deliberately intended to create a recession in order to slow down the inflation rate. This was not the first such policy to induce recession, nor would it be the last; the recessions of 1969–70 and of 1980 were also created by similar policies. Indeed, some economists have argued that all six recessions since the end of World War II can be traced to changes in government budgetary policies (Heilbroner and Thurow 1981, 306). The behavior of industrial economies in the early 1970s merits special attention, however, since it illustrates the response of these economies to deliberate policy measures intended to slow the rate of inflation by reducing the rate of economic growth.

As mentioned earlier, the 1969–70 recession resulted from policy measures aimed at dampening inflationary pressures in the economy. This recession was followed by an expansionary policy that pushed the economy into a sharp rise in 1972 and early 1973. What distinguished this boom from preceding booms was that it happened simultaneously throughout the industrialized world. The coincident impact of the expansionary forces in the major industrialized countries resulted in an unprecedented real annual rate of economic growth of 9.5 percent in the first half of 1973. Such a rate was impossible to sustain, however, as supply constraints began to appear by mid-1973. In addition to the constraints, economic policy was beginning to restrain aggregate demand within the limits of available capacity in order to accomplish the same policy objective. The combination of these two sets of restrictions resulted in a sharp decline in the growth rate, from 9.5 percent in the first half of 1973 to a 2.75 percent annual rate for the second half of that year.[4]

The deceleration of the growth rate in the second half of 1973 was compounded by several other factors. One of these was a crippling coal miners' strike in England that contributed to a fall in output in the first quarter of that year. The poor harvests of 1972 and 1973 further exacerbated matters, leading to major increases in food prices that intensified the inflationary pressures. In addition to the rise in food prices, there was a sharp increase in the prices of raw materials, a fact that contributed to the general rise in prices. It was within this economic context that the prices of crude oil were raised by OPEC and production cutback measures instituted by the Arab oil-producing nations. Needless to say these measures further strained a world economy that was already undergoing a severe deceleration in output.

The effects of the restrictive policies of industrialized countries did not cease with the lifting of the production cutback and embargo measures in early 1974. These policy measures led to virtually no growth in the real gross national product of the industrialized countries. Thus between the second half of 1973 and the first half of 1974 real GNP was declining in these countries at an annual rate of one-half of 1 percent. Yet the cessation of growth failed to dampen the inflationary pressures in these countries as they entered the severe 1974–75 recession. In this regard, the combination of high inflation and high unemployment in economies that showed either an absence of growth or sluggish growth moved Professor Paul Samuelson of Massachusetts Institute of Technology to state that no mixed economy—whether it be the United States, the United Kingdom, Sweden, Switzerland, Germany, Japan, France, or Italy—knows how to sustain full employment with price stability.[5]

In conclusion, the evidence indicates that the economic difficulties of the industrialized countries predated the sudden increase in the price of oil. This is not to say, however, that the increase did not aggravate an already-difficult situation throughout the industrialized world.

THE SECOND OIL-PRICE SHOCK AND STAGFLATION

The events that led to the success of the Iranian Revolution in early 1979 had the effect of introducing certain irreversible changes into the international oil industry. Nowhere were such changes more evident than in the phenomenal increase in the price of crude oil.

The slowdown and virtual stoppage of production of oil in Iran toward the end of 1978 led to a marked increase in the price of crude oil. OPEC, as was discussed earlier, found itself without any control over its own official prices, because the traditional relationship between spot and official prices had been severely ruptured, with the former constantly much higher than the latter. OPEC was thus continually in the position of having to abandon official prices and official formulas in order to align its prices with those in the open market. The new emerging supply/demand imbalance drove prices from a level of $13 per barrel at the end of 1978 to close to $35 per barrel by early 1981.

The significance of this change can be seen by analyzing the payments position of industrialized economies whose current-account balance changed from a surplus of $31 billion in 1978 to a current-account deficit of $10 billion in 1979, and to an even-higher deficit of $44 billion in 1980 (IMF, *World Economic Outlook* 1982, 165). Looking at the cost of imported oil alone, the net oil import cost for the seven major industrialized countries (the United States, the United Kingdom, Japan, Germany, France, Italy, and Canada) increased from $105 billion in 1978 to $217 billion in 1980. Again, in relation to the gross national product of the major oil-importing countries, the second jump in price represented a major reversal in the relative cost of imported oil. Thus in the case of Japan net-oil imports as a percentage of GNP had declined from 4.8 percent in 1974 to 2.6 percent in 1978 but increased to 5.5 percent in 1980. In the case of France, the ratios for these years were 3.9 percent, 2.3 percent, and 4.8 percent, respectively; and for Germany, the corresponding ratios were 2.8 percent, 2 percent, and 5 percent, respectively. But in spite of all these shifts the impact of the second oil shock seems to have been absorbed by the industrialized economies with less severity—in other words, the impact on the economic growth rates and on the inflation rates was much less pronounced—than was the first oil shock of 1973–74.[6]

The second oil shock had differing effects among the industrialized countries in terms of output and prices, for several reasons. In the first place, the industrial countries exhibited differences in the timing and the direction of change of their economic activities. In the United States and Canada, for instance, economic activity declined during the first half of 1980, and was followed by a weak recovery until mid-1981, which turned into a recession later that year. In Europe, on the other hand, output remained stable and at about the level to which it had declined in mid-1980 (IMF, *World Economic Outlook* 1982, 31).

Not only did the pattern of economic activity vary among the major industrial countries but so did the pattern of domestic price response to the change in the price of oil. The price response to an external shock, such as a dramatic rise in the cost of imported oil, cannot be separated from the complex of problems that characterized the economies of the industrialized countries throughout the 1970s. In addition to the major difficulties of inflation and high rates of unemployment, these countries were suffering from high interest rates, lack of growth of world trade, and the impairment of the international purchasing power of the developing countries. These problems might have found some solutions within the traditional combination of fiscal and monetary policies of the industrial economies, had the latter not also been hampered by major rigidities and structural imbalances that had become embedded in their economic systems. Examples of these rigidities may be found in the areas of wage bargaining and price setting, in government subsidies or protection of ailing industries, in structural unemployment, and in fixed government spending and taxation policies. These problems tended to make inflation intractable and economic recovery slow

(IMF, *World Economic Outlook* 1982, 12). Of particular relevance in this context is the fact that oil prices are expressed in dollars and that the value of the U.S. dollar appreciated considerably in 1980 and 1981, so much so that it more than offset the deceleration of domestic inflation as measured by GNP deflator (IMF, *World Economic Outlook* 1982, 7).

In addition to these forces, which either reinforced or weakened the influence of the 1979–80 oil-price rise, there was the changing relationship between economic growth and energy consumption. Although gross national output did increase in many countries between 1974 and 1980, the energy requirements for such increases were lower in the 1970s than in earlier decades. The policies of conservation and more efficient utilization of energy were making their impact felt by the end of the 1970s. Two other forces tended to slow down the rate of growth of oil imports. The first was the increase in the oil output of a number of importing countries. The increase in the price of OPEC oil in the 1970s provided an incentive to bring into the market crude oil from fields with a higher cost of production that had formerly been excluded from the market owing to the relatively cheap price of crude oil from the OPEC region. The other factor was the successful substitution of nonoil sources of energy, particularly coal for oil, in a number of oil-importing countries.

To recapitulate, the OPEC oil-price increases of 1973–74 and 1979–80 represented serious shocks to the economies of the industrialized countries. These external shocks were superimposed on economies that had already entered a period of slow growth or of no growth or that were already experiencing a serious decline in output. These changes in output were also associated with high rates of unemployment and persistent inflation, giving rise to conditions of stagflation. The persistence of stagflation conditions, aggravated at times by exchange-rates movements, was not helped by changes in prices of raw materials, especially oil. The ultimate impact of the rise of crude-oil prices on any one national economy must be judged on the basis of a number of complex relationships and structural features of that economy. These include the degree of dependence on imported oil and/or other energy sources, structural imbalances, economic rigidities (especially with respect to wage bargaining and price setting and the resiliency of the export sector of the economy), as well as the specific objectives of fiscal and monetary policy measures of any particular country.

THE RISE AND FALL OF THE OPEC SURPLUSES

At the time of the 1973–74 OPEC price rise, it was assumed that oil-exporting countries would continue to accumulate financial assets in the years following. Estimates of these financial assets ranged widely. For example, the World Bank, in a study published in 1974, projected that the financial accumulations of OPEC-member countries would reach $653 billion in 1980 and $1.2 trillion by 1985 in current dollars. Exxon, on the other hand, predicted financial accumulations in the range of $300 billion to $350 billion for 1980, while Morgan Guaranty Trust Company foresaw $179 billion for 1980 (Willet 1975, 5–7).

These projections differed of necessity, because they had to be based on a host of variables—such as prices, rates of economic growth, energy-consumption patterns, and new oil discoveries—none of which could be plotted with any accuracy. Underlying these projections were several major assumptions. One such assumption was that demand for energy and/or oil would continue to rise linearly at its historical rates. Another assumption was that the demand for oil would continue to be relatively inelastic even at the higher price range. In addition, it was assumed that the absorptive capacity of oil-producing countries for imports would remain low in spite of the increase in these countries' export earnings. All of these suppositions proved faulty, partly as a result of other factors that could not be predicted at the time. The first of these was that the 1970s proved to be a decade of relatively low economic growth throughout the world. Another factor was the increase in oil production and/or exports from non-OPEC regions such as the North Sea, Alaska, and Mexico. A third factor was the active intervention by the governments of major oil-importing countries in the oil market to influence the behavior of demand and supply. Briefly stated, these governments launched a series of energy policy measures designed to reduce oil consumption and oil imports. These energy policies, which were not contemplated when the projections were made, proved to be effective in reducing the demand for oil. Not only did the policies of oil-importing countries succeed in reducing OPEC current-account surpluses and financial accumulations but the policies of the oil-exporting countries themselves tended to have a similar effect.

With the sudden increase in export earnings, governments of oil-producing countries found themselves embracing certain policies that would have been difficult if not impossible to embrace without such increases. These policies centered around the adoption of two sets of measures dealing with internal and external economic objectives. On the domestic side, oil-producing countries found it necessary to initiate or accelerate the effort to achieve their long-sought objective of economic diversification. The increased earnings from oil were regarded as an important vehicle to attain this objective. And given the limited resource endowments in many of these countries, it was only natural that these countries would increase drastically their imports of goods and services. The attempt at economic diversification not only increased imports considerably; there was also a pent-up demand for consumer goods and military imports. Thus, imports of consumer-good durables and nondurables, as well as essentials and nonessentials, increased considerably in the period following the rise in the price of crude oil. The same observation was true of arms imports, which were considered essential in the process of modernizing and equipping these countries' armed forces.

The provisions for economic diversification, higher levels, of consumption, and the modernization of the armed forces were also accompanied by an expansion in social services that in turn required increased public-sector employment to administer the programs. These changes contributed substantially to the sharp rise in imports.

Externally, OPEC-member countries recognized the importance of creating vehicles for channeling surplus funds to other developing nations as well as to multilateral and other international organizations. The routing of funds to other developing countries took several forms, such as bilateral assistance through national funds for external development, multilateral assistance through the OPEC Fund for International Development, or regional organizations such as the Arab Fund for Economic and Social Development. In addition to these directly or indirectly dispensed but controlled funds, OPEC-member countries provided the International Monetary Fund and the World Bank with loans that were used to augment the lending capacity of these institutions. Most of the surplus, however, was recycled back into the international financial system in the form of bank deposits, acquisitons of government securities, and corporate stocks and bonds in the industrial countries (see table 2).

Two observations are relevant here. First, the current-account surplus of the oil-producing countries, which peaked at $68 billion in 1974, began to decline in 1975 and continued to drop until it reached the vanishing point by 1978. Conversely, industrialized nations' current-account deficit was transformed into a surplus by 1978. Second, it is important to remember that only a few of the thirteen OPEC-member countries—those with low absorptive capacity—were responsible for most of the so-called OPEC surplus. By way of explanation, OPEC-member countries may be classified into two groups. The first group is composed of the six countries that had current-account surplus every year during the 1970s and includes Saudi Arabia, Kuwait, the United Arab Emirates, Iraq, Libya, and Qatar. The second group is composed of the other seven member countries Algeria, Ecuador, Gabon, Indonesia, Iran, Nigeria, and Venezuela, whose current accounts exhibited either a surplus or deficit during this period. The six countries with consistent current-account surpluses were responsible for 92 percent of the accumulated current-account surplus, with Saudi Arabia predominating in that it owned 34 percent of the total surplus of the group.

With the second price shock of 1979, the payments position of the oil-

Table 2. Deployment of OPEC–Member Countries' Foreign Assets, 1974–80 (Billions of U.S. Dollars)

	1974	1975	1976	1977	1978	1979	1980	Cumulative Total
Short-term investment								
United States	9.3	1.1	0.6	(0.4)[a]	(0.2)	8.3	0.2	18.9
Other industrial countries	27.2	8.4	9.5	11.0	3.4	34.9	42.3	136.7
Total short-term investment	36.5	9.5	10.1	10.6	3.2	43.2	42.5	155.6
Percentage of total investment	64.0	27.0	27.0	32.0	24.0	71.0	49.0	48.0
Long-term investment								
United States	2.3	8.9	11.4	9.6	1.5	(1.5)	14.3	46.5
Other industrial countries	8.5	6.8	7.3	6.5	3.9	9.7	18.7	61.4
Developing countries	6.3	6.5	6.4	6.5	4.5	9.6	6.6	46.4
International institutions	3.5	4.0	2.0	0.3	0.1	(0.4)	4.9	14.4
Total long-term investment	20.5	26.2	27.1	22.9	10.0	17.4	44.5	168.6
Percentage of total investment	36.0	73.0	73.0	68.0	76.0	29.0	51.0	52.0
TOTAL INVESTMENT	57.0	35.7	37.2	33.5	13.2	60.6	87.0	324.3

Source: Organization of Arab Petroleum Exporting Countries (OAPEC), *Secretary General's Eighth Annual Report, 1981* (Kuwait: OAPEC, 1982), p. 66.
[a]Data in parens denote a decline in investment.

exporting countries changed drastically, from that of a small surplus of $2 billion in 1978 to a sizable surplus of $69 billion in 1979. This surplus reached a high of $114 billion in 1980, only to decline to $65 billion in 1981 before turning to a deficit in 1982 (see table 3). As would be expected, the payments position of the industrialized countries moved in the opposite direction. Again the development of current-account surplus in the second period reflected a pattern similar to that in the earlier period, in that the surplus found its way to developing countries, imports expenditures, and various forms of financial investments in industrial countries.

According to the IMF, the oil-exporting countries' total accumulated current-account surplus for the period 1974 to 1982 was $421 billion. If net borrowing by these countries and the oil-sector capital transactions are added to this surplus, these countries had a total cash surplus of $471 billion, which was disposed of in the following manner (IMF, World Economic Outlook 1983, 187):

$ 14 billion loans to IMF and purchases of World Bank bonds
$ 72 billion loans and grants to nonoil developing countries
$141 billion bank deposits in industrial countries
$244 billion government securities, corporate bonds and stocks, bilateral lending, real estate, and other direct investment

OPEC AND THE INDUSTRIALIZED COUNTRIES: TRADE

One of the immediate manifestations of the sharp change in crude-oil prices of 1973–74 was a major shift in the relative position of OPEC imports and exports in world trade.[7]

In 1973 OPEC total exports amounted to $39.5 billion, or 7.5 percent of the world total exports. The value of member-country imports in that year was $20.3 billion, or 3.8 percent of the world total. The ratio of OPEC imports to its exports in that year was 51 percent.

In 1974, following the hike in the price of crude oil, OPEC's combined exports jumped to $115.8 billion, or 15 percent of the world total exports. OPEC's imports, on the other hand, increased to $33.1 billion, or 4.2 percent of the world total import trade. The ratio of OPEC imports to its exports had fallen in 1974 to 29 percent.

By 1978, the last full year prior to the second price shock, OPEC total exports had increased to $143.8 billion and its imports to $102.1 billion. Relative to world trade, OPEC exports had declined to 12 percent, while its imports had

Table 3. OPEC-Member Countries' Distribution-of-Payments
Balance on Current Account, 1973–82 (Billions of U.S. Dollars)

Year	Total Current-Account Balance	Share of Six Surplus Countries	Share of Other Seven Countries
1973	6.7	6.8	−0.1
1974	68.3	43.8	24.5
1975	35.4	31.2	4.1
1976	40.3	36.6	3.7
1977	30.3	32.5	−2.3
1978	2.2	18.0	−15.8
1979	68.6	54.5	14.1
1980	114.3	101.0	13.3
1981	65.0	67.4	−2.4
1982	−2.2	10.3	−12.5

Source: Derived from International Monetary Fund, *World Economic Outlook*, 1983, p. 187.

Notes: Surplus countries are defined as the countries that had a current-account surplus each year in the 1970s. These countries included Iraq, Kuwait, Libya, Qatar, Saudi Arabia, and the United Arab Emirates. The other seven countries referred to in the table include Algeria, Ecuador, Gabon, Indonesia, Iran, Nigeria, and Venezuela.

almost doubled their share to 8.1 percent. In that year the ratio of OPEC imports to its exports had climbed to 71 percent. Looking at the same data from the perspective of the growth of both imports and exports, it may be seen that while the value of exports increased by 24 percent between 1974 and 1978, imports increased by 208 percent during the same period (see table 4).

Several factors account for the discrepancy in the rates of growth of exports and imports, as well as for the change in the relative importance of these growth rates within the context of world trade. To begin with, crude-oil prices remained remarkably stable during the period between the two price shocks, except for some fractional changes. As for the volume of oil exports—the other determinant of export earnings—again the period between the two price shocks did not witness any significant increase in OPEC exports of crude oil. Indeed, once the major changes in the prices of crude oil were reflected in the rise of the export value in 1974, subsequent changes reflected either fractional changes in crude-oil prices or the change in demand conditions or both. In other words, once prices were set, the value of exports was determined externally by demand conditions in the world market. And given the fact that most OPEC exports were destined to the economies of the industrialized countries, it followed that OPEC export earnings were determined externally by economic conditions in the industrial economies.

Table 4. OPEC-Member Countries' Exports, Imports, and Trade Balance, 1970–82 (Billions of U.S. Dollars)

	Exports, Imports, and Trade Balance by Year														
	1970			1974			1978			1980			1982		
	X[a]	M[b]	B[c]	X	M	B	X	M	B	X	M	B	X	M	B
Algeria	1.0	1.3	-0.3	4.7	4.0	0.7	6.3	8.7	-2.4	12.4	10.6	1.8	12.5	10.9	1.6
Ecuador	0.2	0.3	-0.1	1.0	1.0	0	1.5	1.6	-0.1	2.4	2.3	0.1	2.7	2.4	0.3
Gabon	0.1	0.1	0	0.8	0.3	0.5	1.1	0.6	0.5	1.9	0.8	1.1	1.9	0.9	1.0
Indonesia	1.1	1.0	0.1	7.4	3.8	3.6	11.6	6.7	4.9	21.4	7.9	13.5	20.0	15.7	4.3
Iran	2.6	1.7	0.9	21.6	5.4	16.2	22.2	13.5	8.7	13.5	10.5	3.0	16.4	11.2	5.2
Iraq	0.8	0.5	0.3	6.6	2.4	4.2	11.1	4.2	6.9	26.4	12.9	13.5	11.2	21.2	-10.2
Kuwait	1.7	0.6	1.1	9.9	1.6	8.3	10.4	4.6	5.8	20.0	7.3	12.7	9.8	8.9	0.9
Libya	2.8	0.6	2.2	7.1	2.8	4.3	9.5	4.6	4.9	22.6	8.8	13.8	12.9	8.2	4.7
Nigeria	1.2	1.1	0.1	9.7	2.8	6.9	10.5	12.8	-2.3	26.7	15.8	10.9	14.9	13.9	1.0
Qatar	0.2	0.1	0.1	2.0	0.3	1.7	2.4	1.2	1.2	5.6	1.4	4.2	4.1	2.1	2.0
Saudi Arabia	2.4	0.7	1.7	31.2	2.9	28.3	37.9	20.4	17.5	102.5	33.1	69.4	77.4	41.0	36.4
United Arab Emirates	0.5	0.3	0.2	6.4	1.7	4.5	9.1	5.4	3.7	20.7	9.4	11.3	18.5	9.8	8.7
Venezuela	2.6	2.0	0.6	11.1	4.2	6.9	9.2	11.8	-2.6	18.8	11.4	7.4	17.0	13.0	4.0
OPEC total	17.4	10.1	7.4	119.4	33.1	86.4	142.9	96.2	46.7	294.8	132.2	162.7	219.3	159.2	60.0

Sources: OPEC, *Annual Statistical Bulletin 1980*, p. xxii; International Monetary Fund, *International Financial Statistics, Supplement on Trade Statistics* (Washington, D.C.: IMF, 1982), pp. 40–43. International Monetary Fund, *Direction of Trade Statistics Yearbook* (Washington, D.C.: 1983), pp. 14–15.

[a] = exports.

[b] = imports.

[c] = trade balance.

Although export earnings were externally determined, imports, on the other hand (again most of which come from industrialized countries), tended to be influenced by the interaction of a number of factors and developments that have characterized oil-producing countries since the change in the price of oil in 1973. First, the sudden rise in export earnings had the effect of removing the foreign-exchange constraint in member countries that had high marginal propensity to import and a high average propensity to import. Again, it should be emphasized that although OPEC as a whole did have a current-account surplus prior to 1974, the surplus was concentrated in only six countries, all of which have relatively low population and low absorptive capacity. Most of the other OPEC-member countries were restricted by lack of foreign-exchange earnings in their ability to finance their current as well as capital spending. Once the foreign-exchange constraint was relaxed and/or removed, it became clear that imports would be allowed to rise in these economies at a relatively high rate. The same can be said, of course, for countries with current-account surplus, in that the marked increase in oil-export earnings provided both an incentive and an opportunity to engage in much-higher levels of spending than would have been possible prior to the increase in oil prices.

Not only did the expansion in oil prices and export earnings permit all OPEC-member countries to increase their imports, but the credit worthiness of member countries was increased, thus leading to a rise in their borrowing capacities in capital markets. This in turn encouraged OPEC-member countries to expand their imports at even faster rates than would have otherwise been the case.

More important is the fact that the dramatic increase in oil-export earnings introduced a qualitative change in the way economic policy makers approached their countries' economic problems. Reduced to its bare essentials, the policy objective adopted by oil-producing countries was that oil-export earnings represented a transient source of wealth that had to be converted into productive assets and infrastructures. Given the paucity of nonoil resource endowment in many of the OPEC countries and the narrowness of the range of these exports, a policy of accelerated development was felt to be essential. In other words, the national objective of many oil-exporting countries became one of attempting to convert as much of the oil earnings as possible in as short a time period as possible into as many income-producing assets as feasible. Having adopted this policy objective, it became clear that foreign markets, especially those of the industrial countries, would be called upon to provide the necessary wide array of goods and services to help the OPEC-member countries achieve their objectives.

The availability of foreign exchange, in addition to enabling these countries to import capital goods and services for industrialization, diversification, and the building of infrastructures, made it possible for these nations to escalate their importation of consumer goods. Increased foreign exchange also allowed these countries to increase expenditures for their militaries; this in turn raised the level of their imports from the industrialized countries with which they had traditional political ties.

The attempt by OPEC-member nations to hasten their economic development led in many instances to serious changes in the composition of their labor force and its sectoral distribution. In countries with an agricultural sector, accelerated public spending generated migration from the countryside to urban centers. This resulted in a lack of growth or even a shrinkage in the size of the agricultural sector, with a consequent increased dependence on the importation of foodstuff from abroad. In countries without a significant agricultural sector, development attempts involved a major influx of foreign labor, which led similarly to a greater dependency on food imports, most of which came from the industrialized countries (see table 5).

To characterize some of the major changes during this period, it can be said that although the trade position of OPEC countries was altered in both absolute and relative terms in the post-1974 period, pattern of trade remained the same as in the pre-1974 period. In other words, the industrial market economies continued to be the main recipients of most of OPEC's oil, as well as the main suppliers of OPEC imports. Indeed, between 1974 and 1978, OPEC imports from the industrial countries increased from 76 percent of their total imports in 1974 to 82 percent of total imports in 1978. Industrialized countries continued to receive, however, roughly three-quarters of OPEC's oil exports over the same period (see table 6).

Within this broad pattern of relationships some significant changes occurred in the post-1974 era. First, OPEC exports between 1974 and 1978 rose by only 24 percent, compared to an increase of 208 percent for OPEC imports during the same period. Thus, while industrialized countries did not overwhelmingly increase their dependence on OPEC oil, OPEC countries' reliance on industrialized countries for commodities they deemed necessary for economic development and political stability rose precipitously. These commodities ranged from agricultural and food products to technical services and capital goods necessary for building infrastructures, factories, plants, and industrial complexes. The dependence of oil-producing countries on the industrialized nations was further intensified by the formers' perceived need to expand their military capabilities, requiring imports of military hardware and software from the industrialized countries. It became increasingly clear that the ties between these two groups of countries could not be easily broken without major economic, social, and political consequences to the oil-producing countries.

Two other forms of linkage tended to cement the reliance of the oil-

Table 5. OPEC-Member Countries' Distribution of Imports by Major Country Groupings, 1970 and 1980 (Percentage of Total)

	1970			1980		
	Industrial Countries	Developing Countries	Other Countries	Industrial Countries	Developing Countries	Other Countries
Algeria	83.0	11.5	5.5	83.6	12.8	3.5
Ecuador	83.4	14.9	1.7	80.6	16.8	2.6
Gabon	91.8	6.0	2.2	81.4	7.6	11.0
Indonesia	71.6	26.1	2.3	64.8	29.9	5.3
Iran	85.1	10.5	4.8	67.0	23.8	9.1
Iraq	51.9	27.8	20.3	76.8	19.7	3.5
Kuwait	69.8	26.0	3.9	74.1	21.3	4.6
Libya	74.1	20.5	5.5	84.2	12.9	2.9
Nigeria	84.5	12.2	3.4	80.3	15.9	3.8
Qatar	66.6	32.3	1.2	77.7	20.5	1.8
Saudi Arabia	64.3	33.4	2.3	79.6	15.6	4.7
United Arab Emirates	70.4	22.8	6.7	70.7	26.9	2.4
Venezuela	92.5	6.9	0.6	86.7	12.0	1.4
OPEC total	79.4	16.3	4.3	77.3	18.5	4.2

Source: International Monetary Fund, *International Financial Statistics, Supplement on Trade Statistics* (Washington, D.C.: IMF, 1982), pp. 80–102.

Table 6. OPEC-Member Countries' Distribution of Exports by Major Country Groupings, 1970 and 1980 (Percentage of Total)

	Year and Country Grouping					
	1970			1980		
	Industrial Countries	Developing Countries	Other Countries	Industrial Countries	Developing Countries	Other Countries
Algeria	82.2	9.5	7.6	90.3	5.4	4.3
Ecuador	75.4	12.5	12.0	49.9	49.4	0.7
Gabon	67.3	31.2	1.5	59.8	24.5	15.7
Indonesia	72.3	25.4	2.4	77.6	20.3	2.2
Iran	77.2	20.5	2.4	61.3	37.2	1.5
Iraq	66.8	32.4	0.8	59.4	40.4	0.2
Kuwait	83.3	14.5	2.2	50.3	36.6	11.1
Libya	96.1	3.9	—a	89.8	9.6	0.6
Nigeria	88.2	9.2	2.6	88.1	11.3	0.6
Qatar	94.3	5.7	—	70.5	28.6	1.0
Saudi Arabia	68.7	22.6	8.7	75.3	21.9	2.8
United Arab Emirates	90.3	9.7	—	81.0	18.4	0.6
Venezuela	64.9	35.0	0.1	58.3	39.4	2.3
OPEC total	77.6	19.8	2.6	73.6	23.9	2.6

Source: International Monetary Fund, *International Financial Statistics, Supplement on Trade Statistics* (Washington, D.C.: IMF, 1982), 80–102.

aDash denotes negligible trade.

producing countries on the industrialized countries. Both of these linkages were touched upon earlier but deserve elaboration here. First, international trade between the two groups of countries is not confined to merchandise. The service component of the current accounts of oil-producing countries shows increasing reliance on imported services from foreign suppliers, mainly industrialized countries. The value of these services ranged from $14 billion in 1974 to $38 billion in 1978, or between 37 percent and 40 percent of the total value of the oil-producing countries' merchandise imports. The supply of services, which is as essential as the availability of merchandise imports, varied from engineering, contracting, and construction, to consulting, military and civilian advice, and the managing of enterprises.

The final linkage to be mentioned here concerns the manner in which current-account surpluses were deployed in the capital markets of industrial countries. Given the paucity of advanced and sophisticated money and capital markets in the oil-producing countries, as well as the small size of their economies, it was natural for countries with surplus funds to place them in the capital markets of the United States and of Western Europe. Another reason why the oil-producing countries elected to invest in the industrialized countries was owing to the traditional monetary, trade, and financial linkages between the two groups of nations. OPEC-member countries were traditionally paid either in American dollars or British sterling for their share of the oil net income. This pattern was altered only slightly in the postwar period when the dollar became the currency in which oil prices were expressed and payments to governments made. Given the convertibility of the American dollar under the provisions of the international monetary system, it was natural that the governments of oil-producing countries would ask and receive from the oil companies an increase in oil prices to compensate for the two official devaluations of the dollar that occurred in the aftermath of the collapse of the international monetary system in August 1971. It is important to note that oil-producing countries were at one time or another members of the monetary blocs of the industrialized countries. Oil-producing countries also had the values of their currencies pegged to those of the industrialized countries. They could naturally, therefore, be expected to channel their surplus funds into the capital markets of the latter group of countries. Another contributing factor was the common economic orientation of portfolio managers in both groups of countries. Assuming that the objective of a portfolio manager is the maximization of return and the minimization of risk, it follows that the capital markets in industrialized countries were wide enough and the economies they were serving were large enough to accommodate the influx of funds from the surplus countries. Although many nonoil developing countries would have certainly preferred to be the primary recipients of these flows, the already-existing financial networks between the oil-exporting countries and the industrialized countries provided a framework that enabled the financial institutions in the latter group to be the primary recipients of these funds. These institutions found themselves engaged in the secondary recycling of funds to those countries with balance-of-payments deficits.

The accumulation of financial assets by the OPEC-surplus countries created a new set of conditions whereby these governments became keenly aware of the importance of any drastic economic shifts in the industrialized countries. Thus, monetary instability, wide exchange-rate fluctuations, and inflationary pressures were recognized as forces that tended to erode the purchasing power of financial assets. In fact, the fear of erosion of the value of OPEC-member investments can be viewed as one explanation for the stability of the price of crude oil between 1974 and 1978. A factor that intensified the surplus countries' dependency on economic conditions in industrialized economies was the realization that the larger the size of their investment, the less freedom they had to manage their portfolios, lest their actions precipitate conditions that might increase the risks of loss. The ultimate loss would occur if the governments of the oil-producing countries were denied access to their financial assets, a situation that materialized in 1980 when the U.S. government froze Iran's assets.

To recapitulate, the period from 1974 to 1978 created conditions that gave rise to numerous economic interrelationships between oil-exporting countries and industrialized countries. These ties, in the areas of exports, imports, services, and investment opportunities, were developed to such an extent that any sudden change in their pattern resulted in serious disruption to the economies of the oil-exporting countries. This increased dependency of the oil-producing countries on the industrialized countries in the aftermath of the first oil shock broadened further as a result of the second oil shock, as will be seen in the section following.

THE 1979 OIL-PRICE SHOCK AND OPEC TRADE

As noted earlier, crude-oil prices remained relatively stable for the period 1974 to 1978. By 1978 OPEC-member countries concluded that crude-oil prices had declined sufficiently in real terms to warrant an upward adjustment in these prices. Toward this end, it was decided to introduce the concept of quarterly upward adjustments for the year 1979, according to which the official price of oil would rise from $12.70 per barrel to $14.50 per barrel during 1979. Yet no sooner had this scheme been adopted than the events of the Iranian Revolution began to unfold, rendering the gradual adjustments irrelevant.

The threat of panic buying, as well as speculation, increased stockpiling, and the deregulation of crude-oil prices in the United States, drove spot-market prices skyward. And with each increase in spot-market prices, OPEC followed the lead of the spot market by raising its prices, with some time lag. Thus by the end of 1979, when the price was supposed to have been $14.50, it actually had reached $26.00 per barrel. And by January 1981 the official price had reached $34.00 per barrel.

This phenomenal and rapid increase in the price of crude oil caused another jump in the export earnings of oil-producing countries. Thus, the value of exports increased from $142.9 billion in 1978 to $209.5 billion in 1979 and to $294.8 billion in 1980 but declined to $215.7 billion in 1982 (see table 7). This surge in export earnings increased the relative share of OPEC exports in world exports from 12 percent in 1978 to 15.5 percent in 1980, although this figure declined to 12.7 percent in 1982. The doubling of export earnings was unaccompanied by a similar rise in imports, as was the case for the years 1974–78. Imports between 1978 and 1980 increased from $96.2 billion to $132.2 billion, or an increase of 37.4 percent. And by 1982, the value of imports reached $159.1 billion, or a 65 percent increase over the 1978 value. This led to a rise in the relative position of OPEC imports from 8.1 percent of world imports in 1978 to 8.9 percent of the world total in 1982.

The main explanation for the behavior of imports in the second period lies in the fact that the capacity of the economies of oil-producing countries to absorb imports was approaching its limit when the second price jump occurred. Another explanation may be found in the way the increase in export earnings was distributed during this period. While the 1973–74 price increase did not change the relative market shares of oil-producing countries, this was not the case with the second price jump. From April 1979 to September 1981, Saudi Arabia charged lower prices for its oil (from $2 lower to $4 lower per barrel) than those of other member countries with similar crude oil. This price differential, which amounted to the functional equivalent of discounting, enabled Saudi Arabia to expand its share of the market at the expense of other member countries. This can be seen by comparing the change in the value of Saudi Arabia's exports relative to OPEC's total exports. Between 1978 and 1982 OPEC total exports increased by $76.4 billion, with Saudi Arabia's share in this increase being 52 percent, or $39.5 billion. This in turn changed the relative position of Saudi Arbia's exports, from 26.4 percent of OPEC total exports in 1978 to 35 percent of OPEC's total by 1982. And of the $63 billion expansion in OPEC imports between 1978 and 1982, 33 percent, or $20.6 billion, went to Saudi Arabia. The change in the share of Saudi Arabia's exports in relation to OPEC's total exports made it possible for that country to have a current-account surplus in 1982 at a time when there was a deficit in the combined current account of all OPEC-member countries.

Table 7. OPEC-Member Countries' Value of
Total Exports and Share of Oil Exports, 1961–80

		Year				
		1961	1970	1974	1978	1980
Algeria	A[a]	0.4	1.0	4.7	6.3	12.4
	B[b]	60.0	66.0	91.0	92.0	92.0
Ecuador	A	0.1	0.2	1.0	1.5	2.4
	B	—[c]	1.0	55.0	35.0	54.0
Gabon	A	0.1	0.1	0.8	1.1	1.9
	B	12.0	35.0	85.0	73.0	95.0
Indonesia	A	0.8	1.1	7.4	11.6	21.4
	B	33.0	40.0	70.0	64.0	62.0
Iran	A	0.9	2.6	21.6	22.2	13.5
	B	85.0	90.0	97.0	98.0	95.0
Iraq	A	0.5	0.8	6.6	11.1	26.4
	B	96.0	93.0	99.0	98.0	99.0
Kuwait	A	1.0	1.7	9.9	10.4	20.0
	B	89.0	94.0	94.0	90.0	92.0
Libya	A	—	2.8	7.1	9.5	22.6
	B	—	100.0	100.0	100.0	100.0
Nigeria	A	0.5	1.2	9.9	10.5	26.7
	B	7.0	58.0	93.0	91.0	95.0
Qatar	A	0.1	0.2	2.0	2.4	5.6
	B	100.0	96.0	98.0	97.0	95.0
Saudi Arabia	A	1.0	2.4	31.2	37.9	102.5
	B	92.0	100.0	100.0	100.0	100.0
United Arab Emirates	A	—	0.5	6.4	9.1	20.7
	B	—	95.0	99.0	95.0	94.0
Venezuela	A	2.2	2.6	11.1	9.2	18.8
	B	91.0	90.0	95.0	95.0	95.0
OPEC total	A	7.5	17.4	119.4	142.9	294.8
	B	75.0	85.0	95.0	93.0	94.0

Source: OPEC, *Annual Statistical Bulletin*, 1980, pp. xvii, xx.

[a] = exports in billions of U.S. dollars

[b] = percentage of oil to total exports

[c] = Dash denotes less than $50 million.

In retrospect, the second price shock appears to have been a major turning point in the position of OPEC with respect to the industrial countries, as well as to other oil-importing countries. This is so because the effects of the second price increase were being felt at a time when the industrial economies were beginning to enter the world-wide recession of the 1980s. One of the major effects of this recession was the marked decline in the demand for OPEC oil. Thus, from total crude-oil exports of 26.1 MBD in 1978 OPEC exports of crude oil plummeted to 22.9 MBD by 1980 and declined again to 16.1 MBD by 1982. In addition to the rise in the price of crude oil and the recession-induced decline in demand, OPEC oil by the end of the 1970s faced serious competition from non-OPEC oil, primarily Mexican and North Sea oils. Within the worldwide network of OPEC exports, industrialized countries continued to remain OPEC's chief importers. The share of OPEC's total exports that found its way to the markets of the industrial economies ranged from a low of 70 percent to a high of 80 percent for the period 1960 to 1982. OPEC's imports from industrialized countries ranged, on the other hand, between 76 percent and 80 percent of their total imports during the same period.

OPEC: INCREASED DEPENDENCY

The question of reliance on industrialized economies has assumed major importance for the economies of the oil-exporting countries ever since the latter assumed responsibility for price and output determination. This section explores the implications of this dependency in light of evidence provided in earlier sections.

As pointed out in earlier chapters, the oil resources of the oil-producing countries were developed historically by major oil companies to meet the rising needs of the industrialized economies for oil. From the time of their inception, the oil sectors in OPEC-member countries were developed as enclave raw-material-producing, export-oriented sectors. The nature of the oil sectors was such that they could not have been integrated into the nonoil economies of member countries. (This would have required planning at the national level at a time when the major decisions affecting the oil sector were outside the policy domain of national authorities.) While the oil sector was by far the most important and developed sector in most OPEC countries, other sectors of the OPEC economies exhibited features and problems similar to nonoil sectors in other developing countries.

Under the guidance of the multinational oil firms, the oil sectors continued to gain in importance relative to the rest of the economy, first as a result of the continued increase in oil output and export and later on owing to the improvement in fiscal terms. But despite the rising status of the oil sector, its isolation from the nonoil economy and its export orientation were undiminished. Indeed, the expanded importance of the oil sector relative to other sectors of the economy meant that policy makers were in a position to acquire revenue and foreign exchange without having to develop the nonoil sectors to their potential.

Yet the whole structure had become dependent on two important conditions. The first condition involved the relationship that had developed between the oil companies and host governments. The second condition focused on the demand conditions for oil in the markets of the industrial countries. As to the first condition, the relationship between oil companies and host governments was such that host governments had to depend ultimately on the good will of the oil companies. The oil companies for their part created a sophisticated system that was intended to regulate output from various supply sources to meet the requirements of their integrated operations. And since these companies were dealing with several governments, the need to balance various claims and demands with each other and with supply requirements became an important force in determining the economic viability of any one oil sector.

The second condition relates to the fact that the primary markets for oil from the OPEC region were and still are the economies of the industrial countries. Whatever economic changes and policy considerations affected the demand for oil automatically affected the entire economy of oil-producing countries. Trade and tariff policies, monetary and tax policies, as well as energy policy in general are examples of policies that directly or indirectly influenced the demand conditions for oil exports from OPEC-member countries. Given these two conditions, it was clear that the size of the oil sector—and by extension that of all economic sectors in oil-producing countries—was determined externally by economic conditions in industrialized countries, by their governments, and by the corporate policies of the major oil companies.

Although the 1973 price revolution and the subsequent transfer of price and output-setting powers to the governments of oil-producing countries did transform the structure of the international oil industry, it failed to alter the dependency of the oil economies on the policies of the industrialized countries and on the profit-maximizing policy objectives of the oil companies. It is true, of course, that the events of 1973–74 resulted in a massive shift of financial resources from the industrialized countries to the OPEC countries, but the shift in and of itself did not change the basic fact that the oil-producing countries were dependent on the export of one raw material, oil, the demand for which was externally determined. While the structure of relationships between the oil companies and the governments did change in favor of the governments, the underlying forces shaping the evolution of the oil sectors in the OPEC countries stayed the same. In other words, the oil companies remained the primary buyers of oil, which they needed for their global marketing network. While the companies in the period prior to 1973 were the producers and the sellers—to their own network of integrated channels—after 1973 they became the primary buyers of oil from the governments.

It can be argued that the sudden increase in oil prices in 1974 and again in 1979 had the net effect of making the oil-producing countries more rather than less dependent on economic conditions in the industrial countries. There are several reasons for this argument. First, the abrupt rise in the price of oil led to a sudden increase in wealth in OPEC-member countries and to the emergence of what might be termed the wealth illusion. Such an illusion encouraged policy makers and economic planners to believe that traditional constraints on public-sector spending, such as foreign exchange and domestic savings, were no longer significant. The implications of such an illusion are serious, since any decline in the growth rate of oil-export earnings tends to force a country into borrowing and/or leads to economic disruptions and dislocations.[8]

Second, the displacement of the oil companies by the oil-producing governments as the agents responsible for output management resulted in the fragmentation of the output control into several components lacking coordination among them. A corollary to this situation would be a multiplant firm that relinquishes control over output to the plant managers who, in turn, choose not to coordinate their output policies and targets. It should be noted that such coordination is not necessary so long as the demand conditions allow all producers to produce at the desirable level without fear of retaliation. But when demand conditions change and capacity is in place, there is always the temptation to expand output at the expense of one or more of the other producers. This danger may be averted if some of the producers choose to absorb the decline in demand by reducing their own output in order to forestall price competition among the few producers. This actually was the case in 1975 when Saudi Arabia decided to reduce its own output in the face of declining demand. However, no such policy was followed by Saudi Arabia after 1975, a fact that led to a decrease in the market shares of other oil-producing countries. The point here is that OPEC did not have a common production policy for its member governments because these governments preferred to retain at the national level the decision to determine output.

Another facet of the absence of production policy coordination among member countries caused OPEC to assume the anamolous position of being the world supplier of residual oil. This meant that OPEC members were expected to gear their production to the level that would fill the gap between the demand for oil and what non-OPEC, oil-producing countries were willing to produce. This position of residual supplier was a logical outgrowth of the way in which the oil sectors were developed originally. The transfer of controlling power from the oil companies to the host governments was not accompanied by the necessary fundamental changes that would reorient the oil sectors toward the respective national economies. Had this reorientation occurred and had there been some kind of coordination among member countries, OPEC would have been able to follow an independent production policy that would have rendered the economies of member countries less vulnerable to policy changes in the industrial countries.

An additional aspect of the increasing dependency of OPEC-member countries on industrialized nations is the rising size of the financial assets of some of the major oil-producing countries in the capital markets of industrialized countries. As touched upon earlier, the linkages created by the accumulation of these assets have tended to limit the freedom of action of these oil-producing countries. This may be attributed to the fear that certain oil production and pricing policies by oil-producing nations might undermine the financial systems in which these nations have considerable investments. The fear of potential policy measures such as the denial of access to these assets, which would result in economic and political difficulties for oil-producing countries, may also be a factor.[9]

The increase in the price of crude oil in the 1970s and the early 1980s focused debate in practically every oil-importing country on the issues of a national energy policy and dependence on foreign suppliers, mainly OPEC-member countries. The changes that had occurred with respect to the price and cost of imported oil concentrated attention not only on balance-of-payments deficits but beyond to the realm of lessening dependence on imported oil. In an effort to become more self-sufficient, a host of measures were adopted by industrialized countries, among them: energy conservation measures; interfuel substitution; placing a cost ceiling on imported oil; accelerating the development of new energy sources; enhancing the output of existing sources; mutual arrangements to help importing countries share inventories in time of supply disruption; and stockpiling of inventories in order to cope with supply interruptions. In all these policy measures the common objective has been, understandably, the ultimate lessening of industrial countries' dependence on oil imports from the OPEC region. Yet these policy measures, while strengthening the position of importing countries, were taken at a time when OPEC-member countries were either unwilling or unable to develop a coordinated production policy. The lack of symmetry in the position of the two groups thus acted to weaken the export position of OPEC-member countries with respect to the industrialized countries. Coordinated policy making by OPEC was furthermore made more difficult by the threat of military intervention by the governments of industrialized countries. Finally, there is the fact that oil is produced to be exported. Consumption by oil-producing countries is only a fraction of total output. As indicated earlier, between 75 percent and 80 percent of OPEC oil is exported to the industrialized countries of North America, Western Europe, and Japan. And since oil constitutes 95 percent of OPEC members' total exports, it follows that any change in the demand for oil, whether caused by deliberate policy actions to reduce imports from OPEC members or by changing economic conditions such as recessions, would have serious economic as well as social and political effects in the oil-producing countries. The situation could hardly be otherwise, given the dependency between oil-producing and industrialized countries that was allowed to develop and to increase.

CHAPTER 6

OPEC, The Third World, and the Rise of Interdependence

The first oil-price shock of 1973–74 inflicted heavy financial burdens on the oil-importing developing countries and contributed to the sharp rise in their external debt. To be sure, Third World countries had a long history of having to resort to the international financial system to meet balance-of-payments needs. However, the magnitude of the crude-oil price increase created a new era in the otherwise stagnant economic relationships between one group of developing countries, that is, OPEC-member countries, and the rest of the Third World.

The new relationships were reflected in a number of developments, including the expansion of trade between the two groups of countries, the flow of economic assistance from OPEC-member countries to other Third World countries, the migration of labor from non-OPEC developing countries to most OPEC-member countries, the inflow of worker remittances from OPEC-member countries to other developing countries, and attempts by the two groups to introduce certain changes in the international economic system. Before discussing each of these developments, a few observations are in order about the role of OPEC members in the Third World.

OPEC COUNTRIES AS DEVELOPING COUNTRIES

Prior to the drastic change in the position of OPEC-member countries in relation to the rest of the world in 1973, it was taken for granted that each OPEC-member country was a developing country. If one cites conventional standards, OPEC-member countries in 1970 had a combined population of 258 million and a combined GNP of $58 billion, resulting in an average per-capita income of $223 (see table 8). Needless to say, there were wide variations among member countries in their respective per-capita GNP. Thus, while Indonesia's per-capita GNP in 1970 was only $78, Kuwait's was close to $3,000. On the other hand, the per-capita GNP in Saudi Arabia in 1970 was $616 and in Iraq,

Table 8. Gross National Product of OPEC-Member Countries
at Current Market Prices, 1970–80 (Billions of U.S. Dollars)

	Year					
	1970	1972	1974	1976	1978	1980
Algeria	4.6	6.1	11.6	16.5	25.4	40.6
Ecuador	1.6	1.8	3.6	5.1	7.4	10.1
Gabon	0.3	0.4	1.4	2.9	2.4	3.4
Indonesia	9.0	10.6	24.6	36.2	48.9	63.2
Iran	10.6	16.3	47.5	71.4	76.1	74.5
Iraq	3.0	3.7	10.6	16.0	22.7	39.7
Kuwait	2.2	3.6	10.6	13.1	15.3	26.7
Libya	3.4	4.6	11.9	14.8	18.3	33.8
Nigeria	7.9	11.7	26.9	39.4	45.5	71.6
Qatar	0.2	0.4	1.5	2.9	2.8	5.6
Saudi Arabia	3.8	5.8	23.2	46.9	66.3	117.6
United Arab Emirates	0.5	1.6	7.9	11.0	13.8	20.8
Venezuela	10.8	13.3	25.6	31.1	39.7	58.5
OPEC total	58	80	207	307	384	566
World total	3,250	4,300	5,800	6,800	8,793	11,026
Ratio of OPEC to world total (%)	1.8	1.9	3.6	4.5	4.4	5.1

Sources: Ruth Leger Sivard, *World Military and Social Expenditures, 1983* (Washington, D.C.: World Priorities, 1983), p. 32; OPEC, *Annual Statistical Bulletin*, 1980, pp. xv–xvi.

Note: The combined population of OPEC countries for the years cited in the table was 260 million in 1970, 289 million in 1974, 303 million in 1976, 318 million in 1978, and 334 million in 1980. As a percentage of the total world population, the OPEC countries comprised 7.2 percent in 1970, 7.4 percent in 1974, 7.5 percent in 1976, 7.6 percent in 1978, and 7.6 percent in 1980.

$322. (By way of reference, per-capita GNP in the United States in 1970 was $4,842.)

The low level of national income in OPEC-member countries was reflected in high rates of unemployment, high rates of illiteracy, and economies that were dependent on one or two sectors (one of which was agriculture).

Ten years after two major price increases, the underlying forces that tended to shape the economies of OPEC-member countries remained relatively the same, yet the overall per-capita national income had increased dramatically, from $223 at the beginning of the 1970s to $1,692 by 1980. In terms of individual country per-capita income by 1980, Kuwait's, for example, had climbed to $19,500; Saudi Arabia's to $14,050; Iraq's to $3,038; and Indonesia's to $445. (Again, for reference, GNP per capita in the United States in 1980 was $11,563.)[1]

When OPEC's per-capita GNP is compared with those of other developing countries, according to the World Bank, low-income developing countries (both OPEC and non-OPEC) in 1980 had a per-capita GNP of $260, while middle-income developing countries had a per-capita GNP of $1,400. Within the latter group, oil exporters (excluding the high-income oil exporters such as Saudi Arabia, Kuwait, Libya, and the United Arab Emirates) had a per-capita GNP of $1,160, while the oil importers had a per-capita GNP of $1,500 (World Bank 1982, 111).

One of the more common features shared by OPEC-member countries and other developing countries is their position in the international economic system. Oil-producing countries have always claimed, with good reason, that they must use oil revenue for economic growth—to build infrastructures, develop industry and agriculture; and provide for social services, training, and employment. The most important objective of oil-producing nations' economic policies has been economic diversification, in view of the realities that oil is a depletable resource and that political independence cannot be meaningful if not accompanied by economic independence. This line of thinking, it should be noted, has been the guiding principle for the developing nations since they began to attain their independence from the colonial powers and has also been the main thrust of the economic philosophy of nonaligned nations as expressed in various international organizations and forums such as the United Nations and the United Nations Conference on Trade and Development (UNCTAD).

In the international arena, a primary argument for this line of reasoning is that the international economic system as it had evolved and functioned over the years has tended to distribute benefits in a pattern that has favored the developed countries (the center countries) at the expense of the developing countries (the periphery). Since international trade (and for that matter all foreign transactions) is not an end in itself but a means for economic development, it is only natural that the extent of any country's participation in the world economy should be governed by strategies and programs relating to national economic and social development. Moreover, since international trade is by definition a multilateral undertaking and involved the interests of more than one economy, such trade should confer benefits among all the participants if mutually beneficial interdependence is to be realized. This is, however, the theory of international trade. In practice, the history of trade has been one of domination by the strong and deprivation of the weak. It has been in general, both an "engine of growth" for developed countries and an instrument of exploitation of the developing countries. For the developing nations of the world's South (the periphery), this statement holds true not only for past economic history but for the contemporary pattern of economic relationships.[2] This certainly has been the case with respect to oil-producing countries from the time that they commenced producing and exporting, with the exception of the years since 1973, when the terms of trade improved in their favor.

For purposes of the present analysis, the developing countries are divided into two groups, the net oil-exporting countries and net oil-importing countries. In the first group are OPEC-member countries and other net oil exporters; in the second group are all the net oil importers.

Although OPEC-member countries are an integral part of the Third World in that they share, as mentioned earlier, similar economic and social characteristics, it is correct to say that OPEC-member countries constitute a special group within the broad designation, *Third World.* However, oil alone is what sets them apart from other developing countries and makes them unique. Within OPEC there is a subgroup of major oil-producing countries that have small populations relative to their export earnings and that therefore tend to generate capital surplus. However, there are also nations within OPEC that find themselves resorting to external borrowing to meet balance-of-payments needs. The public, however, fails to delineate between these two OPEC subgroups, giving rise to erroneous assumptions and conclusions regarding the financial and economic ability of the OPEC countries. In the pages following the pattern of interdependence between OPEC member countries and other Third World countries is dealt with.

OPEC AND THE THIRD WORLD: ENERGY

OPEC-member countries are not the only developing countries that export oil. Other developing net oil exporters include Mexico, Egypt, Oman, Syria, Angola, Bahrain, Bolivia, Congo, Malaysia, Tunisia, Trinidad and Tobago, and Zaire. The remaining developing countries constitute what is referred to as oil-importing developing countries (OIDC).

One of the most striking features of the economies of OIDC over the last three decades has been the marked increase in their energy consumption. In 1955 the total energy consumption of oil-importing developing countries amounted to 3.4 million barrels per day of oil equivalent (MBDOE). By 1970 their consumption had increased to 7.8 MBDOE and by 1980 to 13.7 MBDOE. OIDC domestic production of various sources of energy—oil, natural gas, solid fuels, and primary electricity—supplied 62 percent of the demand in 1960; 60 percent in 1970 and 55 percent in 1980.[3] The gap between domestic output and consumption of energy had to be met, of course, by importing energy—mainly oil, primarily from OPEC-member countries.

On the basis of the energy consumption data of the developing countries, for the period 1960 to 1980, energy consumption increased at an average annual rate of 15.1 percent. Given that the population growth rate for these countries during the same period was 2.4 percent and that their rate of increase in per-capita GNP was 3 percent, it follows that their per-capita energy consumption increased at the rate of 9.7 percent per annum. The rise in per-capita energy consumption may be explained by the fact that as economies moved from one stage to another or their structures altered in the process of economic growth, they participated in more intensive energy economic activities. Another aspect of this process of economic growth was that economies tended to rely less on the traditional noncommercial sources of energy and to increase their reliance on conventional, commercial energy sources such as oil, coal, and natural gas (see table 9).

Although indigenous energy sources succeeded in increasing their share of the energy market from 38 percent in 1960 to 45 percent in 1980, the gap between consumption and production remained wide and had to be filled. As indicated earlier, the gap was filled by imported energy, chiefly oil. Thus in 1960 these countries imported only 1 MBD of oil, or 29 percent of their total consumption of energy. By 1970 these countries' oil imports had climbed to 3 MBD, or 38 percent of total energy consumption, and by 1980 imported oil had reached 5.8 MBD, or 42 percent of total energy consumption.[4] These developments indicate that while oil-importing countries achieved a balance in their consumption and production of nonoil energy sources, this was obviously not the case with respect to oil. Not only did these countries increase their imports of oil but they found themselves meeting 56 percent of the total increase in energy consumption by importing oil (table 9).

It is clear from the data that these countries were able to increase their consumption of oil at a time when oil was affordable and available. But as the volume of imported oil continued to increase, so also did the cost of these countries' oil imports. These countries, in other words, were subject to both price and quantity factors throughout the 1970s.

Thus, in 1972, the last full year prior to the first oil price shock, the value of exports from oil-exporting countries to nonoil developing countries amounted to $9 billion. By 1974 the figure had risen to $23.6 billion and by 1978, the last year before the second oil price shock, the value of oil exports to these countries had reached $29.2 billion. Following the second price shock, the value of exports increased to $44.6 billion in 1979 and again to $66.5 billion in 1980.[5]

There are several ways to measure the burden of the oil-price increases. First, the absolute increase in the cost of oil imports can be analyzed. Second, the incremental cost of imported oil can be compared to the overall increase in the value of imports in general. Third, the burden can be related to the export

Table 9. Total Energy Consumption and
Total Oil Consumption by Country Groupings, 1950–82

	Year					
	1950	1960	1970	1975	1980	1982
Industrial countries						
Total energy consumption (MBDOE)[a]	26.7	37.7	65.5	70.2	76.3	72.0
Oil consumption (MBD)[b]	8.3	15.5	33.2	36.9	38.0	34.1
Share of oil in total consumption (%)	31.0	41.0	50.7	52.7	49.8	47.4
Centrally planned economies						
Total energy consumption (MBDOE)	7.8	18.8	27.5	35.5	42.8	44.6
Oil consumption (MBD)	1.2	2.9	7.0	10.5	12.7	12.8
Share of oil in total consumption (%)	15.4	15.4	25.4	29.6	29.7	28.7
Developing countries						
Total energy consumption (MBDOE)	3.1	6.0	11.0	14.2	18.2	20.8
Oil consumption (MBD)	1.2	3.2	6.3	8.3	11.0	11.6
Share of oil in total consumption (%)	38.7	53.3	57.3	58.5	60.4	55.8
World Total						
Total energy consumption (MBDOE)	37.5	62.4	103.9	119.9	138.3	137.4
Oil consumption (MBD)	10.8	21.6	46.4	55.7	61.7	58.5
Share of oil in total consumption (%)	28.8	34.6	44.7	46.5	44.6	42.6

Sources: Computed from OECD, *Energy Policy: Problems and Objectives*, pp. 148–87; British Petroleum Company, *BP Statistical Review of the World Oil Industry* 1962–77; British Petroleum Company, *BP Statistical Review of World Energy, 1982* (London).

[a]MBDOE = million barrels per day of oil equivalent.

[b]MBD = million barrels per day.

earnings of the oil-importing developing countries. Fourth, one can determine whether there were compensating flows from the oil-exporting countries to the oil-importing countries. Fifth, the balance-of-trade deficit can be analyzed.

In absolute terms the cost of oil imports by the OIDC was increased sharply, from $9 billion to $66.5 billion from 1972 to 1980. But in relation to total imports, the cost of imported oil relative to total imports may be seen to have actually declined, from 15.7 percent in 1972 to 11.8 percent in 1978, but it rose to 14.1 percent in 1979, following the second oil shock and again to 16.4 percent of total imports in 1980.[6]

If the value of oil imports is related to total export earnings of OIDC, one finds that the ratio of oil imports to export earnings in 1972 was 19.4 percent. This ratio declined to 18.1 percent of export earnings in 1978, but it moved upward in 1979 to reach 18.1 percent and was followed by another increase to 21.1 percent in 1980.[7]

It should be noted that following the first oil price shock, OIDC exports to oil-exporting countries began to rise, from $1.4 billion, or 3 percent of their total exports, to $12.8 billion, or 6.7 percent of the total exports by 1978. By 1980 exports reached $22.1 billion, or 7 percent of OIDC oil exports. It is significant that during this period OIDC exports increased from $46.3 billion in 1972 to $314.6 billion in 1980 and that their imports increased from $57.3 billion to $404.6 billion during the same period. In other words, OIDC balance-of-trade deficits increased from $11 billion to $90 billion from 1972 to 1980.[8]

Thus, in 1972 the deficit in the balance of trade between the oil-exporting countries and OIDC amounted to $7.6 billion, or 69 percent of the total trade deficit of OIDC. By 1978 the deficit of OIDC with the oil-exporting countries had reached $16.4 billion. But in relation to OIDC total trade deficit, the ratio had declined to 29 percent. Following the second oil shock the ratio of the OIDC deficit to the oil-producing countries relative to their total trade deficit increased to 40.7 percent; by 1980 it had risen again to 49.3 percent. The ratio of OIDC exports to oil-producing countries relative to their imports from them was 15.5 percent in 1972; by 1982 the ratio had increased to 44.3 percent.

The preceding discussion makes clear that the burden of the oil-price shocks of the 1970s was not of the dimension that might have been expected. Neither the evident worsening payments position of the developing countries nor the rise in the external debt of these countries can be attributed to the rise in the price of crude oil. The rise in the cost of imported oil was offset partially by the rise in the imports of oil-exporting countries from OIDC and in part, also, as will be seen in the next section, by the influx of funds from oil-exporting countries to other developing countries. The remainder of the cost of imported oil of course had to be met either by increased borrowing or by using international reserves or by a combination of both.

It should be mentioned here that although exports from oil-producing countries to OIDC have increased in absolute terms, they have declined in relation to total exports. Thus, between 1972 and 1980, exports to OIDC from the oil-exporting countries increased from $9 billion to $66.5 billion, but their ratio to total exports declined from 35.7 percent in 1972 to 20.3 percent in 1978 and to 23.1 percent in 1980. The declining share of OIDC in the OPEC export market is not surprising, since OIDC imports of crude oil could have not risen at the same rate as that of the developed countries. OPEC exports of crude oil to the nonindustrialized countries increased from 4.7 MBD in 1972 to 5.8 MBD in 1978 and then declined to 5.3 MBD in 1980, resulting in a net increase of 1.1 MBD in OPEC's crude-oil exports to OIDC. By contrast, U.S. imports from

OPEC increased from 1.9 MBD of crude oil in 1972 to 5.1 MBD in 1978, yielding a net increase of 3.2 MBD of crude exports. By 1980 U.S. imports from the OPEC region had declined to 3.8 MBD, resulting in a net gain over 1978 of close to 2 MBD (OPEC, *Annual Statistical Bulletin* 1980).

Finally, the question of the differences in energy dependence by various OIDC members needs to be addressed briefly. Developing countries, as mentioned earlier, vary widely in their energy requirements, their level of economic development, and their dependence on oil imports. Data on net oil imports of developing countries reveal that these imports range from less than 1,000 barrels of crude oil per day in the case of some of the poorer African countries to almost 1 million barrels per day in the case of Brazil. A survey of eighty net oil-importing developing countries found that in 1973 these countries imported a total of 3.7 MBD and that by 1978 their total imports reached 4.1 MBD. Yet out of the eighty countries, the largest nine importers (Brazil, Korea, Turkey, Taiwan, India, Philippines, Singapore, Thailand, and Cuba) were responsible for almost 66 percent of the total imports of the group in 1973 and almost 78 percent of the group's total imports in 1978.[9] This means that although the bulk of OIDC imported oil found its way to those developing countries with a relatively advanced industrial sector, the other seventy-one developing countries received only 22 percent of the group's total oil imports, or 0.9 MBD in 1978, less than Brazil's oil imports.

OPEC AND THE THIRD WORLD: FINANCE

One of the more significant changes in international economic relations as a direct consequence of the first oil-price shock was the emergence of OPEC-member countries as major suppliers of economic assistance to other Third World countries. Flow of funds from certain OPEC-member countries was not a new phenomenon, since economic aid in the form of grants and soft loans had taken place prior to the 1973 oil-price change. Such aid involved the unilateral transfer from certain Arab oil-producing countries to those Arab countries whose territories were occupied by Israel during the 1967 Arab-Israeli war. Another funding route was through the creation by Kuwait in 1961 of the Kuwait Fund for Arab Economic Development. The Kuwait fund had limited impact, in that its resources were small and its scope limited; however, the creation of a national fund for external development by a small country like Kuwait was a pioneering step in what a decade later would become a major effort to transfer resources to other Third World countries.

The flow of economic assistance to other developing countries prior to 1973 was provided principally by Saudi Arabia, Libya, and Kuwait. These three countries together supplied between $380 million and $530 million total per annum between 1970 and 1973. Although the flow of official economic aid may seem modest in absolute terms, it was high relative to the gross national product of these three donor countries at that time. This is demonstrated by the fact that net disbursements (exclusive of military assistance) amounted to between 2.7 percent and 3.6 percent of the GNP of the donor countries. The bulk of the aid, almost 83 percent, went to Egypt, Syria, and Jordan, and the rest found its way to other Arab countries and some countries in sub–Sahara, Africa. Although OPEC countries, such as Iran, Iraq, the United Arab Emirates, and Qatar, supplied economic aid prior to 1973, their aid was of a much smaller scale than that of the other three countries (Gerakis and Thayanithy 1978, 260–62). It was only after the oil-price revolution, however, that economic assistance to other developing countries assumed major importance in the pattern of economic relations between the two groups of countries. In addition to these bilateral government arrangements, which were undertaken initially in the aftermath of the 1967 Arab-Israeli war, there was the already-mentioned Kuwait Fund for Arab Economic Development. During the period 1963 to 1970 the Fund disbursed about $200 million in economic aid, an amount that represented 1.3 percent of that country's income. In 1968 the Arab countries established the first major multilateral funding organization, the Arab Fund for Economic and Social Development. This fund did not begin operation, however, until 1972 (Shihata and Mabro 1978, 2).

The big push to increase economic assistance to developing countries took place soon after the 1973 rise in crude-oil prices. The channeling of OPEC assistance involved several funding mechanisms. In addition to the traditional direct grants and loans, several member countries decided to institutionalize the flow of funds through newly created national funds for external development. Another mechanism was to increase the resources of the World Bank and the International Monetary Fund—for example, through purchase of World Bank bonds and contributions to the IMF Special Oil Facility. Balance-of-payments support was also provided to countries that sought such assistance. Central-bank-to-central-bank deposits on relatively concessional terms were an innovation that provided both liquidity to the recipient bank and an outlet to the lending bank. Another financing mode was the traditional project loan fashioned after World Bank loans to Third World countries. Yet another form of aid was that of cofinancing, which brought OPEC-member countries together with other developing countries and with industrialized countries in multilateral arrangements for project funding. An outstanding illustration of this arrangement was the creation of the International Fund for Agricultural Development, which was designed to ease food problems and stimulate agricultural development in Third World countries. Aid was further provided through the creation of joint enterprises for the purposes of borrowing in capital markets or direct investment in developing countries. OPEC aid also took the form of providing banking guarantees, as well as an underwriting service for commercial loans to developing countries (Shihata and Mabro 1978, 2; OPEC Special Fund 1976).

In addition to the national funds for external development formed by various member countries, OPEC created in 1976 the OPEC Special Fund as its own multilateral agency for distributing loans to developing countries. (This fund was expanded in 1980 and renamed the OPEC Fund for International Development.) Although most of the resources provided by OPEC-member countries have been supplied through their own national funds for external development, the OPEC Fund for International Development provides an important collective vehicle of assistance. The fund's resources are dispensed through four broad activities: (1) loans for balance of payments support, (2) loans for development projects and programs, (3) contributions or loans to international development agencies whose operations benefit developing countries, and (4) the financing of technical assistance. Loans provided by the fund carry no interest rate if the borrowing country belongs to the low-income group of developing countries. Interest rates of 4 percent to 5 percent are applied to the relatively higher-income group of developing countries. The fund, however, imposes a service charge of less than 1 percent and provides a grace period of between five and seven years and a loan repayment period of between ten and fifteen years.

During a five-year period (October 1976–October 1981), the OPEC Fund provided 266 loans to seventy-nine countries, in the amount of $2.5 billion (an annual average outlay of $0.5 billion). In addition to loans to individual countries, the OPEC Fund gave $72 million in technical and research assistance to a number of international and regional organizations, both within and outside of the United Nations system. Equally important to the OPEC Fund's loans have been the grants it has supplied to the Common Fund for Commodities and the contributions made to the International Fund for Agricultural Development. The total of these grants and contributions from October 1976 to October 1981 amounted to $1.1 billion (OPEC Fund for International Development 1980; Shihata 1981b).

The loans and grants provided by the OPEC Fund represent a small part of OPEC's official development assistance (ODA) to developing countries. Between 1975 and 1981 OPEC ODA ranged between $6.1 billion in 1975 and $9.1

billion in 1981. Total OPEC ODA for the entire period was $51.6 billion (an average of $7.4 billion per year). During the same seven-year period, ODA from industrialized countries to developing countries amounted to $139 billion (OECD, *Development Co-Operation* 1981; World Bank 1983). OPEC ODA, in other words, constituted 27 percent of the total ODA received by developing countries. While in absolute terms ODA from the seventeen donor industrial countries was much higher than that from OPEC-member countries, the burden of the financial flow from OPEC-member countries was much heavier than that for the seventeen countries that comprise the OECD Development Assistance Committee (DAC).

This can be seen by relating ODA from both groups of countries to their combined GNP. In 1975 the ratio of ODA from the DAC countries to their combined GNP was 0.36 percent. By 1981 the ratio had declined slightly to 0.35 percent of the GNP. By contrast the relative share of ODA from OPEC member countries to their combined GNP was 2.92 percent in 1975 and 1.5 percent in 1981. The relative share of OPEC ODA would be more realistic if the non-Arab member countries were removed from the data, since the Arab member countries provide 95 percent of OPEC ODA. If this is done, it is found that Arab OPEC ODA averaged $7 billion per year for the period 1975–81 and that the relative share of ODA in this group's GNP fluctuated between close to 3 percent and 5.68 percent of the countries' combined GNP (see table 10).[10] Interestingly enough in 1975 Qatar, for example, had supplied 15.6 percent of its GNP in the form of ODA. The United Arab Emirates contributed 11.7 percent of its GNP to developing countries. As national income in these countries increased by the end of the 1970s, the relative share of ODA to GNP declined, although it continued to increase in absolute terms.[11]

The role assumed by Arab-donor OPEC countries was made possible owing primarily to the favorable balance-of-payments position of certain Arab members of OPEC as compared with other members. A major factor was that the non-Arab countries' aid-giving ability was restricted: Indonesia and Nigeria were too poor to be expected to contribute to OPEC ODA; Gabon's current-account surplus was too insignificant for it to contribute to OPEC aid programs; Ecuador had an erratic current-account balance throughout the 1970s; and both Venezuela and Algeria had relatively high absorptive capacity, a fact that tended to limit severely their contributions to OPEC ODA. This left the Arab countries of the Middle East and Libya as the countries accounting for the bulk of the funds appropriated to developing countries (Iran's contribution was drastically reduced in the aftermath of the Iranian Revolution). The next major question to be addressed relates to the motives behind this relatively high

Table 10.   OPEC and OECD Official Development Assistance (ODA), 1975–81

	Year						
	1975	1976	1977	1978	1979	1980	1981
OPEC ODA (billions of U.S. dollars)	6.2	6.1	6.3	8.3	7.8	9.1	7.8
As percentage of GNP	2.92	2.32	2.03	2.46	1.88	1.74	1.46
Arab OPEC ODA (billions of U.S. dollars)	5.6	5.2	5.9	7.9	7.6	9.0	7.8
As percentage of GNP	5.68	4.20	4.00	4.78	3.56	3.08	2.99
OECD ODA (billions of U.S. dollars)	13.8	13.7	15.7	20.0	22.8	27.3	25.6
As percentage of GNP	0.36	0.33	0.33	0.35	0.35	0.38	0.35

Source: World Bank, *World Development Report*, 1983, pp. 182–83

level of economic assistance flowing from one group of developing countries to another.

OPEC AID: MOTIVES AND ISSUES

OPEC's experiment with economic assistance has not been free of controversy. The main criticisms of OPEC aid center around the fact that aid was never sufficient to offset oil-induced balance-of-payments problems of developing countries and that the aid has not been dispersed widely but has tended to concentrate on Arab and Islamic countries. This latter assertion is supported by data on economic assistance from OPEC countries to other developing countries and was particularly the case during the 1970s and especially with respect to bilateral aid flows (OECD *Development Co-Operation* 1981, 181).

It should be noted, however, that the ratio of total aid to Arab recipient countries declined from over 90 percent of the total OPEC aid by the early 1970s to 53 percent by the end of 1981. Next in line in terms of amount of aid received were the Asian countries, which received close to 26 percent of OPEC's total economic assistance in 1981. They were followed by the African countries, which received 18 percent of the total assistance.[12]

The main reason for the tilt in favor of Arab countries is explained by the historical context in which Arab aid evolved in the first place and by the nature of political developments in the Arab region. It will be recalled that the Kuwait Fund for Arab Economic Development was created in 1961 to provide aid to

Arab countries. The extent of economic assistance provided by the fund between 1961 and 1967 was, however, modest.

The 1967 Arab-Israeli war, in which Egypt, Syria, and Jordan were badly defeated by Israel, led, among other things, to major increases in the amount of Arab aid and to a shift in political power from the nonoil states of Egypt and Syria to the oil states, especially Saudi Arabia. It was in this context that a massive transfer of economic assistance began to take place from Saudi Arabia, Kuwait, and Libya to Egypt, Syria, and Jordan.

The motives for aid giving prior to 1973 included the attempts to deter Israeli expansion in the region; to moderate and influence political currents under the banner of Arab nationalism; to prop up conservative regimes (both Muslim and Arab) in the region; and the general notion that there is a coincidence or at least a compatibility of interests among countries that have a common political and cultural heritage or common religion.

After the 1973 oil-price revolution, several forces combined to provide a quantum jump in the flow of ODA from OPEC countries to other less-developed countries (LDCs). The factors motivating certain oil-producing countries (mainly Arab) to channel funds were still operative, but new factors also emerged to increase the scope, the mechanisms, and the modalities of OPEC ODA.

It should be remembered that the initial jump in the price of oil took place within the context of the October 1973 Arab-Israeli war. Hence, it was only logical and inevitable that funds would be diverted to those Arab countries— Egypt, Syria, and Jordan—that suffered the most from the war.

The solidarity of the Third World countries was sought by OPEC-member countries in their attempt to change the terms of the oil concessions. This is an important point, in that the eventual benefits to OPEC-member countries were made at the expense of multinational oil companies and their home governments. In other words, the nonoil producing countries felt a genuine association with the accomplishments of OPEC. This view was encouraged by member countries, who thought that their success should be regarded as a model worth emulating by other developing countries.

The price revolution of 1973–74 coincided with the movement by many developing countries to establish a New International Economic Order. This attempt was encouraged by OPEC's success in restructuring the pattern of economic relations between countries of the North and the South.

In the same way that decisions to supply economic assistance to nonoil Arab countries have been based on political, economic, and cultural considerations, so also have been decisions about the extension of OPEC economic assistance to other developing countries. The official position stated repeatedly by OPEC-member countries has been that economic assistance to developing countries has been based on moral obligations tempered by political considerations as well as the principle of oneness with other developing countries. Thus, in its *First Annual Report*, the OPEC Special Fund stated its objectives as follows: "The aims of the Fund are to promote, through financial cooperation and assistance, the economic development, as well as the international solidarity of the third world" (OPEC Special Fund 1976, 7). The same principle was reiterated in 1980 when the fund was converted into the OPEC Fund for International Development. The views of individual countries with respect to eligibility criteria for receiving national funds for external development were illustrated by the president of the Iraqi Fund for External Development, as follows: "Those eligible to its aid include all developing countries whose policies are constant with the general policies of OPEC member countries and Iraq, in terms of their attitude to the relationship between industrialized countries and developing countries, and their attitude to the non-aligned movement and so on" (Al-Anbari 1980, 14–20).

The concept of solidarity found expression also in the U.N. system, since OPEC aid represented a major departure from the traditional pattern of donor-recipient in which the donor was a developed country and the recipient a developing country. Under the emerging system of financial solidarity, both donor and recipient countries were developing countries.[13]

It is clear from the foregoing discussion that all developing countries are eligible for OPEC economic assistance. This is true for two interrelated reasons. First, it is understood that all developing countries belong to the nonaligned movement; once this is recognized, differentiation among developing countries loses its meaning. Second, in order to be eligible for assistance, a developing country is expected to share OPEC-member countries' attitudes vis-á-vis the industrialized countries. That there is a consensus among OPEC-member countries and other developing countries on the need for reform of the international economic system in order to make it more beneficial to developing countries is a matter of record. Given this commonality of interests, the term *solidarity* begins to acquire economic as well as political implications so far as developing countries are concerned.

It is important nevertheless to qualify assertions about the extent of solidarity by stating that at certain historical junctures political considerations have overriden the requisites of unity between some OPEC-member countries and other developing countries. This was demonstrated forcefully in 1979 when all OPEC Arab-member countries suspended their economic aid program to Egypt in retaliation for the latter's decision to sign a peace treaty with Israel. Still, it should be underscored that this was a move by a group of countries within OPEC and not by OPEC as a whole. Furthermore, the decision was taken within the framework of the League of Arab States and not within the structure of OPEC.

Another issue that has received some attention has been the contention that OPEC aid should have been distributed on the basis of balance-of-payments difficulties of developing countries. According to this argument, the incremental cost of oil imports should be the guiding principle for the transfer of financial resources from OPEC-member countries to other developing countries. However, this view, though attractive is superficial. As noted earlier, almost 80 percent of oil imported by developing countries finds its way to nine countries only; the remaining oil is imported by the other seventy oil-importing developing countries. Had the criterion of cost compensation been adopted, a disproportionate amount of OPEC ODA would have gone to those countries with relatively high per-capita income and with more-advanced industrialized sectors. Another point against such an argument is that OPEC ODA was not intended to be a compensatory mechanism for higher import cost. Indeed, long before the price revolution of 1973, the flow of economic assistance from donor countries was governed by nonbalance-of-payments considerations. The point that OPEC economic assistance is unrelated to balance of payments was stated unequivocally as follows:

> *The OPEC Special Fund was not established as an instrument of compensation for the difference—or part of the difference—between the new and the old price of petroleum. . . . Yet the member countries of OPEC are deeply aware of the financial burdens of developing countries faced with rising costs of imports—not only crude oil and petroleum products—but food, manufactured goods, and essential raw materials. . . . The OPEC Special Fund's preferred approach has been to consider the resource gap for development in the totality of its causes, and to contribute to its closing, especially in the most affected countries, irrespective of the ways in which the gap rises. (OPEC Special Fund 1976, 7)*

The dispensing of OPEC aid in favor of the least-developed and most seriously affected countries is supported by some empirical studies. Thus according to one study, OPEC aid tended to follow criteria similar to those defined by the DAC, as indicated by the fact that OPEC and DAC donors directed about the same proportion (15 percent) of their aid toward the twenty-nine countries designated by the U.N. as the least developed (Cummings, Askari, and Salehizadeh 1978, 34). The same study also found that the forty-five countries designated by the U.N. as most affected by the major changes in trade balances during the 1970s received almost the same absolute amounts of economic aid in 1976 from the DAC and OPEC-member countries, and that nearly 95 percent of OPEC aid went to countries with per-capita GNP of less than $800, compared with only 70 percent of DAC aid. As to the claim that OPEC aid is biased in the direction of Arab and other Muslim countries, it was found that DAC aid was also heavily concentrated in a relatively small number of current or past associates. Thus it was noted that fifty-nine countries and territories with less than 3 percent of the Third World population received more than 36 percent of DAC economic assistance during 1976 (Cummings et al. 1978, 34).

Another study found that in 1975 and 1976 OPEC bilateral aid financed more than 100 percent of the increase in the oil bills of forty-one very poor countries and that OPEC concessional flows in 1975 financed about 60 percent of the additional financial requirements of oil-importing developing countries as a result of the oil-price increase (OPEC 1979b, i–vi). And for the period 1974 to 1980 OPEC ODA to the thirty-one countries designated as least developed amounted to $4.8 billion ($679 million per year), or about 12.5 percent of all OPEC ODA (Shihata 1981, table 1).

To summarize, like all other donor countries, OPEC-member countries have been guided in their aidgiving by a combination of political and economic considerations that have defined the scope and level of their aid. There are several major differences, however, between OPEC ODA and OECD ODA. First, OPEC ODA was a new and major departure in the pattern of economic assistance, in that no other group of developing countries commanded financial resources to the extent that OPEC ODA was directed to other developing countries. Second, given the membership makeup of OPEC and the dominant economic position occupied by the Arab-member countries in it, it was inevitable that most of the economic assistance from OPEC actually came from a few Arab-member countries. This was made possible by the availability to these countries of sizable financial assets, due to their current-account surplus during the period 1974 to 1982. Third, OPEC ODA, in contrast to economic assistance from the industrialized countries, was untied. Indeed, it had to be since developing countries did not have much else to spend the proceeds of a loan or a grant on except oil. Fourth, OPEC aid-giving countries provided a much higher ratio of their GNP in the form of ODA than did the industrialized countries. Finally, OPEC aid should be differentiated from other forms of aid from other donor countries by virtue of the fact that the flow of financial resources from OPEC-member countries represents an irreversible depletion of national wealth, that being oil.

OPEC AND THE THIRD WORLD: LABOR MOVEMENT

One of the more striking manifestations of the growing interdependence between OPEC-member countries and other Third World countries has been the movement of workers to labor-deficient, capital-surplus countries in the aftermath of oil-price increases and the resultant decisions by capital-surplus countries to accelerate economic growth. The consequences of labor movement to OPEC-member countries—mainly Saudi Arabia, Kuwait, the United Arab Emirates, Qatar, and Libya—have been multifaceted both for countries who gained workers and those who lost them.

In the case of the five countries just mentioned, the indigenous labor force was either small or lacked the necessary skills, or both. In another case, that of Iraq, although the labor force was large and skilled, the acceleration in development resulted in massive migration from rural areas to the urban centers, which in turn made it necessary to import rural and agricultural workers from abroad.

The initial rise in the demand for labor caused an increase in the flow of labor from traditional sources of surplus labor. In Arab labor-deficient countries and long before the onset of the increase in oil wealth, most imported workers have traditionally been Palestinians and Egyptians and most of these have been skilled workers. The importance of these expatriate workers may be seen in the Kuwait census of 1975. In that year the census reported that 41,836 persons were classified as professionals, technicians, or managers (categories that include scientists, engineers, physicians, dentists, nurses, statisticians, economists, accountants, teachers, clergy, jurists, artists, managers, government civil servants, and all types of technical workers). Of the 41,836 persons 26 percent were Kuwaitis; 13 percent were non-Arab and the remaining 61 percent came from Arab countries. Of the Arab technical workers, there were 12,614 Palestinians—comprising 44 percent of the Arab component of this group of professionals and managers—with the balance coming mainly from Egypt (Government of Kuwait 1977).

The ability of the oil-exporting, labor-importing countries to bid up the price of labor provided a powerful incentive to workers in the labor-exporting countries to seek employment opportunities in the oil-producing countries. And when the traditional labor-exporting countries could not meet the labor demand, new sources of labor were found. So in addition to the Egyptians and Palestinians, oil-producing countries found themselves importing labor from Jordan, Sudan, North Yemen, South Yemen, Lebanon, Pakistan, Bangladesh, India, the Philippines, and Korea. So great was the migration of foreign workers into some of the oil-producing countries that by 1978 foreign workers constituted between 40 percent and 80 percent of the total labor force in the countries of Saudi Arabia, Libya, Kuwait, the United Arab Emirates, and Qatar.[14]

Of equal if not greater significance is the fact that migrant workers comprised significant portions of the total labor force in their own countries of origin. For example, in 1975 the ratio of migrant workers to the domestic labor force in five labor-exporting countries amounted to 28 percent in the case of Jordan; 27 percent for North Yemen; 3.8 percent for Egypt; 8.7 percent for Lebanon; and 91 percent in the case of South Yemen.[15] On the positive side is that the remittances that nonnational workers transfer to their countries of origin constitute a major source of foreign-exchange earnings to the labor-exporting countries. In 1978, for example, the total amount of remittances that were transferred to seven countries—Egypt, Pakistan, India, Bangladesh, Jordan, South Yemen, and North Yemen—amounted to $6.5 billion. Of these, Egypt was the largest recipient of remittances, with $1.8 billion, which financed 46 percent of Egypt's merchandise imports, constituted more than 10 percent of its GNP, and were the equivalent of 89 percent of its merchandise exports. In the case of Jordan the remittance inflow was the equivalent of 175 percent of that country's merchandise exports and 22 percent of its GNP, and it financed 35 percent of that country's merchandise imports. In North Yemen, which virtually had no exports, the workers' remittance inflow, amounting to $1.3 billion in 1978, financed all of that country's imports that year and contributed almost 56 percent of its GNP. In Pakistan, worker remittance inflow in 1978 contributed 7 percent of that country's GNP, financed 40 percent of its imports, and was the equivalent of 93 percent of its merchandise exports (World Bank 1981; 1982).

As stated earlier, these major movements of personnel and finance among the two groups of countries had a number of economic benefits and economic and social costs. For the labor-exporting country, the benefits include, of course, an increase in the inflow of funds from abroad as the migrant workers remit part of their earnings to their country of origin. Another advantage is the reduction in unemployment in the labor-exporting country in the early stages of the outflow of workers. For labor-importing countries the most obvious benefit is that the country's needs for particular skills are met immediately and at no capital investment.

Opposed to these benefits are diseconomies or costs. One such cost to labor-exporting countries is that as the pool of skilled workers begins to shrink, the wages of the remaining workers begin to rise, a fact that tends to add to whatever inflationary pressures exist in these countries. Furthermore as a result of the outflow of workers, the labor-exporting country may find itself compelled to change its pattern of investment in response to external forces rather than the imperatives of its own needs and objectives.

Another aspect of this flow of labor is that the availability of foreign exchange to the labor-surplus countries encouraged these countries to increase their imports of durable and nondurable consumer goods. The extent of the rise in imports is determined by several variables, including the number of workers involved, the amount of remittances they send to the home country, and the extent of the impact of the demonstration effect on consumption patterns.

While the economic and social problems of labor-exporting countries of course existed long before the oil-price revolution, the impact of this revolution on the freedom of action by policy makers should not be underestimated. In the case of Egypt, for instance, it has been estimated that within a three-year period, 1973–76, the number of Egyptian workers who migrated to oil-exporting countries increased from 0.1 million to 0.6 million. Regardless of the importance of the last figure relative to the total labor force, the mere fact that the number of migrant workers increased by five times was bound to have economic and social consequences that policy makers had not anticipated. One such economic problem, for instance, was the emergence of shortages in certain segments of the labor markets from which these workers were pulled.

Another problem that was observed in Egypt and other labor-exporting countries was the tendency of migrant workers to leave their families in their home countries, a fact that resulted in certain economic and social problems.[16]

Labor-receiving countries also had to contend with a variety of problems. One of these was the decline in the productivity of certain migrant workers. The main explanation for this decline is the lack of a similar technical infrastructure in the labor-receiving country that would help workers attain levels of productivity comparable to those in their countries of origin.[17]

In the period prior to the sudden increase in wealth and income, the dependency of the labor-receiving countries on foreign labor was much smaller in scope. However, the rise in income and the decision to accelerate the rate of economic growth by building infrastructures and industries made it necessary to rely heavily on foreign labor almost permanently.[18] This was so because none of these countries has the demographic base to generate the required labor force to run an expanding economy. The significance of this observation can be more fully appreciated when it is realized that in 1975 foreign labor represented 43 percent of total employment in Saudi Arabia and Libya; 69 percent in Kuwait; and 85 percent in United Arab Emirates. Again, the rising dependence of Saudi Arabia on foreign labor can be appreciated by looking at the evolution of the Saudi Arabian development plans. The 1975–80 Five Year Development Plan, for example, envisaged the expenditure of $140 billion, or $28 billion per year, compared with only $2.5 billion per year under the preceding five-year plan of 1970 to 1975. It is important to note that the 1975–80 Plan aimed to generate 730,000 jobs, with only 232,000, or 32 percent, of these jobs to be filled by nationals and the balance of 498,000 jobs to be filled by nonnationals (Alnasrawi 1979, 1–27). And there is no reason to expect that the 1980–85 plan, which forecast expenditures of $57 billion per year, will lessen Saudi Arabian dependence on foreign labor, given that country's small population and its relatively low participation rate in the labor force. The presence of a large number of foreign workers inevitably creates a number of serious political, social, and economic problems, including erosion of indigenous cultural values, social discontent, accentuation of inequitable income distribution, and the decline of work ethics (Ibrahim 1982, 53–58).

OPEC AND THE QUEST FOR A
NEW INTERNATIONAL ECONOMIC ORDER

The oil-price increase of 1973 and the consequent change in the world balance of economic forces thrust OPEC in to the then-ongoing debate on the international economic system. From the perspective of Third World countries, important structural changes in the system were necessary if the benefits of trade and investment were to be shared equitably among all participants. The position of the developing countries, as expressed in numerous documents, was that the existing international economic order tended to perpetuate the developing countries' dependency on and exploitation by industrial countries. For the developing countries of the South, the existing international economic order brought with it a number of burdens, including the oppressive trade policies of industrialized countries, debt burden, insufficient flow of resources, and general indifference to the plight of the developing countries. In short, these nations recognized that, having little power, they were at the losing end of the international economic system.[19]

Although several attempts were made to change or modify some of the more objectionable aspects of the international economic system through the activities of the United Nations Conference on Trade and Development and other international bodies, none of these attempts brought about any meaningful change. The efforts of the developing countries in this regard were continued within the U.N. and resulted in the adoption in 1974 by the U.N. General Assembly of the Declaration on the Establishment of a New International Economic Order and Action Programme and similar pronouncements. But again no success from the standpoint of developing countries could be recorded.

OPEC's decisions, however, to alter the terms of trade between its member countries and the industrial countries and to change the distribution of income in favor of OPEC members provided a major boost to the push for a new economic order and contributed, as well, to the continuing debate on the subject. OPEC, in other words was transformed from being an instrument for pressuring the multinational oil companies to being an instrument for pressuring industrialized economies to accept changes in the international economic system for the benefit of the developing countries.

Although the sudden increase in the price of oil was a more serious problem to the developing countries than to the industrialized countries, the former group considered its long-term interests as conforming more with those of OPEC-member countries than with those of the industrialized countries. This perception was strengthened by several considerations. First, the mere act by a number of developing countries of raising the price of oil was interpreted as signaling a new era in the pattern of relationships between the countries of the South on the one hand and those of the North on the other. The ability, in other words, of a number of developing countries to act in collusion to raise the price of a raw material and to maintain the price at the new level was considered an achievement of major proportion. One observer at the time described the meaning of OPEC's decisions as the first time since Vasco da Gama that the peripheral countries had wrested the mastery of a crucial area of economic policy from the major industrialized countries (quoted in Barraclough 1976, 31).

Second, the developing countries of the South had no illusion about the ability of the countries of the North to weather the oil crisis. Although in the industrial countries the price increase affected the upper layers of consumption (in other words, nonessential consumption), the entire economy and especially the productive capacity of developing countries was affected. The countries of the North, in contrast to those of the South, also had the purchasing power to pay for their imported oil, as well as the backing of the entire international monetary and financial system to help them meet the price rise. The countries of the South, however, had to incur higher debt burdens to pay for their imported oil, a plight made worse by the 300 percent rise in the cost of imported wheat between 1972 and 1974. It should be noted that this burden did not evoke concern and protest in developed countries on a scale similar to their response to the oil-price increases (Parmer 1975, 17–22).

A third consideration that tended to discourage developing countries from associating themselves with the countries of the North was the systematic effort by industrialized countries to organize and create their own International Energy Agency, as well as to enter into bilateral arrangements with oil-exporting countries to secure oil supplies.

The fourth and most important consideration was that OPEC-member countries themselves identified with the demands of Third World countries for a different international economic order. Indeed, this commonality of beliefs had been in the making long before the oil-price revolution, and a leading OPEC-member country, Algeria, had played a key role in the Third World movement toward the establishment of a new international economic order.

Algeria, owing to its role in the summit conference of the Non-Aligned Coordinating Council in September 1973 and its linkages with both Arab and OPEC policies and politics was a logical linkage between the two groups of developing countries and an important articulator of the general economic objectives of the South. Thus, when the oil-price and output decisions were made immediately after the 1973 Non-Aligned summit in Algeria, it was only logical that Algeria's position within the two groups of countries would be enhanced and that both sets of countries would be united in their attempt to challenge industrial countries' monopoly in the international economy. Algeria's special position enabled it to request and obtain the convening of a U.N. Sixth Special Session in April 1974 to consider raw materials problems of all types, not just energy. This special session adopted, in May 1974, the earlier-mentioned Declaration on the Establishment of a New International Economic Order and the Programme of Action on the Establishment of A New International Economic Order.[20] The joining of forces between OPEC-member countries and other Third World countries in an undertaking that resulted in the resolutions of the Sixth Special Session led one observer to comment: "OPEC's bold stroke, which had brought energy resources to the fore as a worldwide problem, gave the Third World activists an opportunity to transform the oil crisis into a means for pursuing the goals they had elaborated at Algiers prior to the oil crisis" (Wiggins and Adler-Kartsson 1978, 69).

The resolutions adopted by the Sixth Special Session were either opposed by or did not receive the support of industrialized countries. In December 1974 the developing countries as a group urged the U.N. General Assembly to adopt the Charter of Economic Rights and Duties of States. But, even though the charter was adopted, the industrialized countries again either opposed or failed to support the charter. Those who opposed the charter objected to provisions in it that reaffirmed not only the principle of the sovereignty of the state over natural resources and wealth, but the power of the states to regulate and supervise the activities of multinational corporations, as well as a provision providing for the nationalization of the companies' assets as appropriate compensation. Industrial countries also disliked the charter's endorsement of the beliefs that primary commodity producers should form producers' organizations and that all states should cooperate to adjust the export prices of developing countries in relation to their import prices.[21]

In February 1975, two months after the passage of the charter, the Dakar (Senegal) Declaration and Action Programme of the Conference of Developing Countries on Raw Materials was adopted by 110 developing countries. The Dakar declaration reaffirmed the principles adopted by the United Nations in 1974 as contained in both the Sixth Special Session and the just-described charter and elaborated on the concept of collective "self reliance" embodied in these documents.

The significance of the Dakar conference in relation to OPEC–Third World interdependence is that it emphasized the importance of collective action by the developing countries vis-à-vis the developed countries. In the words of the declaration: ". . . the developing countries must undertake common action to strengthen their bargaining position in relation to the developed countries" (Erb and Kallab 1975, 217). As to the 1973 price hike, the declaration maintained that the increase was justified, since it was in reaction to a long period of deterioration in the terms of trade of the developing countries (Erb and Kallab 1975, 216).

In March 1975, prompted by the unstable international economic system and the new role of OPEC in stimulating change, OPEC-member countries held their own summit conference in Algeria and issued the "Solemn Declaration of the Algiers Conference of Sovereigns and Heads of State of the OPEC Member Countries."[22] This conference and its declaration were important for several reasons. First, the conference was the first (and so far the only) summit meeting held by OPEC-member countries. So urgent were the issues at hand that by the time of the conference, OPEC-member countries not only had succeeded in asserting their economic interests with respect to the industrialized countries but they had effectively mobilized development assistance programs to other developing countries. They had managed, moreover to press for international discussion with industrialized countries on issues of immediate concern to other developing countries. The conference thus served as a catalyst for action.

The worth of the conference declaration derives from the broad policy outlines that the participating countries enumerated in light of their understanding of the international economic system and of their perception of their new place in it, as well as the extent of their commitment to other developing countries and to the industrial countries. They accepted, first, the principles espoused in the resolutions of the Sixth Special Session of the U.N. Siding with other developing countries, the declaration reiterated the view that the world economic crisis stems largely from economic and social inequalities caused by foreign exploitation. Wary of foreign intervention, the declaration advocated that heads of state: " . . . denounce any grouping of consumer nations with the aim of confrontation, and condemn any plan or strategy designed for aggression, economic or military, by such grouping or otherwise against any OPEC Member Country."[23]

After reaffirming the solidarity of OPEC-member countries with other developing countries and pledging continued financial assistance to these countries, the declaration proceeded to link the energy problem with other problems facing the world economy. It stated:

> *The Sovereigns and Heads of State agree in principle to holding an international conference bringing together the developed and developing countries.*
> *They consider that the objective of such a conference should be to make a significant advance in action designed to alleviate the major difficulties existing in the world economy, and that consequently the conference should pay equal attention to the problems facing both the developed and developing countries.*
> *Therefore, the agenda of the aforementioned conference can in no case be confined to an examination of the question of energy; it evidently includes the question of raw materials of the developing countries, the reform of the international monetary system and international cooperation in favor of development in order to achieve world stability.*[24]

The declaration furthermore stated that such a conference might be convened within a limited framework, provided that all of the nations affected were adequately and genuinely represented. One point made in the declaration that influenced official OPEC thinking in subsequent years pertained to the issue of the price of oil. The declaration's position was that the price of petroleum had to be maintained by linking it to certain objective criteria, including the price of manufactured goods, the rate of inflation, and the terms of transfer of goods and technology for the development of OPEC-member countries.[25]

The declaration's call for a conference between developed and developing countries materialized later in 1975 when the Conference on International Economic Cooperation (CIEC) was held in Paris to address issues raised by developing countries. But prior to the opening of the CIEC the U.N. held the Seventh Special Session in September 1975.

At the time of the convening of the Seventh Special Session, some of the important changes of the preceding years seemed no longer of immediate significance. For instance, the oil crisis of October 1973 had proved to be short-lived and manageable in terms of its consequences. To the industrial countries neither the cost nor the availability of oil were commanding the attention they had commanded at the time of the Sixth Special Session in 1974. Put another way, the dire after-effects that were predicted for the economies of the industrialized countries at the time of the oil-price increase failed to occur. As a result, OPEC-member countries lost their leverage to influence events and effect changes in the international economic system.

Another factor that diminished the urgency of events of the previous years was the change in the food situation, as shortages and higher prices gave way to higher output and lower prices. And within the ranks of the Third World, Saudi Arabia was beginning to assume a more assertive role within OPEC; by extention, so also was the entire Third World strategy vis-à-vis the industrial countries.

Thus, by the time of the Seventh Special Session the key issues had become commodity agreements, the functioning of the international monetary system, and the assertion by developing countries of their rights to control their own resources and their own economic development without hindrance from the West.[26] At the session's end the demand for a new international economic order was side-stepped and it was decided to engage the industrial countries in negotiations outside of the framework of the U.N. General Assembly. The framework selected turned out to be the Conference on International Economic Cooperation, also known as the North-South Dialogue, in which OPEC was to play a prominent but unsuccessful role, as discussed in the next section.

OPEC AND THE CIEC NEGOTIATIONS

The Conference on International Economic Cooperation was launched in December 1975 and ended in June 1977. Three elements led to its convening. The first was the French government's call in 1974 for a conference to deal with the issue of energy in light of the new conditions created by the 1973 OPEC decisions. The second was the acceptance of the French initiative by the OPEC summit of April 1975 provided that energy would be only one of several issues discussed. In other words, energy was seen as linked to all matters of economic concern in developing countries. This issue linkage was one of the most significant contributions of OPEC to the attempt by developing countries to change the international economic order.

The third element that led to the convening of the CIEC was a change in U.S. policy—from one of confrontation to one of negotiation—in regard to the demands of the Third World. This change took place during the Seventh Special Session of the U.N. in 1975. As one observer noted:

> *The North was finally brought to the bargaining table by the South when the United States failed to drive a wedge between OPEC and the rest of the developing countries in the spring of 1975. Only the energy issue was deemed important enough by the North to produce the switch from confrontation to "dialogue"; only after the United States plan to isolate OPEC and deal with the energy question alone failed did it [the North] agree to "discuss" other NIEO issues at CIEC in order to open an exchange on energy. (Hansen 1979, 104)*

The participants at the Conference on International Economic Cooperation included nineteen developing countries—seven of which were OPEC-member countries and seven were developed countries—plus the European

Economic Community. The conference created four commissions to deal individually with energy, raw materials, development, and finance. The concept of issue linkage was reflected in the fact that the commissions were to work in parallel, and progress in any one commission had to be matched by progress in the others. A safeguard was therefore provided against the conferences concentrating exclusively on energy (Seymour 1980, 261).

No sooner had the work of the conference started, however, than it became apparent that no progress would be made. The reappearance of surplus conditions in the oil market and the decline in the real price of crude oil led the developed countries to adopt the position that there was no need to concede anything either to OPEC or to the rest of the Third World (Seymour 1980, 261). After almost eighteen months of negotiations, the CIEC was thus concluded. The participating developing countries acknowledged the failure of the North-South Dialogue when they noted that most of their proposals failed to receive the support of the rich countries and that the accomplishments of the dialogue fell short of the objectives envisaged for a comprehensive and equitable program of action designed to create a new international economic order. The developed countries concurred with this appraisal when they stated that the conference had not been able to agree on some important areas of the dialogue, such as certain aspects of energy cooperation.[27] In assessing the CIEC, Roger D. Hansen said that the conference terminated with a singular lack of positive results, having failed to reach agreement on a single issue of importance to either set of participants. He further stated:

> *The only cost to the North of 2 years of dialogue was a promise of a $1 billion Special Action program to meet the most urgent foreign-exchange needs of the least developed countries. And since Northern economic assistance bookkeeping practices will determine whether this $1 billion actually involves* additional *funds or simply a shifting of previously appropriated foreign aid expenditures, it is highly unlikely that anywhere near the full $1 billion will be, in the aid jargon, "additive" (Hansen 1979, 283–84)*

The failure of CIEC effectively ended attempts by developing countries to introduce major changes into the international economic system. The efforts to change the pattern of international economic relations had begun with the creation of UNCTAD in 1964 and received its major support from Third World governments at the Algiers meeting of the Non-Aligned conference in September 1973. The success of OPEC during this time and the challenge that it represented to the industrial countries encouraged developing countries to call upon the U.N.—through two special sessions—to issue a number of resolutions and declarations favoring the establishment of a new international economic order. Even with the help that OPEC provided when it insisted that energy issues could not be separated from other concerns of developing countries the results of the CIEC were marginal and inconsequential at best.

And so by June 1977 both OPEC and other Third World countries found themselves back where they were in 1973, prior to the increase in the price of crude oil so far as their attempts to change the international economic system were concerned. The major difference was that by 1977 OPEC-member countries had succeeded in changing the terms of trade and the distribution of income in their favor.

SUMMARY

This chapter has reviewed a number of changes that occurred in the pattern of economic relations between OPEC-member countries and other Third World countries in the aftermath of the oil-price revolution. Several points bear reemphasizing here.

In the first place, OPEC-member countries instituted mechanisms to provide financial assistance to a large number of developing countries through bilateral, regional, and multilateral vehicles. Most of the financial flows from OPEC-member countries were channeled through bilateral agreements. And most of OPEC financial flows came from a few capital-surplus countries.

Second, OPEC-member countries, especially the labor-deficient countries, attracted large numbers of workers from other developing countries. The remittances of these workers constituted a major source of foreign-exchange earnings to the labor-exporting countries. Of course, important economic and social costs were also incurred by these labor-exporting countries.

Another area of economic interactions between the two groups of countries that expanded rapidly following the rise in the price of crude oil was that of foreign trade. In their attempt to pay for the rise in the cost of imported oil, developing countries succeeded in increasing their own exports to OPEC-member countries.

On the other side of the ledger, it can be said that OPEC failed to exercise its new-found power and resources to benefit Third World countries in their attempts either to change the international economic system to their advantage or to pursue the ambitious objectives of Third World collective reliance. As to the attempt to establish a new international economic order, OPEC-member countries elected not to use their resources to that end. Instead, they found themselves and other developing countries engaged with the industrialized countries in discussions and negotiations that failed to yield any significant benefits to the Third World. OPEC's position on the principle of self-reliance did not go beyond a political endorsement. In the view of developing countries OPEC failed to marshal its economic and political resources to move self-reliance from being a call to being a policy. The mere fact that OPEC-member countries with financial resources opted to place these funds in the existing money and capital markets instead of using them to promote economic development and economic independence was seen by non-OPEC developing countries as testifying to where OPEC members' allegiance lies.

Finally, the experience of OPEC-member countries during this time was unique and could not have been duplicated by any other country or group of developing countries. The conditions that made the OPEC coalition workable included the fact that oil is a highly essential commodity; the capability of oil-producing countries to regulate output; the difficulty of developing substitutes; and the ease of storing the commodity for so long as necessary.[28] No other commodity has all these features and no other commodity is more depended upon by the international economy.

CHAPTER 7

OPEC in the 1980s:
Historical Reversals and Prospects

Any examination of OPEC's role in the world economy is problematic because the conditions affecting the way in which OPEC operates change constantly. These conditions include the internal workings of the economies of member countries; their oil reserve endowments; their absorptive capacity; the stability of their political structures; and their demographic base. Other sources of change are intra-OPEC conflicts, economic change and growth in industrial countries, the availability of oil from sources outside the OPEC region, interfuel substitution, the development of nonconventional energy sources, conservation and efficient use of energy, and elasticity of demand for oil at different price ranges. In addition to these economic factors, political and strategic considerations which may be national, regional, or global in nature, impinge directly on the availability of oil and its price.

CONTEXTUAL EVOLUTION OF OPEC

No study of OPEC and its behavior and impact on the world economy can ignore the fact that the petroleum history in most OPEC-member countries was shaped to a considerable extent by political forces outside and beyond the control of their governments. It was during the period that first Europe and then America expanded their direct investment in the Third World that the oil sectors emerged in the oil-producing countries.[1] It was in this era that the governments of the oil-producing countries were either supported, protected, or dominated by one or another of the major industrialized powers of the day and the concession agreements were granted or obtained. These concessions were signed by governments and/or rulers who did not or could not appreciate the value of their countries' natural resources.

The system of oil concessions was born moreover, at a time when the power of the host governments in relation to the industrialized countries was either nonexistent or inconsequential. The concession system that in most cases gave virtually the entire territory of the state to foreign capital also gave the oil companies exclusive control over output and prices. The asymmetry between the power and the technical resources of the state and those of the foreign enterprise was of such proportion that it was almost impossible for any one host government to present a serious challenge to the multinational oil corporations. The concession system was made impenetrable by the very nature of the rise and evolution of the operating companies in the oil-producing countries. Bargaining and negotiations, if they were ever allowed to occur, had to be conducted between one government and a number of multinational oil companies that owned the operating company in that country. And behind the combined power of the oil companies, was the collective power of their respective home governments. Even when a concession was granted to one foreign enterprise, as in the case of British Petroleum in Iran, the government of that country found it impossible to sell its oil to foreign buyers, owing to a British Petroleum boycott against Iranian oil (aided by the British government).

The role of the governments of the oil companies was not the only political dimension shaping the petroleum history of oil-producing countries. Political changes and upheavals within the oil-producing countries had an enormous impact both on the evolution of the international oil industry and on the rise of OPEC. The Iranian experiment in nationalization in 1951 was carried out against a backdrop of rising nationalism in the Middle East. Although the nationalization failed, it forced the oil companies in the region to alter the fiscal terms of their concession agreements in favor of the oil-producing countries. In Iraq the revolutionary government of Abdul-Karim Qassem, which came to power in 1958, demanded new terms for the exploitation of Iraq's oil resources. When the negotiations failed to reach an agreement, the government expropriated the entire concession area except for the oil-producing plots. The companies then retaliated by not allowing Iraq's output to rise in tandem with the rise in oil output in other producing countries. Similarly, when the revolutionary government of Muammar Qadhafi came to power in Libya in 1969, a new era in the petroleum history of that country and in the concession system throughout the Middle East was inaugurated.

Aside from national political changes, regional conflicts also affected the course of oil developments in the OPEC region. Both the closure of the Suez Canal in the aftermath of the 1956 invasion of Egypt and the 1967 Arab-Israeli war directly affected the pattern of oil flow from Arab oil-producing countries to the major centers of consumption.

The period of the Arab-Israeli conflict that coincided with the big push for the expansion of oil output in the Middle East had its own impact on output and price decisions and, in certain instances, on supply as well. In each of the Arab-Israeli wars during this time, oil was used an an instrument of economic pressure, either officially or unofficially. The most dramatic illustration of this point is, of course, the 1973 price revolution. It was in the context of the October War that oil was deliberately used an an instrument of foreign policy. Although OPEC itself was not directly involved in the oil events of that period, the majority of its members and the bulk of its output were affected. The embargo measures imposed by OPEC's Arab members on oil exports to the United States and the Netherlands and the decision to reduce oil output in order to persuade the United States to exert pressure on Israel created the artificial shortage that persuaded the non-Arab members to push for a second increase in the price of crude oil. Thus, the second price increase, which was made effective in January 1974, can be considered a direct result of the Arab-Israeli conflict of 1973.

The economies of the industrial countries added another dimension to the strategic importance of oil. It is no secret that military planners and strategists in industrial countries pay close attention to the security of the oil fields of OPEC-member countries as well as to the sea routes that oil travels from these countries to the major centers of consumption. The point here is that the international oil industry in the OPEC region has always played a role in the strategic and national interests of one or another of the major industrial countries—Great Britain, United States, France, Germany, and so forth. And the creation of Israel and the consequent Arab-Israeli conflict furthermore enhanced the political dimension of oil.

Although when OPEC was created in 1960 its founders conceived of it as an instrument to pressure the oil companies into improving the fiscal benefits of member governments, it was not until 1973 that OPEC began to be perceived as a power to be reckoned with. Yet this perception was not rooted in the realities of the organization and of its evolution to that point. For example, commodity price data shows that OPEC failed during the 1960s to keep the price of its major export in line with the prices of other internationally traded commodities. (It is not without justification that the oil-price revolution of 1973–74 is referred to sometimes as a price adjustment.) The explosion in the terms of trade in favor of OPEC-member countries as a result of the oil-price revolution brought the depressed price level of oil in line with the prices of other commodities.[2] The combination of significant price increases with politically motivated output reductions led the overwhelming majority of observers to attribute to OPEC market powers that it did not have. OPEC was founded, after all, on the premise that every member country can do as it wishes; this means that the ultimate arbiter as to how much oil OPEC-member countries can sell is the market.

It should be noted that the elaborate output-control mechanisms and formulas that were adhered to by the oil companies prior to 1973 were not only abandoned by OPEC but were not replaced by any system that would relate world oil demand to output in member countries. This major deficiency in the structure of OPEC was not important so long as the demand for OPEC oil was high enough to meet the fiscal requirements of member countries. A downward movement in demand, however, which occurred in 1974–75, had the effect of unmasking OPEC's weakness in administering prices. This weakness, which neither OPEC nor its critics seem to have appreciated, stemmed from the fact that OPEC, like any seller, could not control both the price charged and the quantity bought, since OPEC-member countries retain the right to set output volume individually rather than collectively. The dispersion of the output control mechanism meant that the cartel function that was performed collectively by the multinational oil corporations was allowed to be fragmented by OPEC-member countries. The fragmentation of the output control mechanism was to be expected, of course, given the nature of the state system that replaced the concession system as the mechanism for the development of oil resources. The difference between the former and the latter is rooted in the divergent purposes of the two systems.

Under the concession system the producer was interested in the commercial terms of the enterprise, with profit maximization the governing principle. In order to ensure that profits were maximized, long-term collective planning was utilized in order to reconcile supply with projected demand targets and to iron out differences among partners. Moreover, for each of the oil companies, production of crude oil represented but one phase in the totality of the integrated operations of the corporation.

Under the state system, which was instituted by OPEC-member countries following the transfer of controlling power to the governments, the objectives of oil policy were no longer purely commercial but became integrated in the overall economic, social, and political goals of the state. This meant that any collective power that OPEC exerted against the oil companies or might have exerted in the market was eventually dissipated by the individual actions of sovereign states that constitute the membership of OPEC. For example, although Saudi Arabia attempted to articulate a set of principles to guide OPEC pricing policies, no effort was made to integrate output allocation into the pricing system. The consequences of the failure to develop an output allocation system to replace the one used by the oil companies were driven home in the aftermath of the second price shock after the Iranian Revolution.

By the time the second price shock was felt, the demand for oil had not only stopped growing but had declined in absolute terms. The higher price of oil, together with the steep and long recession in the industrial countries for whose economies OPEC oil was destined, forced OPEC-member countries to the realization that the promising projections of a few years earlier with respect to oil demand would not materialize. With no supply-controlling mechanism within OPEC, it was inevitable that a condition of excess supply would arise in the international market. In fact, the excess supply was the result of forces that had been at work for a decade, including significant structural changes in the energy economy, structural changes in the international oil industry, and the drive by the industrial countries to lessen their dependence on OPEC-member countries as their major supplier of oil. These forces and their implications for OPEC and its future in the world economy are examined in the sections following.

STRUCTURAL CHANGES IN THE ENERGY ECONOMY

The importance of oil for the functioning of a modern economy is summarized in *The Geopolitics of Oil*: "The problem is that human society in the 20th Century has developed around easy-to-use, cheap oil, and most of our major institutions, including our military, are heavily dependent upon this particular form of energy. Oil is the lifeblood of the modern world. Without oil no modern economy can presently exist" (U.S. Senate, Committe on Energy and Natural Resources 1980, iii).

The indispensability of oil to the modern industrial economies can be appreciated by examining a number of indicators, one of which is the ratio of oil consumption to total energy consumption. Thus for the OECD countries total consumption of energy increased from 25.2 MBDOE in 1950 to 66 MBDOE in 1973, or an increase of 162 percent. Oil consumption for the same group of countries on the other hand, increased from 8.1 MBD to 37.2 MBD, or a 362 percent increase during the same period. This difference in the respective growth rates of energy and oil consumption resulted in a major change in the structure of energy demand and in the role of oil as the primary component of energy. In 1950 oil supplied 32 percent of total energy consumption in the OECD countries. Ten years later the share of oil had increased to 42 percent, and in 1970 it increased again to 53 percent (see table 9). The share of oil in total energy consumption in OECD countries peaked at 56 percent in 1973. It should be noted that the combined real gross domestic product (GDP) of the OECD countries increased during the period 1950 to 1973 from $1.4 trillion to $4.1 trillion, or by 193 percent.

Another indicator of the rising importance of oil in the industrial economies is the energy and/or oil-intensity ratios that measure the amount of energy and/or oil consumed per unit of GDP. In 1950 energy requirements per $1,000 of real GDP in OECD countries was computed to be 6.6 barrels of oil equivalent. This ratio declined to 5.93 barrels of oil equivalent by 1973. The oil-intensity ratio, by contrast, increased from 2.12 barrels per $1,000 GDP to 3.35 barrels in 1973.[3] It is clear from these indicators that the rate of growth in oil consumption considerably exceeded the rate of growth of GDP, a situation that reflected two major trends. The first was the fact that the increase in the demand for energy was met primarily by one source: oil. The second trend was the interfuel substitution in favor of oil, a trend that was enhanced by environmental considerations in the 1960s and 1970s in the industrialized economies.

Two important factors contributing to the enhancement of the role of oil in total energy consumption were the cost of oil and its availability. As was indicated earlier in this book, government revenue from oil was about 85¢ to 90¢ per barrel for almost two decades prior to the conclusion of the Tehran Agreement of 1971. Taking into account the constant erosion in the terms of trade of the oil-exporting countries, the variable cost of oil to the economies of the consuming countries was in fact negligible.

The quadrupling of the price of crude oil and the assumption of controlling power over prices and output by OPEC-member countries introduced certain key changes that in time led to the restructuring of the energy market. Thus, in 1974, instead of paying about $1 per barrel of oil the consuming countries found themselves paying about $11 per barrel. This was owing to the fact that prior to 1973 the governments received only part of the economic rent, with the rest going to the oil companies, while in the post-1973 era the governments were in a position to appropriate to themselves the entire difference between the cost of production and the posted price of crude oil. In the post-1973 price revolution the cost of oil as a variable input ceased to be unimportant from the perspective of the importing countries. The phenomenal and sudden increase in the cost of oil and the resultant balance-of-payments difficulties forced the consuming countries to reexamine their energy policies with an eye to reducing both the cost of imported oil and their quantitative dependence on it. This in turn meant that energy consumption in general and oil consumption in particular had to be decreased.

The central focus of energy policies in OECD countries was to stimulate certain structural changes in the energy economy, in order to reduce energy consumption without damaging economic growth prospects. This view was summarized by the International Energy Agency as follows:

> *The two oil crises have illustrated the threat which energy can represent to the economy. But they have also awakened the world to the challenge of structural adjustment in the energy economy. Structural change is necessary to remove*

energy as a major constraint to sustained, noninflationary economic growth and to reduce oil supply vulnerability. The main objectives of structural change are to use energy more efficiently and to reduce dependence on oil so as to achieve a more balanced mix of energy sources that is less exposed to supply security. (IEA 1982, 21)

In order to attain the objective of removing the energy constraint, the IEA adopted and implemented several policy objectives that led ultimately to the reduction in demand for energy and oil. The most important of these policies were intended to achieve, among other things, the following: energy conservation and the development of alternative sources of energy, by allowing domestic energy prices to reach a level that would encourage such actions; adoption of minimum energy-efficiency standards; encouragement and expansion of investment in energy-saving equipment and techniques; progressive replacement of oil in electricity generation as well as in space heating and industrial activity; a strong coal utilization strategy; steady expansion of nuclear-generating capacity as a main and indispensable element in attaining energy objectives.[4]

The implementation of these policies by the industrialized countries and the rise in the price of oil led to major structural changes in the pattern of energy and oil consumption. According to the IEA's own asessment, between 1973 and 1980 the following changes in the energy economy occurred for the OECD group of countries (IEA 1982, 22).

1. Real GDP increased by 19 percent but the increase in total energy requirements was only 4 percent, reflecting a significant historical reversal in the relationship between energy consumption and GDP growth. This historical change was evidenced by the 13 percent decline in the energy used to produce one unit of GDP.

2. Of greater significance from OPEC's perspective, the successful energy policies of the OECD countries resulted in a reduction in their oil imports from all sources by 14 percent, and the oil used to produce one unit of GDP declined by 20 percent.

3. Domestic energy production increased by 13 percent, with oil rising by 9 percent, coal by 23 percent, and nuclear energy by 206 percent.

As stated, these changes in the energy and oil intensity ratios resulted in a shift in the structure of energy consumption. In 1973 the share of oil in total energy consumption in the OECD area was 53.3 percent. By 1982 the contribution of oil to total energy consumption had declined to 45.2 percent, reflecting a major shift away from oil in favor of other forms of energy, particularly coal and nuclear energy. The efficient utilization of energy, which was prompted by the rise in energy cost, was achieved in all sectors of the energy economy. If 1973 is used as the base year, by 1980 energy consumption per unit of industrial output had declined by 18 pecent in the OECD region; and another 18 percent decline was achieved in the residential/commercial sector as measured by energy use per unit of private consumption expenditure..Even in the transportation sector it was found that in the major industrial economies, gasoline consumption for road transport per car declined by 19 percent between 1973 and 1980 (IEA 1982, 22).

In summary, in the period since 1973 the energy economy has undergone key structural changes, the most important of which has been the reduction in energy requirements per unit of output. The demand for oil in the OECD countries has actually declined, reflecting, first, considerable improvement in the efficiency of energy utilization in general and in utilization of oil in particular, due to the phenomenal increase in its price; and second, the rise in the cost of oil has encouraged fuel substitution away from oil and in favor of other forms of energy, especially coal and nuclear energy. Energy policies both at the national level and among governments of the industrialized countries have been aimed at reducing energy and oil consumption so as to lessen their economies' dependence on oil imports. Available statistical evidence published by OECD and OPEC indicates that the industrial countries have succeeded in accomplishing their objectives. The reduction of OECD dependence on oil is reflected in the decline in oil consumption in the OECD area from 40.9 MBD in 1979 to 33.8 MBD in 1982, a decline of 17.3 percent. Net oil imports also declined during the same period by 30 percent, from 26.8 MBD to 17.6 MBD, and the ratio of net imports to consumption was reduced from 65.5 percent to 52.1 percent during the same period.[5]

STRUCTURAL CHANGES IN THE OIL INDUSTRY

The sharp increase in the price of crude oil and the transfer of pricing and production policies to the oil-exporting countries, together with other changes in the world economy and the energy markets, precipitated important alterations in the international oil industry and in OPEC's position in it.

An early change that was a direct outgrowth of the expanding role of the governments of oil-producing countries was the increase in the number of sellers and buyers in the international oil markets. This occurred because as individual states assumed controlling power over their oil sectors, they created state-owned companies and entrusted them with the task of producing and marketing crude oil. Yet there was a lack of coordination among the national oil companies, owing to the absence of integrated policies governing the level of output in member countries.

The emergence of national oil companies in the oil-importing countries that were organized for the purpose of securing favorable terms from oil sellers added another new dimension to the international oil industry. This rise in the number of sellers and buyers had the effect of diluting the monopoly elements in the industry and increasing competition.

Another major change in the world oil market was the increase in the level of output outside the OPEC area. The rise in the price of OPEC oil made it profitable to increase output from higher-cost existing oil fields and to provide strong fiscal incentive to develop high-cost, new-oil resources. For example, oil output was increased in the United States, the United Kingdom, Norway, Egypt, and Mexico. The expansion of output in these producing countries, as well as others, had the effect of reducing the demand for OPEC oil. This was reflected in the decline of OPEC oil output from close to 31 MBD in 1979 to 19.1 MBD in 1982 (see table 11).

It will be recalled that one of the major aspects of the oil industry under the concession system in the Middle East was the long-term supply contracts among the major oil companies. It was the combination of joint ownership and long-term supply contracts that strengthened the oil companies' ability to regulate the supply of oil to meet projected demand. Although the entry of independent oil companies had the effect of weakening the system to some extent, the share of the major oil companies in the oil market remained high enough to ensure the continued domination of the major oil companies over the international oil industry. Such domination was totally undermined when OPEC-member countries and other producers found themselves producing independently of each other and when long-term contracts that provided an element of stability were replaced by short-term contracts, in turn increasing the competitive dimension of the industry. The deregulation of the U.S. oil market strengthened competitive tendencies in the world oil market, because the U.S. oil sector is the world's largest oil sector in terms of consumption.

The growth of large numbers of buyers and sellers in the world oil market also gave rise to the emergence of the spot market as a prime indicator of the underlying forces of demand. As pointed out in an earlier chapter, it was the spot market that provided OPEC with the rationale to raise its prices between 1979 and 1981. The importance of this market was a direct result of the significant increase in the number of buyers and sellers in search of transactions outside the traditional integrated channels of major oil companies and outside the large-size transactions normally associated with government contracts.

Table 11. OPEC-Member Countries' Crude-Oil Output and Exports, 1961–82 (Millions of Barrels per Day)

		Year					
		1961	1970	1974	1978	1980	1982
Algeria	A[a]	0.3	1.0	1.0	1.2	1.0	0.8
	B[b]	0.3	1.0	0.9	1.0	0.7	0.6
Ecuador	A	*[c]	a	0.2	0.2	0.2	0.2
	B	—[d]	a	0.2	0.2	0.2	0.1
Gabon	A	*	0.1	0.2	0.2	0.2	0.2
	B	*	0.1	0.2	0.2	0.2	0.1
Indonesia	A	0.4	0.9	1.4	1.6	1.6	1.3
	B	0.2	0.6	1.0	1.3	1.0	0.9
Iran	A	1.2	3.8	6.0	5.2	1.5	2.0
	B	0.8	3.3	5.4	4.4	0.8	1.6
Iraq	A	1.0	1.5	2.0	2.6	2.6	1.0
	B	1.0	1.5	1.8	2.4	2.5	0.8
Kuwait	A	1.7	3.0	2.5	2.1	1.7	0.9
	B	1.5	2.6	2.2	1.8	1.3	0.8
Libya	A	a	3.3	1.5	2.0	1.8	1.2
	B	a	3.3	1.5	1.9	1.7	1.1
Nigeria	A	a	1.1	2.3	1.9	2.1	1.3
	B	a	1.1	2.2	1.8	2.0	1.0

Qatar	A	0.2	0.4	0.5	0.5	0.5	0.3
	B	0.2	0.4	0.5	0.5	0.5	0.3
Saudi Arabia	A	1.5	3.8	8.5	8.3	9.9	6.8
	B	1.2	3.2	7.9	7.7	9.2	6.1
United Arab Emirates	A	—	0.8	1.7	1.8	1.7	1.2
	B	—	0.8	1.7	1.8	1.7	1.1
Venezuela	A	2.9	3.7	3.0	2.2	2.2	1.9
	B	2.0	2.4	1.8	1.2	1.3	1.5
OPEC total	A	9.4	23.4	30.7	29.8	26.9	19.1
	B	7.4	20.2	27.3	26.1	22.9	14.3[e]
World total	A	22.3	45.7	56.1	60.1	59.7	53.8
	B	8.2	23.4	31.3	31.3	30.6	22.4
OPEC share in world total (%)	A	41.9	49.0	52.4	46.4	42.9	35.3
	B	90.9	86.3	87.0	83.4	74.8	63.9

Sources: OPEC, *Annual Statistical Bulletin,* 1980, pp. xxvii, xxviii, LI, and LII; OPEC, *Annual Report,* 1982, p. 65.

[a] = Output

[b] = Exports

[c] = Asterisk denotes less than 50,000 barrels per day.

[d] = Dash denotes no output or export.

[e] = Consumption data for 1982 were estimated on the basis of 1981 data.

*Having regained their sovereignty over oil resources and having become auton-
omous producers/sellers, most OPEC countries have diversified their sales outlets.
Until a few years ago the eight major companies lifted 80–90% of OPEC exports.
The number of lifters has now increased manyfold to some 150. A typical OPEC
country has between 20 and 40 customers, including previous concessionaires,
U.S. independents, European and Japanese companies, Third World companies,
refiners, traders and governments. . . . This means greater competition between
buyers in tight markets; also lesser commitment by the buyers to their supply
sources when the market is slack.*[6]

In addition to these changes in the market the direct involvement of the
governments of oil-importing countries contributed to the erosion of OPEC's
position in the international oil industry. The energy policies of the oil-
consuming countries, as was discussed earlier, directly influenced the international oil industry. Another aspect of the role of the governments of the oil-
consuming countries that was destined to have a serious impact on the oil
market was the collective resolution of these governments through the IEA to
increase their inventories of crude oil and petroleum products to meet emergency supply conditions. The size and behavior of these inventories became an
important determinant of crude-oil supply and prices in the years 1980–82, and
consequently of the price-determining power of OPEC, as discussed in the next
section.

OPEC, OECD, AND THE 1983 PRICE REDUCTION

One of the more important historic reversals that OPEC had to contend with
was the March 1983 price reduction, in which OPEC-member countries were
compelled by the changing market conditions to reduce the official price of the
marker crude, Arabian Light 34°, by $5 per barrel—from $34 to $29 per barrel.
All other prices were adjusted to reflect this official price. It is important to
understand some of the conditions that led to the price reduction. The ostensi-
ble reason for the reduction was, of course, the imbalance between supply and
demand: the continued decline in the demand for OPEC crude oil resulted in an
excess supply. Since OPEC was not prepared to deal with a continued decline in
demand, it found itself adopting a series of ad hoc measures that were not
complied with under the developing new realities in the energy markets.

There are several explanations for the emergence of the supply imbalance
and for OPEC's behavior in the period prior to the historical reversal of March
1983. Immediately after the 1973 price revolution, when supply and cost became matters of national and international energy policy, the prevailing consensus was that a shortage in oil supply relative to demand was bound to
emerge in the 1980s. The thrust of policy and focus of attention was not on

whether an oil glut might develop but on how to curb the demand in order to allow the world economy to move from an oil-based economy to an economy that would be less dependent on oil. The concern in the 1970s was not whether the price of oil would go up but whether OPEC-member countries would be able to fill the gap between what the world economy was predicted to need and the amount of oil that could be expected to be supplied from OPEC and non-OPEC sources for the remainder of the twentieth century.

The perception that the world would continue to need an ever-rising volume of OPEC oil, at least for the balance of this century, was strengthened by several studies that concluded that the 1980s would experience a major oil shortage. Thus in 1978 the U.S. Central Intelligence Agency (CIA) forecast that the world would require OPEC to produce in excess of 30 MBD of oil by 1982 (actual output by OPEC-member countries in 1982 was about 18.4 MBD). In a similar vein, the International Energy Agency predicted in 1978 that oil consumption in 1985 would require OPEC to produce close to 43 MBD in that year. (Two years later, the IEA revised its projection for 1985 from 43 MBD to 31 MBD.)[7] Not only were the CIA and the IEA predictions wide of the mark, but a host of other agencies and corporations issued prognoses that were not much less conservative. Most of these studies were conducted in 1977–78, following the recovery from the 1974–75 recession. The underlying assumption in all these studies was that the economies of industrial countries, and by extension those of the Third World countries, would continue their upward movement. These forecasts also unanimously agreed that a condition of world energy imbalance was ahead that would give rise to shortages and that OPEC-member countries would not be in a position to fill the gap between supply and demand due to the physical constraints on their productive capacity. It was assumed that such a shortage would in turn exert an upward pressure on the prices of crude oil. Given that these forecasts were produced by a range of organizations, many unrelated to each other—such as the CIA, the IEA, oil companies, the U.S. Department of Energy, U.S. Congressional Research Service, Congressional Budget Office, and the European Economic Community—it was difficult for OPEC-member countries to take exception to such forecasts. Indeed, OPEC-member countries began to advocate that industrial countries reduce their rate of growth of demand for OPEC oil. OPEC also had already agreed to fund energy development efforts in developing countries in order to ease the perceived pressure of demand for oil.[8]

Not only was it the emerging consensus among forecasters that an oil shortage was in the making, but the drastic decline in Iranian oil output in the context of that country's revolution strengthened the belief that an oil shortage in the 1980s was virtually unavoidable. OPEC's Long-Term Strategy Committee seemed to accept these forecasts without any serious questioning. Indeed, on the premise that there would be no decline in demand for OPEC oil, the committee concentrated its efforts on devising a formula that would adjust the price of crude oil upward. Although the committee recognized that there might be excess supply conditions, these were predicted to be of a short-term nature only. As late as September 1980 when oil output of OPEC had declined by 13 percent relative to the 1979 output, the Long-Term Strategy Committee was still focusing its final report on price-related issues.[9]

It is relevant to note here that subsequent studies (since 1980) tended to show progressive reductions in the demand for energy and therefore a downward revision in the demand for OPEC oil. Although such revisions occurred as early as 1979–80, OPEC member-countries did not take these downward revisions seriously.[10] Why did OPEC fail to take note of these emerging trends and fashion its policies accordingly? Several explanations may be offered, the most important being that OPEC was organized to deal with pricing, not with oil-production management. Indeed OPEC's most significant accomplishment during the 1960s was to freeze crude-oil prices and, consequently, the per-barrel revenue throughout that decade. This preoccupation with the price of crude oil continued after OPEC-member countries assumed the controlling power over their respective oil sectors. And, in the aftermath of the 1973 price revolution, prices and fiscal matters remained the major focus of OPEC-member countries, owing to the massive distribution of income and financial resources between OPEC-member countries on the one hand and oil-importing countries on the other.

The continued preoccupation with price rather than output can also be attributed to the fact that demand for oil was sufficiently high to meet all the fiscal needs of member countries. And given the consensus among forecasters that the demand for oil would continue to rise, OPEC-member countries did not find it necessary to engage in output distribution among themselves.

Another factor that caused OPEC to avoid confronting the issue of output regulation was the political upheavals in the Middle East between 1978 and 1980. OPEC-member countries would have recognized the effect of the decline in the demand for energy and the resultant decline in the demand for their oil had it not been for the events that led to the ultimate collapse of the monarchy in Iran. The last quarter of 1978 and the first quarter of 1979 witnessed a severe decline in the production and export of Iranian oil. This decline and the subsequent policy decision by the Khomeini regime in Iran to reduce oil output below its traditional levels led other OPEC-member countries to increase their output to offset the permanent decline in the Iranian output. This made any advocacy of production-control mechanisms seem unnecessary and irrelevant.

Another development of major importance in 1979 and 1980 was the decision by the governments of the OECD countries to increase their oil inventories. This decision had the effect of increasing the demand for OPEC oil above the normal pattern of demand and had serious consequences in terms of OPEC's ability to maintain its leading position in the oil market. The first consequence of the increase in OECD demand for oil was a sharp escalation in the spot-market prices, which after a time lag forced OPEC-member countries to raise their official prices. Yet the rise in spot prices continued unabated well into 1981. The panic buying that was triggered by the events of the Iranian Revolution also created an upward spiral of price increases. So great was the increase in OECD stocks of petroleum that when the Iraq-Iran war errupted in September of 1980 its impact on the oil market was both temporary and marginal.

The increase in oil stocks in OECD countries was associated with three other economic developments that led these countries to liquidate some of their oil inventories. These changes included the worldwide decline in economic activity; the abnormally high interest rates; and the actual decline in the demand for oil as energy conservation measures and policies began to show serious results. It was clear by 1981 that the realities of the market simply would not support further price increases by OPEC-member countries. Once it was realized that OPEC could not or would not raise its prices, a process of destocking was initiated, since there was no incentive to hold these stocks at abnormally high levels at a time of emerging glut conditions and a downward pressure on the price structure. The high interest rates that prevailed in 1981 caused the opportunity cost of holding these oil stocks to be high. The high cost of investing in oil inventories, together with the expectations that prices would be ultimately reduced or at least held constant, further weakened OPEC's positon in the world oil market.

It should be reemphasized that OPEC's position of control in the world oil market was deteriorating due to the general decline in demand for energy and oil; the substitution of nonoil sources of energy for oil; and the displacement of OPEC oil by non-OPEC oil. To all these forces of change was added the reentry into the world market of previously purchased oil that had the same displacement effect as that of non-OPEC oil. Taken together, these factors have been held responsible for the 12-MBD reduction in the production of OPEC crude oil between 1979 and 1982, from 31 MBD to 19 MBD. The distribution of this reduction among these four sources of decline was estimated to be as follows:[11]

Reduction in inventories	3.5 MBD
Decline in energy demand	3.5 MBD
Displacement by non-OPEC oil	2.0 MBD
Substitution by nonoil fuels	3.0 MBD

Another estimate of the reduction in inventories for the year 1982 revealed that destocking for the whole year amounted to 1.9 MBD but fluctuated between a low of 0.7 MBD in the third quarter and a high of 3.8 MBD in the first quarter of that year.[12]

Regardless of the actual volume of destocking, these actions were superimposed on a market that was already characterized by an oil glut and declining demand. Furthermore, the destocking was taking place at a time when some OPEC-member countries were resorting either to hidden or open price discounting. Iran, for instance, maintained that due to war conditions in the Gulf it was forced to sell its oil at less than the official price in order to compensate oil buyers for the high insurance premiums. Other countries found themselves resorting to other forms of price discounts, including lower differentials for higher-quality oil, longer credit terms, and barter deals at which prices of the nonoil commodities were set above open market prices. Accompanying the downward pressure on the prices of OPEC oil was a clear shift in price leadership to the non-OPEC oil producers.

The rise in oil exports from new, non-OPEC sources of crude oil such as the North Sea (the United Kingdom and Norway), Mexico, and Egypt in the 1970s happened at a time when the prices of and demand for oil were high. The pricing behavior of these newcomers was typical of any newcomer: they tended to follow the price leadership of the established firms when the demand was high and to sell at lower prices when the market was soft. For the newcomers the goal was to capture and keep part of the market even if this meant selling oil at lower prices. From the perspective of the established sellers the newcomers presented no threat so long as demand for oil remained high. But although the newcomers' encroachment upon the markets of OPEC-member countries initially was unimportant, its effect began to be demonstrated when the production and exports of OPEC-member countries shrank from 31 MBD to 19 MBD. The ratio of the newcomers' exports to total oil exports and thus also price changes by these newcomers became extremely important during this period, because any reduction in price meant a loss of the share of the market by OPEC-member countries. The newcomers were, moreover, not bound by a collective decision to set and keep the prices at certain levels. OPEC-member countries, by contrast, were called upon to observe and respect their own collective pricing decisions.

The freedom of action enjoyed by the newcomers manifested itself in the series of price cuts that the North Sea producers instituted in 1982 and 1983. In early 1982 the price of North Sea oil of a quality comparable to that of Arabian Light was $36.50 a barrel, or $2.50 above the price of Arabian Light. By early 1983 the North Sea oil price was reduced to $30.50, or $3.50 below the price of

Arabian Light. The significance of the reduction for future OPEC prices stems from a number of considerations.

First, price reductions during the period 1982–83 indicated beyond any doubt that the market conditions were weak enough to justify such price cuts. Second, the 1982 price reduction reversed the traditional price alignment between the North Sea oil and OPEC oil, in that this was the first time that the price of North Sea oil was set below that of Arabian Light. Third, the North Sea price reductions, which were followed by other reductions by the Soviet Union, Mexico, and Egypt, signaled a shift away from OPEC power in world oil.

These price reductions in a shrinking market directly affected the market shares of other sellers. For example, in the case of Nigerian oil, following the 1982 North Sea price cut the oil companies buying Nigerian oil pressured Nigeria to reduce the price of its oil. Nigeria's refusal prompted the companies to take their business elsewhere, causing 50 percent reduction in Nigeria's output in a matter of days.[13] This drastic reduction forced Nigeria eventually to reduce its price by reducing the premium it normally charged above the price of Arabian Light. This in turn led the other African members of OPEC—Libya and Algeria—to do the same. But the narrowing of the gap between the price of the African crudes and that prevailing in the Gulf had the effect of displacing Gulf oil in favor of the relatively cheaper African crudes.

In order to defend its share of the market, Iran announced a three-phase price reduction of $4.00 a barrel (to $30.20 a barrel) in February 1982. Other member countries in addition to Iran, such as Venezuela and Indonesia, also reduced their prices in one form or another. Although OPEC-member countries attempted to stabilize the official price of oil at $34.00 a barrel by adopting a production program that would limit total OPEC output to 18 MBD, the attempt was not taken seriously, and many OPEC-member countries continued to disregard their collective price and output decisions. This meant in effect that only a small number of OPEC-member countries, notably Saudi Arabia, were observing the official price of $34.00 a barrel. But in so doing they had to accept a reduction in their output and sales, since the official price represented the upper tier of a multitier price structure. In the case of Saudi Arabia, its output declined 4.2 MBD between January 1982 and January 1983, from 8.7 MBD to 4.5 MBD—a decline that equaled the decrease in the combined output of OPEC-member countries from 20.8 MBD to 16.6 MBD during the same time period. The sharp decline in Saudi Arabia's output led to a decline in that country's share of OPEC combined output, from 42 percent in January 1982 to 27 percent in January 1983. By early 1983 it was clear that if member countries continued to charge the official price, their market position as well as their development plans and even their national economies would become unstable. The destabilizing effects of declining demand and competitive price cutting thus led OPEC-member countries to embark upon their first collective experiment in price reduction in March 1983.

The most important and novel provision of the OPEC March 1983 agreement was the reduction in the official OPEC price from $34 per barrel to $29 per barrel. This reduction was a historical reversal for a group of oil-producing countries that had seen only price increases for the ten years previous. The other provisions of the March 1983 agreement that were intended to stabilize the new price included a pledge by member countries not to reduce their prices below the agreed OPEC levels; another pledge to retaliate against nonmember countries who might attempt to undermine the new price structure; and specific prohibitions against various forms of price discounting by member countries.[14]

THE 1983 OUTPUT QUOTA
SYSTEM: BIRTH OF A NEW CARTEL

In addition to agreeing to reduce prices, OPEC-member countries reached an agreement on a quota system that allocated to each country an output ceiling within a combined OPEC-wide output of 17.5 MBD. This quota system was important for several reasons. First, in a reversal of its traditional position, Saudi Arabia decided this time to participate in the new production-allocation system. It will be recalled that one of the reasons for the failure of the 1982 production agreement was Saudi Arabia's refusal to be a party to it. However, the changing market conditions and the loss of control by OPEC seemed to convince Saudi Arabia in 1983 that a link between price stability and stable supply conditions was essential. Not only was Saudi Arabia convinced that a production plan was necessary, but it also agreed to become the "swing," or the residual, producer within OPEC. In other words, Saudi Arabia agreed that its output would be allowed to vary in order to fill the gap between the 12.5 MBD combined quotas of the other twelve member countries and whatever demand there was for OPEC oil, even if such demand were to fall below the 17.5 MBD ceiling. This agreement, which gave birth to a new oil cartel, placed Saudi Arabia in a position similar to that of the state of Texas during the years when the prorationing system of oil output was in effect in the United States.

The significance of the output management arrangement stems also from the realization by OPEC-member countries that in order to be able to administer crude-oil prices, they also had to be able to administer the oil supply. In other words, the output-regulating mechanism that worked well for the oil companies prior to 1973 had to be replaced in 1983 by an OPEC-devised mechanism. The newly adopted OPEC mechanism is neither as sophisticated as was that of the oil companies, nor has it been in place long enough to merit evaluation. Suffice it to say that the prerogatives of sovereignty that governed the behavior of OPEC-member countries for over two decades have had to yield to the realities of the market for at least the predictable future.

OPEC'S PROSPECTS IN
A CHANGING WORLD ECONOMY

Any assessment of the prospects for OPEC and the oil of its member countries in the world economy hinges on at least three prospective developments: the economic growth prospects of the world economy; the prospects for unified OPEC-wide action in the face of changing demand conditions; and the impact on the availability of oil of internal changes in OPEC-member countries.

As to the prospects of a world economic recovery, evidence seems to indicate that the rates of economic growth of the 1950s and the 1960s will not be repeated in the foreseeable future. Economic growth rates of 5 percent, which were considered attainable only a few years ago, have now been replaced by growth rates in the range of 2.4 percent to 3.2 percent for the remainder of this century. The lower rate of economic growth for the OECD countries implies an oil-import demand of 18 MBD in the year 2000, while the higher growth rate implies a demand of 30 MBD of imported oil. In 1980 the countries of the OECD imported 24.2 MBD. The difference between 18 MBD and 30 MBD of imported oil has far-reaching implications for the position of OPEC oil in the world economy and for OPEC's ability to set oil prices.

Whereas the rates of economic growth currently projected for industrialized countries are low, the future rates of economic growth in developing countries may prove to be relatively high, judging by the experience of recent years. According to the International Energy Agency, developing countries are projected to increase their demand for oil from close to 8 MBD in 1980 to between 11 MBD and 13 MBD in 1990 and to between 17 MBD and 22 MBD in the year 2000, depending on the assumed rate of economic growth and the industrialization and urbanization movements associated with developing countries' economic growth. Although developing countries are projected to increase their own output of oil, such increase will not be sufficient to meet the increased demand. Thus it is projected that non-OPEC developing countries will have to face an oil gap ranging from 2 MBD to 3 MBD in 1990 and from 8 MBD to 11 MBD in the year 2000.[15]

A third important source of demand for oil will be determined by the rate of industrialization in OPEC-member countries themselves. Demand for oil in these countries is projected to rise from 2.9 MBD in 1980 to between 5 MBD and 6 MBD in 1990 and to between 8 MBD and 9 MBD in the year 2000. Such increases in the demand by OPEC-member countries for their own oil will have the effect of reducing the amount of oil exported to other countries.[16]

If the assumptions on which the IEA's projection were based prove correct, then the oil glut of the early 1980s will be replaced by a possible shortage by 1990, to be followed by a serious shortage in the year 2000, ranging from 9 MBD to 21 MBD. Accordingly, OPEC-member countries will find themselves before the end of this decade in a position of having to resume the upward trend of price increases.

While it is beyond the scope of this study to challenge the IEA's assumptions relating to various economic growth rates, the IEA's projections of OPEC future oil supply are of questionable accuracy and are discussed here. The IEA study projects that OPEC oil output will reach, given the assumed higher rate of economic growth, 26 MBD in 1985, 29 MBD in 1990, and 28 MBD in the year 2000. These production data are rather low in light of OPEC's recent experience and the availability of crude-oil reserves in the OPEC region. During the period 1971 to 1980 OPEC total annual output exceeded 30 MBD for five of the ten years. And in the other years in which OPEC output fell below 30 MBD, it was in response to changing demand conditions rather than supply constraints. For the entire decade, OPEC-member countries produced 106 billion barrels of crude oil. Yet the crude-oil reserves of member countries increased during the same period, from 431 billion barrels in 1971 to 434 billion barrels in 1980. This means that additions to crude-oil reserves in OPEC-member countries exceeded the amount of oil produced during the same period.

Not only do the IEA projections of OPEC's future oil output seem low given the nature of supply, reserves, and demand conditions that have so far characterized the 1980s, but other considerations would tend to encourage OPEC-member countries to expand their output should the demand conditions change. In the first place it should be recognized that the Iraq-Iran war has excluded from the world market a major portion of OPEC oil. The combined output of these two countries under normal conditions is close to 10 MBD. In 1982 their combined output was around 3 MBD. It is axiomatic to assume that once the hostilities are ended both countries will seek outlets for larger volumes of output. The need for more funds for reconstruction and development will motivate Iran and Iraq to produce at even-higher levels should demand conditions permit.

Another consideration that would encourage OPEC-member countries to expand output beyond the IEA's projections is that the decline in demand for oil in the first part of the 1980s created a number of financial and economic problems that need rectifying. The increase in the exernal public debt of a number of oil-producing countries is a case in point. The need to resume work on development projects that had to be abandoned or curtailed for lack of funds is another reason why oil output should be expected to increase if demand conditions allow. Even countries with accumulated foreign assets such as Saudi Arabia and Kuwait cannot be assumed to be insulated from the need to expand their output above historical levels, should world demand conditions allow them to do that. The central question is not whether OPEC-member countries can increase their output, but whether the state of the world economy will be such that these countries would be in a position to expand their output.

Another question to be dealt with is whether OPEC-member countries will be able to forge a unified position in their dealings with the rest of the world, especially with the industrialized countries. In other words, will member countries be able to abide by their own decisions and thus form a successful cartel? There is no inherent reason why OPEC-member countries should not be able to translate their 1983 quota system into a functioning cartel arrangement. Indeed, the history of oil both in the United States and throughout the world is of an industry that developed under cartel or cartellike arrangements administered by private enterprises and public authorities. Yet given the nature of OPEC's make-up, it is hard to envisage OPEC engaged in a successful cartel arrangement unless the demand for oil continues to be soft.

As to the issue of internal changes that might occur in one or more of the OPEC-member countries, it is difficult to see how the world economy can be seriously affected by change in any one country. One can go even further and say it is difficult to see how the world economy can be affected so long as the present pattern of economic linkages remains unaltered. Change in one country or in a number of member countries will not affect the hard reality of the dependence of each one of these countries on the industrialized economies for markets for their exports. Indeed, the market conditions prevailing in the 1980s were such that the simultaneous removal of two major oil-exporting countries—Iraq and Iran—did not seem to affect availability of oil in the world market. Oil in OPEC-member countries is the mainstay of their economies. It is not produced for local consumption but to be exported. And without export markets oil loses much of its significance to the oil-producing countries. Attempts have been made to regulate the outflow of oil by one or more countries, but none has succeeded for more than a short period of time and there is no reason to expect any deliberate attempt to regulate the outflow of oil to succeed in the future.

To recapitulate, oil will continue to be a major source of energy and OPEC-member countries will continue to be the major oil-exporting group of countries in the foreseeable future. Much of OPEC's importance is derived from the status of oil in the world economy. And since the demand for oil is derived demand, the importance of oil will in the last analysis continue to be a function of the rate of growth of the world economy. Given the current and projected state of the world economy, OPEC-member countries can be expected to play a vital, if somewhat reduced, role in the world economy.

Appendix

Table A-1. OPEC-Member Countries' Proven Crude-Oil Reserves, 1961–82 (Billions of Barrels)

	Year					
	1961	1970	1974	1978	1980	1982
Algeria	5.5	8.1	7.7	6.3	8.2	9.4
Ecuador	*[a]	0.8	2.5	1.2	1.1	1.4
Gabon	0.2	0.7	1.8	2.0	0.5	0.5
Indonesia	9.5	10.0	15.0	10.2	9.5	9.6
Iran	35.0	70.0	66.0	59.0	57.5	55.3
Iraq	26.5	32.0	35.0	32.1	30.0	41.0
Kuwait	65.0	80.0	81.5	69.4	67.9	67.2
Libya	3.0	29.2	26.6	24.3	23.0	21.5
Nigeria	0.3	9.3	20.9	18.2	16.7	16.8
Qatar	3.0	4.3	6.0	4.0	3.6	3.4
Saudi Arabia	55.0	141.4	173.2	168.9	168.0	165.3
United Arab Emirates	—[b]	12.8	33.9	31.3	30.4	32.4
Venezuela	17.6	14.0	15.0	18.0	18.0	21.5
OPEC total	220.0	412.0	485.0	445.0	434.0	445.0
World total	310.0	611.0	716.0	642.0	649.0	672.0
Ratio of OPEC to world total (%)	71.1	67.5	67.8	69.3	67.0	66.0

Source: OPEC, *Annual Statistical Bulletin,* 1980, p. xxiii.

[a]Asterisk denotes less than 50,000 barrels per day.

[b]Dash denotes no data available.

Table A-2. OPEC Oil Production of Crude Oil: Government
and Company Shares, 1970–80

Year	Total Output (MBD)[a]	Share of OPEC Governments (%)	Share of Major Oil Companies (%)	Share of Other Foreign Companies (%)
1970	23.4	2.3	81.8	15.9
1972	27.1	8.3	80.0	11.7
1974	30.7	59.5	33.3	7.2
1976	30.7	74.6	19.9	5.5
1978	29.8	75.5	18.8	5.7
1980	26.9	87.7	7.3	5.0

Source: Computed from OPEC, *Annual Statistical Bulletin,* 1970–80.

Note: The major oil companies are British Petroleum, Exxon, Gulf, Mobil, Shell, Texaco, Standard Oil of California, and Compagnie Française des Pétroles.

[a]MBD = million barrels per day.

Notes

1. OPEC AND ITS MEMBER COUNTRIES

1. The Tehran Agreement is dealt with more fully in chapter 2.

2. OIL-PRICE BEHAVIOR UNDER OPEC

1. For more detailed treatment of these points, see Alnasrawi 1975, 368–412.
2. OPEC was founded by Iraq, Iran, Kuwait, Saudi Arabia, and Venezuela. Qatar joined OPEC in 1961, Indonesia and Libya in 1962, Abu Dhabi in 1967, Algeria in 1969, Nigeria in 1971, Ecuador in 1973, and Gabon in 1975.
3. See Shell 1968, and, for the articulation of OPEC arguments concerning royalties, see OPEC 1962. As to the course of negotiations, see "OPEC and the Oil Companies," *Middle East Economic Survey* (*MEES*), August 28, 1964 (Suppl.); OPEC 1965, 7–17; and Rouhani 1971, 217–43.
4. For a detailed analysis of the Tehran price agreement see Alnasrawi 1973, 188–207.
5. For a good survey of the struggle to acquire the concession for the development of Iraq's oil resources see U.S. Congress, Senate Select Committee on Small Business, Subcommittee on Monopoly, *The International Petroleum Cartel*, 82d Cong., 2d sess., 1952, Committee Print 6, Ch. 4.
6. For the text of the Tehran Agreement see OPEC 1973a.
7. *Petroleum Intelligence Weekly* (*PIW*), March 27, 1972, pp. 5–6.
8. *MEES*, September 21, 1973, p. 3.
9. *MEES*, December 28, 1973, pp. 1–3.
10. OPEC, *Annual Review and Record, 1974* (Vienna: n.d.), 28–29.
11. See *MEES*, June 21, 1974, pp. 1–4.
12. OPEC, *Annual Review and Record, 1974* (Vienna: n.d.), 34; *MEES*, September 13, 1974 (Suppl.), pp. 1–4.
13. OPEC, *Annual Review and Record, 1974* (Vienna: n.d.), 36; *MEES*, November 15, 1974 (Suppl.), 1–5. The $10.12 per-barrel government take was arrived at as follows: ($9.60 × 40%) + ($10.34 × 60%) = $10.12, where $9.80 is government take on equity oil (40 percent of total output) and the $10.34 is the buy-back price (93 percent of the $11.25 posted price minus 12¢ production cost).
14. *MEES*, December 13, 1974 (Suppl.), pp. 1–5.
15. OPEC, *Annual Review and Record, 1975* (Vienna: n.d.), 77.

16. *MEES*, September 19–26, 1975, pp. 1–5. The price of $11.51 was 10 percent higher than the pre-October market price of $10.46. The latter consisted of three elements: (1) government take of $10.12 per barrel, (2) cost of production of 12¢ per barrel, and (3) company margin of 22¢ per barrel.
17. Ibid., p. 2.
18. *PIW*, February 28, 1977, p. 11.
19. *MEES*, December 26, 1975, p. 2.
20. *MEES*, June 7, 1976 (Suppl.), 1–3.
21. For a criticism of the Saudi position by the Libyan government see *MEES* June 21, 1976, 2–4. It should be mentioned in this connection that the Libyan government raised its sale prices effective July 1, 1976, in order to bridge the gap between these prices on the one hand and spot-market prices and the prices of other African crudes on the other. See *MEES* July 5, 1976, 1–2.
22. See interview with Saudi oil minister Ahmad Z. Yamani in *MEES* March 7, 1977, 2–3.
23. It is useful to note that OPEC was very much interested at that time in the outcome of the North-South Dialogue. See *MEES* November 29, 1976, 1–2.
24. *MEES*, December 20, 1976 (Suppl.), p. 2.
25. Ibid., December 27, 1976, p. 1.
26. See Yamani 1977, 2–7.
27. See *MEES*, December 20, 1976 (Suppl.), p. 7.
28. *PIW*, March 7, 1977, pp. 3–4.
29. *PIW*, May 2, 1977, p. 11.
30. *MEES*, January 17, 1977, 1–2.
31. *Arab Oil & Gas (AOG)*, December 16, 1976, p. 5a.
32. See *MEES*, May 16, 1977, 1–2.
33. See *MEES*, July 11, 1977, 1–3.
34. *MEES*, December 19–26, 1977, 1–3.
35. For a good survey of price changes during this period see Al-Chalabi 1980, 87–90.
36. *PIW*, April 12, 1982, p. 11.
37. *MEES*, December 24, 1979 (Suppl.), 1–2.
38. *MEES*, June 16, 1980, 1–3.
39. *MEES*, September 22, 1980, 1–3.
40. *MEES*, December 22, 1980, 1–4.

3. CRUDE-OIL PRICE DETERMINATION BEFORE AND AFTER THE EMERGENCE OF OPEC

1. See Clark 1938, 477–89; Kaysen 1949, 289–314; and Landon 1950, 125–40.
2. This is further reinforced by the production policies of the American oil industry, which were designed to protect the small producer. This aspect of the industry is dealt with later in the chapter.
3. Most European imports from the Western Hemisphere were actually drawn from the Caribbean region (Venezuela). This does not affect this analysis, however, since the Caribbean oil was priced in such a way as to make it competitive with the U.S. Gulf oil to all consuming centers. This was achieved by pricing the Venezuelan crude oil f.o.b. Caribbean at the same U.S. Gulf price for crude oil of comparable quality, minus the U.S. import tax. Because the transportation costs from the Caribbean and the U.S. Gulf to the U.S. eastern seaboard were the same, this resulted in identical delivered prices for the oils of these two regions. The same price for the Caribbean oil was also quoted for shipments to other destinations. See U.S. Congress, Joint Select Committee on Small Business, *The Third World Petroleum Congress, A Report to the Joint Select Committee on Small Business*, ch. 2, by Walter J. Levy, "The Past, Present and Likely Future Price Structure for the International Oil Trade," 82d Cong., 2d sess., 1952, 25.

4. *Oil and Gas Journal*, July 15, 1948, 56.
5. U.S. Congress, Senate Select Committee on Small Business, Statement by Mutual Security Administration, *Hearings, Monopoly and Cartels*, Pt. 1, 82d Cong., 2d sess., 1952, 154.
6. U.S. Congress, Senate Select Committee on Small Business, Statement by Mutual Security Administration 1952, 144.
7. As William Fellner has observed, "It is also conceivable, however, that leadership is required for technical-administrative reasons—someone must set the pace in the event of changes—and that such leadership rotates" (Fellner 1960, 129).
8. *Petroleum Times*, June 1958, 504.
9. *Oil and Gas Journal*, December 7, 1950, 67.
10. Ibid., December 14, 1950, 68.
11. Ibid., June 10, 1951, 81.
12. Ibid., February 16, 1953, 106.
13. Ibid., July 27, 1953, 218.
14. Ibid., August 3, 1953, 46.
15. Ibid., August 10, 1953, 96.
16. Ibid.
17. Ibid., February 20, 1956, 102.
18. *Petroleum Press Service*, January 1957, 38; April 1957, 158.
19. *Oil and Gas Journal*, June 3, 1957, 81. This increase was the outcome of the negotiations between the government and the oil companies, according to which the discount offered to the companies was reduced from 2 percent to 1 percent of the posted price of oil.
20. *Petroleum Press Service*, October 1957.
21. Ibid., February 1958.
22. Ibid., March 1959.
23. *The Economist* (London), February 28, 1959, 59.
24. *Oil and Gas Journal*, August 15, 1960, 83.
25. Ibid., September 19, 1960, 81.
26. See Issawi and Yeganeh 1962, table 33, 112.
27. Neil H. Jacoby, *Multinational Oil: A Study in Industrial Dynamics* (New York: Macmillan Co., 1976), 230.
28. Ibid., 226–27.
29. See Johany 1980, 8.
30. For the full text of the Declaratory Statement of Petroleum Policy, see OPEC, *Resolutions Adopted*, 11–15. See also Zakariya 1969, 1–16.
31. OPEC, *Annual Review and Record, 1968* (Vienna: 1969), 17–22.
32. For the text of the Solemn Declaration see *MEES*, March 7, 1975, i–vii.
33. It has been estimated that the technical cost of production in the North Sea is about five to seven times the cost of production in the Middle East. See Shell 1980, 8.
34. It is interesting to note in this connection that long-range economic planners in some of the producing countries look at higher prices as a means for more efficient use of energy and as a way to stimulate development of alternative sources that would be essential regardless of what happened to conventional fuels. See *MEES*, September 21, 1973, 4.
35. This has always been the position of Saudi Arabia within OPEC.

4. OPEC AND THE MANAGEMENT OF OIL OUTPUT

1. "Problems of Prorationing," *Petroleum Press Service*, October 1960, 368–71.
2. Ibid.
3. "Problems of Prorationing," 368–71.
4. See Allen, 1979, 41–42.
5. *MEES*, April 5, 1968, 1.

6. *MEES,* March 22, 1968, 2a.
7. See "An Open Letter from Abd Allah al-Tariki," *MEES,* May 23, 1969, 2–4. Al-Tariki was the predecessor of Saudi oil minister Ahmad Z. Yamani and was a moving force behind the creation of OPEC.
8. *MEES,* June 7, 1968 (Suppl.), 8.
9. *MEES,* July 18, 1977, 2.
10. Ibid., May 15, 1978, 3.
11. Ibid., May 22, 1978, 7.
12. Ibid., November 20, 1978, 7.
13. Ibid., June 1, 1981, 1–3.
14. Ibid., March 29, 1982, 1–8.
15. Ibid., July 19, 1982, 1.
16. This section draws heavily on Abbas Alnasrawi, "OPEC: The Cartel That Is Not," *OPEC Bulletin,* February 1981, 1–6. See also Mansfield 1976; and Samuelson 1976.
17. See, for instance, C. Fred Bergsten, "A New OPEC in Bauxite," *Challenge,* July–August 1976, 12–20.
18. See, for instance, Boulding 1966; Edward N. Chamberlain 1950; and Stigler 1966.

5. OPEC AND THE INDUSTRIALIZED COUNTRIES: THE INCREASED DEPENDENCY

1. In addition to the discussion in chapter 4 on the inapplicability of the term *cartel* to OPEC, see Johany 1980.
2. For some of these arguments, see Enders 1975, 625–37; and Chenery 1978, 55–77.
3. See Enders 1975, 625–37.
4. For a good analysis of economic developments in this period, see "Impact of Rising Oil Prices" 1980, 817–24.
5. See Samuelson 1974, 69.
6. See "Impact of Rising Oil Prices" 1980, 817–24.
7. Data in this and the next section were computed from trade tables for the appropriate years in OPEC, *Annual Statistical Bulletin;* and International Monetary Fund (IMF), *Direction of Trade Statistics Yearbook.*
8. For the relevance of the concept of wealth illusion to Nigeria, see Ojo 1982, 210–25.
9. It is interesting to note that only a fraction of Arab investible funds is managed by Arab banks operating in the international market. Thus, according to one observer, it was estimated that in 1979 Arab banks managed only $30 billion of the $300 billion in Arab money identified as the accumulated gross foreign assets of OPEC members. The observer went on to say that "Arab banks had yet to convince their own finance ministries that they offered as secure and well managed a portfolio deposit outlet for OPEC surplus funds as the large U.S. and European banks" (see Saudi 1982, 15–23).

6. OPEC, THE THIRD WORLD, AND RISE OF INTERDEPENDENCE

1. For data on OPEC-member countries' population and gross national product, see OPEC, *Annual Statistical Bulletin.*
2. For an elaboration on these views from the perspective of developing countries, see "The Dakar Declaration and Action Programme of the Conference of Developing Countries on Raw Materials," conference statement in Erb and Kallab 1975, 213–28.
3. For data on production and consumption of energy, see World Bank 1981, 36; British Petroleum Company 1965–80, various issues. 1982, 5–9.
4. Ibid.

5. Derived from IMF, *Direction of Trade Statistics Yearbook* 1970–83.
6. Ibid.
7. Ibid.
8. Data on exports, imports and balance of trade are derived from IMF, ibid.
9. "Oil Consumption, Production and Trade in Developing Countries," *OPEC Review*, Autumn 1979, tables 1 and 2.
10. Derived from World Bank 1983, 183.
11. Ibid.; United Nations Conference on Trade and Development (UNCTAD), *Financial Solidarity for Development: Efforts and Institutions of the Members of OPEC, 1973–1976 Review* (New York: UNCTAD, 1979).
12. MEES, January 3, 1983, B3–B5.
13. UNCTAD, *Financial Solidarity*.
14. For a statistical analysis of labor movements, see Hallwood and Sinclair 1981, 148–57.
15. Ibid., 150.
16. For a more detailed discussion of some of these implications for Egypt, see Ibrahim 1982, 38–53.
17. Ibid., 47.
18. Ibid., 31.
19. See Parmer 1975, 17–22.
20. For the texts of these documents, see United Nations General Assembly 1981, 19–37.
21. For the text of the Charter of Economic Rights and Duties of States, see Erb and Kallab 1975, 203–12, especially charter articles 2, 5, and 28.
22. For the text of this declaration, see *MEES*, March 7, 1975 (Suppl.), i–viii.
23. Ibid.
24. Ibid.
25. Ibid.
26. See Barraclough 1976, 32.
27. See Amuzegar 1977, 136–59.
28. Some of the conditions that have made the OPEC coalition workable may be found in Wiggins and Adler-Karlson 1978, 52.

7. OPEC IN THE 1980s: HISTORICAL REVERSALS AND PROSPECTS

1. For a detailed study of the evolution of concession agreements, see Stocking 1970.
2. For changes in the terms of trade, see IMF, *International Financial Statistics,* 1981.
3. "Energy Indicators," *OPEC Review* 6, no. 4 (Winter 1982): 374–407.
4. The articulation of the IEA's energy policies was expressed in a number of policy sttements. For some of the more important pronouncements, see IEA 1982, 46–59. See also IEA 1978.
5. *OECD Economic Outlook*, December 1982, 141.
6. See Mabro 1982, 4.
7. See Seymour 1980, 215.
8. A rare exception to the general consensus was voiced in 1977 by Fadhel Al-Chalabi. See his "Energy Conservation Policies of the Consuming Countries: A Producer's Point of View," *OPEC Review*, December 1977, 19–30.
9. *MEES*, September 22, 1980, 5–8.
10. For a good analysis of these forecasts and the assumptions used, see Deagle, Mossavar-Rahmani, and Huff 1981.
11. See The Research Group on Petroleum Exporters' Policies, "Oil Prices in 1983: A Critical Year," *MEES*, December 6, 1982 (Suppl.), 7.
12. See *Petroleum Times Price Report*, November 1, 1982, 2; and *OECD Economic Outlook*, December 1982, 141.

13. *MEES*, March 29, 1982, 1-2.
14. *MEES*, March 21, 1983, A1-A8.
15. For a good summary of the assumptions and projections made by the IEA, see "The Deceptive Glut," *The OECD Observer*, November 1982, 31-32.
16. Ibid.

Bibliography

Adelman, M. A. *The World Petroleum Market*. Baltimore: Johns Hopkins University Press, 1972.

Al-Anbari, Abdul Amir. "OPEC and the Third World." *OPEC Bulletin*, September 1980, 14–20.

Al-Chalabi, Fadhil J. *OPEC and the International Oil Industry: A Changing Structure*. Oxford: Oxford University Press, 1980.

Al-Chalabi, Fadhil, and Al-Janabi, Addan. "Optimum Production and Pricing Policies." In *Energy in the Arab World, Proceedings of the First Arab Energy Conference*. Vol. 3. Kuwait: Organization of Arab Petroleum Exporting Countries, 1980.

Al-Janabi, A. "Production and Depletion Policies in OPEC." *OPEC Review* 3, no. 1 (1979): 34–44.

Allen, Loring. *OPEC Oil*. Cambridge, Mass.: Oelgeschlager, Gunn & Hain, 1979.

Alnasrawi, Abbas. "Collective Bargaining Power in OPEC." *Journal of World Trade Law* 7, no. 2 (1973): 188–207.

Alnasrawi, Abbas. "The Petrodollar Energy Crisis: An Overview and Interpretation." *Syracuse Journal of International Law and Commerce*, 3, no. 2 (1975): 369–412.

Alnasrawi, Abbas. "Arab Oil and the Industrial Countries: The Paradox of Oil Dependency." *Arab Studies Quarterly* 1, no. 1 (1979): 1–27.

Alnasrawi, Abbas. *Arab Oil and U.S. Energy Requirements*. Belmont, Mass.: AAUG Press, 1982.

Al-Pachachi, Nadim. "The Development of Concession Arrangements and Taxation in the Middle East." *Middle East Economic Survey*, March 29, 1968, 2.

Amuzegar, Jahangir. "A Requiem for the North-South Conference." *Foreign Affairs*, October 1977, 136–59.

Askari H., and Cummings, J. T. *Oil, OECD, and the Third World: A Vicious Triangle*. Austin: Center for Middle Eastern Studies, 1978.

Ayoub, Antoine. "Associations of Raw Material Producers: The Desirable Conditions for the Possible." *OPEC Review* 3, no. 4/4, no. 1 (1979/1980): 93–104.

Bain, Joe S. *The Economics of the Pacific Coast Petroleum Industry*. Berkeley and Los Angeles: University of California Press, 1944.

Barraclough, Geoffrey. "The Haves and the Have Nots." *New York Review of Books*, May 13, 1976, 31–41.

Barraclough, Geoffrey. "The Struggle for the Third World." *New York Review of Books*, November 9, 1978, 47–58.

Bergsten, C. Fred. "The New Era in World Commodity Markets." In *Changing Patterns in Foreign Trade and Payments*. 3rd ed., ed. Bala Balassa. New York: W. W. Norton & Co., 1978.

Blair, John M. *The Control of Oil*. New York: Pantheon Books, 1976.

Boulding, Kenneth E. *Economic Analysis*. 3rd ed. New York: Harper & Row, 1966.

British Petroleum Company. *BP Statistical Review of the World Oil Industry* (Annual). London: 1962–82.

Central Intelligence Agency (CIA). *The World Oil Market in the Years Ahead*. Washington, D.C.: CIA, 1979.

Chamberlain, Edward N. *The Theory of Monopolistic Competition*. 6th ed. Cambridge, Mass.: Harvard University Press, 1950.

Chenery, Hollis B. "Restructuring the World Economy." In *Changing Patterns in Foreign Trade and Payments*. 3rd ed., ed. Bela Balassa. New York: W. W. Norton & Co., 1978.

Clark, J. M. "Basing Point Methods of Price Quoting." *The Canadian Journal of Economic and Political Science* 4, no. 4 (1938): 477–89.

Cummings, John T.; Askari, Hossein; and Salehizadeh, Mehdi. "An Economic Analysis of OPEC Aid." *OPEC Bulletin Supplement*, September 25, 1978.

"The Dakar Declaration and Action Programme of the Conference of Developing Countries on Raw Materials." In *Beyond Dependency: The Developing World Speaks Out*, ed. Guy F. Erb and Valeriana Kallab, 213–28. Washington, D.C.: Overseas Development Council, 1975.

Darmstadter, Joel; Dunkerley, Joy; and Alterman, Jack. *How Industrial Societies Use Energy: A Comparative Analysis*. Baltimore: Johns Hopkins University Press, 1977.

Deagle, Edwin A., Jr.; Mossavar-Rahmani, Bijan; and Huff, Richard. *Energy in the 1980s: An Analysis of Recent Studies*. New York: Group of Thirty, 1981.

Dunkerley, Joy et al. *Energy Strategies for Developing Nations*. Baltimore: Johns Hopkins University Press, 1981.

El Mallakh, Ragaei. "Oil in the 1980s: Some Issues of Supply and Demand." *OPEC Review* 2, no. 3 (1977): 37–45.

Enders, Thomas O. "OPEC and the Industrial Countries: The Next Ten Years." *Foreign Affairs* 53, no. 4 (1975): 625–37.

Engler, Robert. *The Politics of Oil: Private Power and Democratic Directions*. Chicago: University of Chicago Press, 1961.

Erb, Guy F., and Kallab, Valeriana, eds. *Beyond Dependency: The Developing World Speaks Out*. Washington, D.C.: Overseas Development Council, 1975.

Erickson, E. W., and Waverman, L., eds. *The Energy Question: An International Failure of Policy*. 2 vols. Toronto: University of Toronto Press, 1974.

Exxon Corporation. *World Energy Outlook*. New York: 1977; 1980.

Federal Trade Commission. *International Petroleum Cartel*. Staff report submitted to U.S. Senate Subcommittee on Monopoly of the Select Committee on Small Business. Washington, D.C.: 1952.

Fellner, William. "Collusion and Its Limits under Oligopoly." *American Economic Review* 40 (May 1950): 54–62.

Fellner, William. *Competition Among the Few*. New York: Augustus M. Kelly, 1960.

Frank, Helmut J. *Crude Oil Prices in the Middle East: A Study in Oligopolistic Price Behavior*. New York: Praeger, 1966.

Fransen, Herman. "Energy Demand and Supply in the 1980s." *Journal of Energy and Development* 6, no. 2 (1981): 213–24.

Fried, Edward R., and Schultze, Charles L. *Higher Oil Prices and the World Economy: The Adjustment Problem.* Washington, D.C.: Brookings Institution, 1975.

Georgescu-Roegen, Nicholas. *Energy and Economic Myths: Institutional and Analytical Economic Essays.* New York: Pergamon Press, 1976.

Gerakis, Andrea S., and Thayanithy S. "Wave of Middle East Migration Raises Questions of Policy in Many Countries." *IMF Survey*, September 4, 1978, pp. 260–62.

Griffin, James M., and Teece, David J. *OPEC Behavior and World Oil Prices.* London: Allen & Unwin, 1982.

Hallwood, Paul, and Sinclair, Stuart. *Oil, Debt, and Development: OPEC in the Third World.* London: Allen & Unwin, 1981.

Hansen, Herbert E. "OPEC's Role in a Global Energy and Development Conference." *Journal of Energy and Development* 5, no. 2 (1980): 182–93.

Hansen, Roger D. *Beyond the North-South Stalemate.* New York: McGraw-Hill Book Co., 1979.

Hartshorn, J. E. *Politics and World Oil Economics.* New York: Praeger, 1962.

Hartshorn, J. E. *Objectives of the Petroleum Exporting Countries.* Nicosia: Middle East Petroleum and Economic Publications, 1978.

Hashim, Jawad. "The Future Relationship Among Energy Demand, OPEC, and the Value of the Dollar." *Journal of Energy and Development* 6, no. 1 (1980): 61–71.

Heilbroner, Robert L., and Thurow, Lester C. *The Economic Problem.* 6th ed. Englewood Cliffs, N.J.: Prentice-Hall, 1981.

Hirst, D. *Oil and Public Opinion in the Middle East.* New York: Praeger, 1966.

Howe, Chárles W. *Natural Resource Economics: Issues, Analysis, and Policy.* New York: John Wiley & Sons, 1979.

Ibrahim, Saad Eddin. "Oil, Migration, and the New Arab Social Order." In *Rich and Poor States in the Middle East*, ed. Malcolm H. Kerr and El Sayed Yassin, Boulder, Colo.: Westview Press, 1982.

IEA. *See under* International Energy Agency.

IMF. *See under* International Monetary Fund.

"The Impact of Rising Oil Prices on the Major Foreign Industrial Countries." *Federal Reserve Bulletin* 66 (October 1980): 817–24.

"Inflation and Stagflation in Major Foreign Industrial Countries." *Federal Reserve Bulletin* 60 (October 1974): 683–98.

International Energy Agency. *Energy Policies and Programmes of IEA Countries, 1977 Review.* Paris: IEA, 1978.

International Energy Agency. *World Energy Outlook.* Paris: IEA, 1982.

International Monetary Fund. *Annual Report.* Washington, D.C.: IMF, 1972–82.

International Monetary Fund. *Balance of Payments Statistics Yearbook* (Annual). Washington, D.C.: IMF, 1972–82.

International Monetary Fund. *Direction of Trade Statistics Yearbook* (Annual). Washington, D.C.: IMF, 1972–82.

International Monetary Fund. *International Financial Statistics Supplement on Trade Statistics, 1981.* Washington, D.C.: IMF, 1981.

International Monetary Fund. *World Economic Outlook* (Annual). Washington, D.C.: IMF, 1980–83.

Issawi, Charles. *Oil, The Middle East, and the World.* New York: Liberty Press, 1972.

Issawi, Charles, and Yeganeh, Mohammed. *The Economics of Middle Eastern Oil.* New York: Praeger, 1962.

Johany, Ali D. *The Myth of the OPEC Cartel: The Role of Saudi Arabia.* New York: John Wiley & Sons, 1980.

Kaysen, Carl. "Basing Point Pricing and Public Policy." *Quarterly Journal of Economics* 62, no. 3 (1949): 289–314.

Kubbah, A. A. *OPEC Past and Present.* Vienna: Petro-Economic Research Centre, 1974.

Kuwait, Government of. *Population Census, 1975.* Kuwait: Government of Kuwait, 1977.

Lambertini, A. *Energy and Petroleum in Non-OPEC Developing Countries, 1974–1980.* Staff Working Paper no. 229. Washington, D.C.: World Bank, 1976.

Landon, Clark E. "Geographic Price Structure." *Law and Contemporary Problems* 15, no. 2 (1950): 125–40.

Leeman, Wayne A. *The Price of Middle East Oil: An Essay in Political Economy.* Ithaca, N.Y.: Cornell University Press, 1962.

McLean, J. G., and Haigh, R. W., *The Growth of Integrated Oil Companies.* Boston: Graduate School of Business Administration, Harvard University, 1954.

Mabro, Robert. "The Changing Nature of the Oil Market and OPEC Policies." *Middle East Economic Survey*, September 20, 1982 (Suppl.).

Mansfield, Edwin. *Microeconomics: Theory and Application.* 4th ed. New York: W. W. Norton & Co., 1982.

Mead, Walter J. "An Economic Analysis of Crude Oil Price Behavior in the 1970s." *Journal of Energy and Development* 4, no. 2 (1979): 212–28.

Melmaid, Alexander. "Geography of World Petroleum Price Structure." *Economic Geography* 38, no. 4 (1962): 283–98.

Mendershausen, Horst. *Coping with the Oil Crisis: French and German Experiences.* Baltimore: Johns Hopkins University Press, 1976.

Mikdashi, Zuhayr. *A Financial Analysis of Middle Eastern Oil Concessions: 1901–65.* New York: Praeger, 1966.

Mikesell, Raymond F. et al. *Foreign Investment in the Petroleum and Mineral Industries: Case Studies of Investor-Host Country Relations.* Baltimore: Johns Hopkins University Press, 1971.

MNC report. *See under* U.S. Senate, Committee on Foreign Relations, 1975.

Moran, Theodore, H. *Oil Prices and the Future of OPEC.* Washington, D.C.: Resources for the Future, 1978.

Neil, Jacoby, H. *Multinational Oil.* New York: Macmillan Co., 1974.

Noreng, Oystein. *Oil Politics in the 1980s: Patterns of International Cooperation.* New York: McGraw Hill Book Co., 1978.

Noreng, Oystein. "The Western World and the Oil Exporters: An Historical Analogy." *OPEC Review* 3, no. 3 (1979): 46–55.

Odell, P. R. *Oil and World Power.* Harmondsworth, England: Penguin Books, 1979.

OECD (Organization for Economic Co-Operation and Development). *Energy Policy: Problems and Objectives.* Paris: OECD, 1966.

OECD. *Oil, The Present Situation and Future Prospects.* Paris: OECD, 1973.

OECD. *Energy Prospects to 1985.* 2 vols. Paris: OECD, 1974.

OECD. *Export Cartels*. Paris: OECD, 1974.

OECD. *World Energy Outlook*. Paris: OECD, 1977.

OECD. *Development Co-Operation* (Annual) Paris: OECD, 1981.

Ojo, Ade T. "Oil Wealth Illusion and Problems for Economic and Financial Management in Nigeria." *OPEC Review* 6, no. 2 (1982): 210–25.

OPEC. *Explanatory Memoranda on the OPEC Resolutions*. Vienna: OPEC, 1962.

OPEC. *OPEC and the Principles of Negotiation*. Vienna: OPEC, 1965.

OPEC. *Selected Documents of the International Petroleum Industry, 1971*. Vienna: OPEC, 1973a.

OPEC. *Selected Documents of the International Petroleum Industry, 1972*. Vienna: OPEC, 1973b.

OPEC. *Selected Documents of the International Petroleum Industry, 1973*. Vienna: OPEC, 1975.

OPEC. *Annual Review and Record*. Vienna: 1968–75.

OPEC. "Oil Consumption, Production, and Trade in Developing Countries." *OPEC Review*, Autumn 1979a.

OPEC. *Annual Statistical Bulletin*. Vienna: 1972–80.

OPEC. *Annual Report*. Vienna: 1976–82.

OPEC. *Resolutions Adopted at the Conferences of the Organization of the Petroleum Exporting Countries*. 3 vols. Vienna: n.d.

OPEC. "An Evaluation of OPEC Aid to LDCs." *OPEC Review*, Summer 1979b, i–xxiv.

OPEC. *OPEC & Future Energy Markets*. London: Macmillan & Co., 1980.

OPEC Fund for International Development. *Basic Information*. Vienna: OPEC, 1980.

OPEC Special Fund. *First Annual Report*. Vienna: OPEC, 1976.

Ortiz, Rene G. *Viewpoint*. Vienna: OPEC, 1981.

Parmer, Samuel L. "Self-Reliant Development in an 'Interdependent' World." In *Beyond Dependency: The Developing World Speaks Out*, ed. Guy F. Erb and Valeriana Kallab. Washington, D.C.: Overseas Development Council, 1975.

Penrose, Edith T., *The Large International Firm in Developing Countries: The International Petroleum Industry*. London: Allen & Unwin, 1968.

Penrose, Edith. *The Growth of the Firms, Middle East Oil, and Other Essays*. London: Frank Cass & Co., 1971.

Pindyck, Robert S. *Advances in the Economics of Energy and Resources*. 2 vols. Greenwich, Conn.: JAI Press, 1979.

Pindyck, Robert S. *The Structure of World Energy Demand*. Cambridge, Mass.: MIT Press, 1979.

Powelson, John P. "The Oil Price Increase: Impacts on Industrial and Less-Developed Countries." *Journal of Energy and Development* 3, no. 1 (1977): 10–25.

Quandt, William B. *Saudi Arabia in the 1980s: Foreign Policy, Security, and Oil*. Washington, D.C.: Brookings Institution, 1981.

Rifai, Taki. *The Pricing of Crude Oil: Economics and Strategic Guidelines for an International Energy Policy*. New York: Praeger, 1974.

Rouhani, Fuad. *A History of OPEC*. New York: Praeger, 1971.

Sampson, A. *The Seven Sisters*. New York: Bantam Books, 1975.

Samuelson, Paul A. "Coping with Stagflation." *Newsweek*, August 19, 1974, p. 69.

Samuelson, Paul A. *Economics* 10th ed. New York: McGraw-Hill Book Co., 1976.

Sarkis, N. "The Role of Oil in the Development of European-Arab Economic and Political Relations." *Arab Oil & Gas*, February 16, 1977, pp. 24–30.

Saudi, Abdulla A. "Arab Banking and the Eurocurrency Market." *OAPEC Bulletin*, August/September 1982, pp. 15–23.

Schurr, Sam H. et al. *Energy in America's Future: The Choices Before Us.* Baltimore: Johns Hopkins University Press, 1979.

Seymour, Ian. *OPEC, Instrument of Change.* London: Macmillan & Co., 1980.

Shell Briefing Service. *The OPEC Allowances.* London: Shell Briefing Service, 1968.

Shell Briefing Service. *Energy Profile.* London: Shell Briefing Service, 1980.

Sherbiny, N. A., and Tessler, M. A., eds. *Arab Oil: Impact on the Arab Countries and Global Implications.* New York: Praeger, 1976.

Shihata, Ibrahim F. I. *The OPEC Fund and the Least Developed Countries.* Vienna: OPEC Fund for International Development, 1981a.

Shihata, Ibrahim. *The OPEC Fund for International Development: The First Five Years (October 1976–October 1981).* Vienna: OPEC Fund for International Development, 1981b.

Shihata, Ibrahim F. I., and Mabro, Robert. *The OPEC Aid Record.* Vienna: OPEC Special Fund, 1978.

Smith, V. Kerry. *Scarcity and Growth Reconsidered.* Baltimore: Johns Hopkins University Press, 1979.

Smithies, Arthur. "Economic Consequences of the Basing Point Decisions." *Harvard Law Review* 62, no. 2 (1949): 308–18.

"Solemn Declaration: Conference of the Sovereigns and Heads of State of the OPEC Member Countries" (Algiers, March 4–6, 1975). In *Annual Review and Record*, published by OPEC, 56–70. Vienna: 1975.

Solow, R. M. "The Economics of Resources or the Resources of Economics." *American Economic Review*, May 1974, pp. 1–14.

Stigler, George J. *The Theory of Price.* 3rd ed. New York: Macmillan Co., 1966.

Stocking, George W. "The Economics of Basing Point System." *Law and Contemporary Problems* 15, no. 2 (1950): 159–80.

Stocking, George W. *Middle East Oil: A Study in Political and Economic Controversy.* Nashville: Vanderbilt University Press, 1970.

U.N. Economic Commission for Europe. *The Price of Oil in Western Europe.* Geneva: U.N., 1955.

United Nations General Assembly. "Resolutions on the NIEO." In *The Challenge of the New International Economic Order*, ed. Edwin Reubens. Boulder, Colo.: Westview Press, 1981.

U.S. Congress. Joint Economic Committee. *Economic Consequences of the Revolution in Iran.* 96th Cong., 1st sess., 1980.

U.S. Congress. Senate. Committee on Energy and Natural Resources. *Access to Oil— The United States' Relationships with Saudi Arabia and Iran.* 95th Cong., 1st sess., 1977. Publication 95–70.

U.S. Congress. Senate. Committee on Foreign Relations. Subcommittee on Multinational Corporations. *The International Petroleum Cartel, The Iranian Consortium, and U.S. National Security.* 93d Cong., 2d sess., 1974.

U.S. Congress. Senate. Committee on Foreign Relations. Subcommittee on Multinational Corporations. *Multinational Oil Corporations and U.S. Foreign Policy* (*MNC* report). 93d Cong., 2d sess., 1975.

U.S. Congress. Senate. Committee on Foreign Relations. Subcommittee on International Economic Policy. *The Future of Saudi Arabian Oil Production.* 96th Cong., 1st sess., 1979.

U.S. Congress. Senate. Committee on Interior and Insular Affairs. *Presidential Energy Statements.* 93d Cong., 1st sess., 1973.

U.S. Congress. Senate. Committee on Interior and Insular Affairs. *Implications of Recent Organization of Petroleum Exporting Countries (OPEC) Oil Price Increases.* 93d Cong., 2d sess., 1974.

U.S. Congress. Senate. Committee on Energy and Natural Resources. *The Geopolitics of Oil.* 96th Cong., 2d sess., 1980.

U.S. Department of Energy. *Annual Report to Congress, Vol. 3, 1977.* Washington, D.C.: U.S. Department of Energy, 1978.

U.S. President. *Economic Report of the President, 1975.* Washington, D.C.: 1976.

Van Vactor, S. A. "Energy Conservation in the OECD: Progress and Results." *Journal of Energy and Development* 3, no. 2 (1978): 239–59.

Waterbury, John, and El Mallakh, Ragaei. *The Middle East in the Coming Decade: From Wellhead to Well-Being?* New York: McGraw-Hill Book Co., 1978.

Weisberg, Richard C. *The Politics of Crude Oil Pricing in the Middle East, 1970–1975.* Berkeley: Institute of International Studies, 1977.

Wiggins, W. Howard, and Adler-Karlsson, Gunar. *Reducing Global Inequalities.* New York: McGraw-Hill Book Co., 1978.

Willet, Thomas D. *The Oil-Transfer Problem and International Economic Stability.* Princeton, N.J.: Princeton University, 1975.

World Bank. *World Development Report* (Annual). Washington, D.C.: World Bank, 1979–83.

Yamani, A. Z. "Arab Oil and World Politics." *Middle East Economic Survey,* January 3, 1977 (Suppl.).

Zakariya, Hasan S. "Some Analytical Comments on OPEC's Declaratory Statement of Petroleum Policy." *Middle East Economic Survey,* February 14, 1969 (Suppl.).

Index